An Anthropologist's Arrival

An Anthropologist's Arrival

A Memoir

Ruth M. Underhill

Edited by
Chip Colwell-Chanthaphonh
and Stephen E. Nash

THE UNIVERSITY OF
ARIZONA PRESS
TUCSON

The University of Arizona Press
© 2014 The Arizona Board of Regents
All rights reserved

www.uapress.arizona.edu

Library of Congress Cataloging-in-Publication Data
Underhill, Ruth, 1883–1984.
   An anthropologist's arrival : a memoir / Ruth M. Underhill ; edited by
Chip Colwell-Chanthaphonh and Stephen E. Nash.
      pages cm
   Includes bibliographical references and index.
   ISBN 978-0-8165-3060-1 (pbk. : alk. paper)
      1. Underhill, Ruth, 1883–1984. 2. Women anthropologists—United States—
Biography. 3. Tohono O'odham Indians—Social life and customs. 4. Pueblo
Indians—Social life and customs. I. Title.
   GN21.U48A3 2014
   301.092—dc23
   [B]

                                                      2013039476

Manufactured in the United States of America on acid-free, archival-quality paper
containing a minimum of 30% post-consumer waste and processed chlorine free.

19 18 17 16 15 14   6 5 4 3 2 1

Contents

Timeline

1883	Born in Ossining, New York
1890–1901	Ossining School for Girls, with several trips to Europe
1901–1905	Vassar College, AB (1905), Phi Beta Kappa
1906–1908	Travel in Europe, with one term each at the London School of Economics and University of Munich
1909–1913	Massachusetts Society for Prevention of Cruelty to Children, Boston, agent in charge of Italian cases
1912–1918	Begins writing articles and book reviews
1914–1915	Charity Organization Society, New York City, agent for Italian cases
1916	National Committee for Mental Hygiene, survey field worker
1917–1919	American Red Cross, in charge of Italian orphanages during World War I; after war employed by the Rockefeller Foundation
1919–1929	Continues writing, occasionally travels, and marries
1930–1937	Columbia University, PhD; assistant in anthropology, Barnard College
1931–1935	Research fellowships from Columbia University Social Science Council and Humanities Council
1935–1937	US Department of Agriculture, consulting anthropologist
1937–1948	US Office of Indian Affairs (later Bureau of Indian Affairs), associate supervisor of Indian education, then supervisor of Indian education
1948	University of Denver, visiting lecturer in anthropology
1949–1952	University of Denver, professor of anthropology
1953	Formally retires, but continues to travel, teach, and write
1957–1958	Television program *Red Man's America*
1984	Dies in Denver, Colorado

Genealogy

Maternal Grandfather: Robert Lindley Murray (1824–1874), born in Flushing, New York, a wool merchant, insurance agent, and Society of Friends minister.

Maternal Grandmother: Ruth Sherman Taber Murray (1827–1907), born in New Bedford, Massachusetts, and gave birth to eight children.

Paternal Grandfather: Jesse Haight Underhill (1812–1896), a Quaker farmer descended from Captain John Underhill, who settled in New England in 1630.

Paternal Grandmother: Eliza Sutton Underhill (1821–1906), lived in Ossining, New York, and had two children.

Mother: Anna Taber Murray Underhill (1854–1919), from a prominent Quaker family after which New York City's Murray Hill was named.

Father: Abram Sutton Underhill (1852–1942), grew up on a farm near Chappaqua, New York, and became a successful lawyer.

Sister: Margaret Underhill (1886–1970), Ruth's beautiful sister, married Edward F. Barron and had a child.

Brother: Robert Lindley Murray Underhill (1889–1983), earned a PhD from Harvard in 1916 and became a professor there with a specialty in logic; celebrated as a pioneering alpine mountaineer; married Miriam O'Brien in 1932 and had two sons, Robert and Brian.

Sister: Elizabeth Sutton Underhill (1892–1982), a suffrage activist, graduated New York University Law School in 1921 and became first female bank director in Westchester County; unmarried.

Monographs

1918   Provision for War Cripples in Germany. Publications of the Red Cross Institute for Crippled and Disabled Men.

1918   Provision for War Cripples in Italy. Publications of the Red Cross Institute for Crippled and Disabled Men.

1919   Child Labor in Italy. Tipografia Nazionale Bertero.

1920   The White Moth. Moffat, Yard, and Company. [fiction]

1934   Southwestern Indians: An Outline and Ceremonial Organization. US Office of Indian Affairs.

1935   Ethnobiological Studies in the American Southwest (with Edward F. Castetter). University of New Mexico Press.

1936   The Autobiography of a Papago Woman. American Anthropological Association.

1937   Social Organization of the Papago Indians. Columbia University Press.

1938   A Papago Calendar Record. University of New Mexico Press.

1938   Singing for Power: The Song Magic of the Papago Indians of Southern Arizona. University of California Press.

1938   First Penthouse Dwellers of America. J. J. Augustin.

1940   Hawk over Whirlpools. J. J. Augustin. [fiction]

1941   The Papago Indians of Arizona and Their Relatives the Pima. US Office of Indian Affairs.

1941   The Northern Paiute Indians of California and Nevada. US Office of Indian Affairs.

1941   Indians of Southern California. US Office of Indian Affairs.

1944   Navajo Weaving. US Office of Indian Affairs.

1945   Indians of the Pacific Northwest. US Office of Indian Affairs.

1945   Pueblo Crafts. US Office of Indians Affairs.

1946   Papago Indian Religion. Columbia University Press.

1946   Work a Day Life of the Pueblos. US Office of Indian Affairs.

1948   Ceremonial Patterns in the Greater Southwest (with David Heath French). Monographs of the American Ethnological Society.

1951   People of the Crimson Evening. US Bureau of Indian Affairs.

1953   Here Come the Navajo! US Bureau of Indian Affairs.

1953   Red Man's America: A History of Indians in the United States. University of Chicago Press.

1956   The Navajos. University of Oklahoma Press.

1958   First Came the Family. Morrow.

1959   Beaverbird. Coward-McCann. [fiction]

1961   Antelope Singer. Penguin. [fiction]

1965   Red Man's Religion: Beliefs and Practices of the Indians North of Mexico. University of Chicago Press.

1970   Youth Problems on Indian Reservations. Educational Resources Information Center.

1971   So Many Kinds of Navajos. Gallup-McKinley County Schools.

1974   Papago Indians I (with Robert A. Hackenberg and Gwyneth H. Xavier). Garland.

1979   Rainhouse and Ocean: Speeches for the Papago Year (with Donald M. Bahr, Baptisto Lopez, Jose Pancho, David Lopez). Museum of Northern Arizona Press.

An Anthropologist's Arrival

The world, I thought, must have its goods to sell
And lo, within my house, I have my gold,
Enough for satisfactions manifold
A glimpse of Heaven and a taste of Hell.

Yet no one spoke in that vast citadel
Upon the floor my golden pieces rolled
My bursting youth, the dreams I would have told
None paused, none answered. So the slow years fell

Into the past. Then, by me, someone strolled
And smiled to notice that I had grown old
While holding out my purchase money. "Well,"
Death said to me, with accents frolicsome,

"Life is not paid for. Life is lived. Now come."

—Ruth M. Underhill, "Buying Life"

Introduction

PERHAPS ONE OF THE MOST striking images from Hollywood about the adventure of anthropology is the final scene of *Raiders of the Lost Ark*, in which the biblical Ark of the Covenant, finally discovered, is once again secreted away as it is taken to a cavernous warehouse filled with countless boxes of treasures.

We are not suggesting that Ruth M. Underhill's unpublished and largely unknown archives are exactly equivalent to Moses's lost tablets. But, for us, maybe they come close.

We had both been at the Denver Museum of Nature & Science for several years before we learned in detail about the Ruth M. Underhill Collection. Rumor had it that this legendary anthropologist's papers were donated to the museum, but amid our other duties we never quite found the free hours to explore them. In 2009, however, when we applied for a Save America's Treasures grant, which sought financial support to garner intellectual and physical control of the museum's North American ethnography collection, we were sure to include the Underhill collection.* The grant would be our chance to finally explore this neglected historical resource—the mislaid tablets made by one of anthropology's own progenitors—half-archived but entirely unstudied and unpublished since the materials were donated twenty-five years earlier.

When the grant proposal was funded, the museum hired Aly Jabrocki to archive the papers and produce a finding aid.† We were astounded by the result of Aly's efforts. The rumors of the archive's historical wealth proved to be true. The Ruth M. Underhill Collection

---

* On the larger collection see: Colwell-Chanthaphonh, Chip, Stephen E. Nash, and Steven R. Holen. 2010. *Crossroads of Culture: Anthropology Collections at the Denver Museum of Nature & Science.* Boulder: University Press of Colorado.

† NEH Grant Number ST-03–06–0024–09. See: Jabrocki, Aly. 2012. Finding Aid to the Ruth Underhill Papers. Ms. on file, DMNS Archives.

runs eighty-five linear-feet and includes such finds as original ethnographic notes from her work with Native Americans, syllabi and class notes from 1930s Columbia University, hand-corrected manuscript drafts, nearly three thousand photographs, and original sound recordings—all created during a life spanning more than ten decades.*

As we worked to grasp the breadth of the collection, Aly pointed us to a particularly unique set of papers: about one hundred typed pages Underhill wrote of what she surely intended to be her autobiography. Our DMNS colleague Carla Bradmon carefully retyped Underhill's memoir into digital format. When we read the product, although it was disordered and at times sketchy, we were immediately taken by Underhill's candor and thoughtful self-reflection. As importantly, we saw that her life provided historically rich insights into the struggles of a woman to break free from the Victorian age and become one of her generation's great anthropologists. Quite simply, Ruth Underhill had a remarkable story to tell.

However, despite the memoir's significance, once we went through our first set of edits, we could see that it was incomplete. Key periods in Underhill's life were missing; key people went unmentioned. The memoir could not hold together by itself.

But, luckily, we could draw history from another archival well. Also in the archives were a string of interviews Underhill conducted—mostly with the museum's staff—between 1979 and 1982. Luckily for us, too, Underhill remained lucid as she neared one hundred years of age, and she answered questions in long paragraphs of sharp, candid, droll, and pensive reflections on her life. Underhill always spoke as if she were writing. With more than a thousand pages of additional material from interviews, we could fill in the voids left in Underhill's rough draft of a memoir. This book is the result.

᠁

Ruth Murray Underhill was born August 22, 1883, some forty miles north of New York City, in a world radically different from the one she departed more than one hundred years later, on August 15, 1984,

---

* Additional though substantially smaller Underhill collections can be found at the Special Collections and Archives of the University of Denver and also the Special Collections and University Archives, University of Oregon Libraries.

Figure 1. Ruth M. Underhill, circa 1960.

in Denver, Colorado.* Underhill's century witnessed the inventions of the steam turbine, zipper, bicycle, Coca-Cola, radio, teddy bear, airplane, automobile, crossword puzzle, telephone, television, polio vaccine, credit card, oral contraceptive, space flight, and Macintosh computer. Underhill lived under eighteen US presidents. She was thirty-six years old when all American women got the vote; fifty-eight years old when the United States entered World War II; and ninety-nine years old when Michael Jackson's *Thriller* started its run to become the best-selling album of all time. The world was utterly remade during Ruth M. Underhill's own storied life.

Underhill had a privileged but unhappy youth. Her father escaped his humble farmer roots by becoming a lawyer. Her mother grew up baked in New York City's upper crust. Ruth Underhill faced constant deflating challenges as a bright, brazen, and analytically inclined girl struggling to come to terms with her existence in a stifling Victorian society. Her stilted Quaker family provided no quarter, much less support, for such attributes in a young girl. While her parents clearly loved her, they did not understand her. Underhill casts herself as an awkward and homely girl, seeking a life of adventure when her culture asked her to seek only a life of domestic delight, marriage, and religious fidelity.

---

* There is confusion about both Underhill's date of birth and death. Some obituaries and biographies incorrectly state that Ruth's birth was in 1884 (see, e.g.: Ruth M. Underhill, 99; Expert on Indian Lore. 1984. *New York Times*, 18 August: 10; Cervi, Clé, and Nancy M. Peterson. 1998. *The Women Who Made the Headlines.* Denver: Denver Woman's Press Club. Pg. 44). But a copy of her birth certificate and her certificate of baptism in the DMNS Archives prove that 1883 is the correct year. Also of note, for Underhill's birthplace the birth certificate copy gives Sing Sing, New York, while the baptism certificate gives Ossining, New York; however, they are essentially the same place, as the name Sing Sing was formally changed to Ossining in 1901 (Cheli, Guy. 2003. *Sing Sing Prison.* Charleston, SC: Arcadia. Pg. 15).

For the exact date of her death, the *Rocky Mountain News* gives Wednesday, August 15 (Melrose, Frances. 1984. Ruth M. Underhill, Anthropologist, Dies. *Rocky Mountain News*, 16 August: 26–27). The *Denver Post* gives "Tuesday night," August 14—although this might be a vague way of saying the early morning hours of Wednesday (Eicher, Daiane. 1984. Ruth Underhill, Noted Writer, Dies. *The Denver Post.* 16 August: 6A). The *New York Times* article cited above indicates it was on Wednesday, August 15, although this source was wrong about her birth date. Most other obituaries give August 15 (e.g., Woodbury, Nathalie F. S. 1984. Past is Present: Ruth Underhill, Centenarian. *Anthropology News* 25(6):3). In Denver County, death records become public only after seventy years, and so the coroner's office could not confirm the exact date of Underhill's death.

Figure 2. Ruth in her college years, circa 1900.

After graduating from Vassar College in 1905 with a bachelor's degree, Underhill at last secured her first true sense of freedom by traveling across Europe for two years without her family. When she returned to New York, rather than settling down to marry, Underhill chose to become a social worker. First, she found work in Boston, helping Italian girls who were victims of sexual crimes. Then, she continued her work in New York City, trying to lift Italian-American immigrant families out of poverty.

This period of Underhill's life largely presaged her later anthropological career. Underhill was greatly moved by the humanity of the people she worked with, and she began to write about their experiences in popular magazines and newspapers. Underhill developed an ethic of cultural and emotional immersion, a hallmark of the anthropological endeavor. As she would reflect in her draft memoir, through social work with these impoverished communities, "I left my world and dwelt completely, for a time, in theirs. I have been, in that way, an Italian factory worker, an Irish laundress. I could understand such a girl's fears and hatreds, why she could not do the normal, reasonable thing the 'office' recommended. I was comfortable and happy in this other life as the girls were with me."

When the Great War broke out, Underhill was thirty years old. A few years later she was able to make her way to the war's theater; in Italy she worked for the American Red Cross, caring for orphans. When she returned to New York, she decided that she could marry. After a brief love affair that resulted in an abortion, Underhill met Cecil Crawford when hanging with a modish Greenwich Village crowd. Underhill spent the Roaring Twenties married to Crawford, living mostly at her family farm outside New York City. Crawford was handsome and charming but unemployed, an engineer who contributed little joy or capital to the household. A sad yet humorous ending marked the conclusion to Underhill's listless marriage. The couple decided to divorce, but under the law it could happen only after they recruited their friends and a private detective for a ruse to "catch" Cecil in the act of cheating.

At the age of forty-six, Underhill entered graduate school, surrounded mostly by men half her age, at Columbia University. Mentored by Franz Boas, Ruth Benedict, and Gladys Reichard, Underhill joined the venerable university just as anthropology was solidifying its role as a major discipline in the social sciences. Underhill would become colleagues with some of the most prominent anthropologists of the twentieth century, including Margaret Mead, Jules Henry, Elsie Clews Parsons, and Edward A. Kennard. After her first year of graduate school, Boas secured $500 and assigned Underhill to study the Tohono O'odham (then called the Papago Indians).* When Underhill inquired

---

* In 1986 the Papago Tribe formally changed its name to the Tohono O'odham Nation. "Tohono O'odham" refers to the particular tribe, while "O'odham" more broadly refers to the language and/or all of the related O'odham groups of southern Arizona. Underhill consistently referred to the people of southern Arizona as "Papago," which is often translated as "Bean Eaters." Although the use of "Tohono O'odham" is perhaps not as historically accurate for Underhill's autobiography, the phrase "Tohono O'odham" is more respectful. Also, we believe that had Underhill

about what methods she should use, Boas would only instruct her to "just find out how those people live and come tell us about it."

Underhill made the most of it. She immersed herself in O'odham life, as she had with her Italian wards a decade before. She began to learn the language and cleverly started making O'odham friends, first through the children and then, their mothers. In a chance encounter Underhill met the extraordinary woman Maria Chona. Chona was born around 1845 in the village of Mesquite Root, located at the center of the Tohono O'odham reservation, and raised in the traditional O'odham manner. She thus had extensive knowledge of O'odham cultural practices, particularly in the realm of ritual medicine. Through their unique friendship Chona would become one of Underhill's primary "informants" (as Native collaborators were then called).* Chona would also become the center of Underhill's pioneering 1936 book *The Autobiography of a Papago Woman*, which has been aptly described as "a striking and lyrical narrative of a woman . . . [who seeks] to satisfy her personal goals and desires within the limits of her culture. The published text was hailed as a breakthrough in ethnographic life history for its literary style and depiction of a complex narrative persona."[†]

After formally receiving her PhD from Columbia University, as the Great Depression lingered on in the 1930s, Underhill struggled to find a secure job. The odds were against her, not only as a woman but also as a middle-aged one embarking on a new career. In her draft memoir and interviews Underhill elides over this period, perhaps revealing, by omission, her disappointment in not finding an academic position.[‡]

---

lived to see this change, she would have followed it out of her deep reverence for this community. However, in several instances, to preserve the accuracy of the historical moment, "Papago" is kept in the text that follows.

* Significantly, Underhill's translation work was aided by collaboration with Ella Lopez Antone, then a fourteen-year-old Tohono O'odham student at the Phoenix Indian School. See: Rios, Theodore, and Kathleen Mullen Sands. 2000. *Telling a Good One: The Process of a Native American Collaborative Biography.* Lincoln: University of Nebraska Press. Pg. 143.

† Bataille, Gretchen M., and Laurie Lisa, eds. 2001. *Native American Women: A Biographical Dictionary.* 2nd ed. New York: Routledge. Pg. 68.

‡ Griffen provides one of the best summaries of Underhill's job prospects during this time. See: Griffen, Joyce. 1989. Ruth Murray Underhill. In *Women Anthropologists: Selected Biographies.* U. Gacs, A. Khan, J. McIntyre, and R. Weinberg, eds. Pp. 355–360. Westport, CT: Greenwood Press. Pgs. 357–359.

Starting in 1934, Underhill worked a series of odd jobs—first partic-ipating in Reichard's Hogan School, which sought to formally teach Navajos their language, and then lecturing workers of the US Office of Indian Affairs (later renamed the Bureau of Indian Affairs) at the Sherman Indian Institute in Riverside, California. In 1935, the bureau reassigned Underhill to Arizona to review a proposed constitution for the Tohono O'odham Nation. She objected to it, arguing that it was divorced from the tribe's social organization. Consequently, Under-hill was removed and never again allowed to work on government projects with the Native peoples she knew best. After this setback, Underhill soon passed the civil service examine and began researching southwestern cultures for the Soil Conservation Service, under the US Department of Agriculture, but was again removed, purport-edly because an assistant to John Collier—then the commissioner for the Bureau of Indian Affairs—feared employees would resent advice from highly educated outsiders and also because Underhill supposed he had had bad experiences with women in administrative posts. These episodes did not portend well for Underhill's career in government service.

In 1936, Underhill was temporarily transferred from the Soil Con-servation Service to the Office of Indian Affairs, so that she could complete a series of instructional pamphlets on Indian history and culture. She was permanently transferred the next year and by 1938 held the title of associate supervisor of Indian education. Based out of the Branch of Education, Underhill worked as an instructor to teachers heading out to Indian country and as a writer of educational booklets. She would come to know the Mojave and Navajo well, but also conducted research on the Pueblo Indians of New Mexico, the Northern Paiute Indians of California and Nevada, the Indians of Southern California, and the Indians of the Pacific Northwest. In 1944, she was promoted to supervisor of Indian education, mov-ing from her base in Santa Fe, New Mexico, to Denver, Colorado. Although intensely grateful that the job allowed her to become financially self-sufficient, Underhill was ultimately frustrated by the bureau's mechanical bureaucracy and mindless intransigence.

Following in the Boasian tradition—and in association with Ruth Benedict, three years her junior but nevertheless a trusted Colum-bia University professor, mentor, and confidant—Underhill sought to control the "facts" of Indian cultures while garnering synthetic anthropological insights that might help solve societal problems. Also, following in the footsteps of Margaret Mead—who preceded her at Columbia by several years and became a renowned curator at the American Museum of Natural History—Underhill worked tirelessly to make anthropology accessible to popular audiences while grounding her work in scholarly research.* Over the course of her career, Underhill published thirty-three popular and scholarly monographs and more than one hundred articles and other contributions.

Through her friendship with another pioneering anthropologist, H. Marie Wormington, Underhill was finally offered the opportunity to leave the bureau with a professorship at the University of Denver in 1948. She accepted the position but quickly found the students languid, and she resented the anthropology department's marginalization within the university. After less than five years, she left the university for a solo trip around the world, at the age of seventy. Believing that she had only a few years left to live, Underhill then settled into retirement and began to write up a few "last" projects. Her 1953 book *Red Man's America*, a seminal textbook on Native American history and cultures, became a hit and even led to a television program of the same name in 1957. She taught again, briefly, at the New York State Teachers College in New Paltz and the Colorado Women's College.[†] A few last books and articles trickled out over the years, like a leaky faucet that refuses to stop. To her surprise—though perhaps not to that of her friends, who knew her tenacity and vigor—Underhill lived just a week short of her hundred and first birthday.

In her final years, Underhill received only a few modest accolades from her colleagues.[‡] But more important to her were the honors she

---

* As Cynthia Irwin-Williams sharply observed, "In a literature today in anthropology characterized by a kind of desiccated, dried up, technical verbiage and obscure jargon, Ruth's contributions stand absolutely alone in the beauty of their language and their lyric quality" (Irwin-Williams, Cynthia. 1983. SWAA Distinguished Scholarly Award for 1983 Presented to Dr. Ruth Murray Underhill. *SWAA News* 22(2/3):17–18. Pg. 18).

† Colorado Women's College merged with the University of Denver in 1982.

‡ Such as an honorary LLD degree by the University of Denver in 1962 and an honorary DSc degree from the University of Colorado at Boulder in 1965. She received the rather obscure Foothills Art Center's Heritage Award in 1980 and the Southwest Anthropological Association's Distinguished Scholarship Award in 1983, as well as a special citation by the American Anthropological Association in 1984, just several

received from the people she had studied—perhaps the most coveted distinction for any anthropologist. In 1980, Underhill was honored at a banquet and in a parade on the Tohono O'odham reservation, and tribal chairman Max H. Norris wrote in a tribal resolution, "It was through your works on the Papago People that many of our young Papagos, in search of themselves, their past, their spirit, have recaptured part of their identities. Your works will continue to reinforce the true identity of many more young people, as well as the old. It is with this in mind that we wish to express our deep sense of appreciation."* His statement was joined by 150 testimonials from other tribal members. She called these honors "the crowning point of my life."† The next year the Gila River Indian Community passed its own tribal resolution thanking Underhill, and the year after that the Colorado River Indian Tribes presented her with a plaque recognizing her work in keeping the memories of the Mojave people alive.

Some readers may be tempted to see the first part of this book about Underhill's years of Victorian servitude as unrelated to the story of her years after she met Franz Boas. Readers who are most interested in the history of anthropology may be especially anxious to skip ahead. But to do so would miss the value of a memoir: the attempt to understand a life holistically, to trace the line between the experiences of youth and the outcomes of adulthood.

---

months before her death. See: Underhill, Ruth M. 1985. *Papago Woman.* Originally published 1936. Prospect Heights, IL: Waveland Press. Pg. v; Tisdale, Shelby J. 1993. Women on the Periphery of the Ivory Tower. In *Hidden Scholars: Women Anthropologists and the Native American Southwest.* N. J. Parezo, ed. Pp. 311–333. Albuquerque: University of New Mexico Press. Pg. 330; Melrose, Frances. 1984. Ruth M. Underhill, Anthropologist, Dies. *Rocky Mountain News,* 16 August: 26–27; Irwin-Williams, Cynthia. 1983. SWAA Distinguished Scholarly Award for 1983 Presented to Dr. Ruth Murray Underhill. *SWAA News* 22(2/3):17–18.

* For description of these honors, see: Lavender, Catherine J., and Nancy J. Parezo. 2008. Ruth Murray Underhill: Ethnohistorian and Ethnographer for the Native Peoples. In *Their Own Frontier: Women Intellectuals Re-Visioning the American West.* S. A. Leckie and N. J. Parezo, eds. Pp. 335–372. Lincoln: University of Nebraska Press. Pgs. 337–338.

† Quoted in: Herold, Joyce. 1980. Papago Tribe Honors Ruth Murray Underhill. *Anthropology News* 21(3):3.

Figure 3. Waving to celebrants, Ruth leads the annual rodeo parade in Sells, Arizona, 1980.

For example, an early vignette about Underhill's education of how babies are birthed at first appears jejune, yet it provides telling insights into the beginning of her gnawing doubts about the role of women in the world, her struggles to reject Victorian expectations, her later, sometimes awkward, interactions with men, and the decision not to have children. Underhill's childhood religion, her family's class, her loneliness among her own kin, her uneasy sense of being a rebel without a cause—all make up the swirling waves that finally swept Underhill to the crest of anthropology, when suddenly she could use her quiet Quaker culture, her rejection of Western gender roles, her willingness to live as a stranger in conditions others would consider hardship, and her love of poetry and language to help reveal the lives of American Indians. The second act of Underhill's life, becoming an anthropologist, is inseparable from the first act of her becoming Ruth Underhill.

Perhaps the single most defining aspect of Underhill's early years was the constant reminder of the limits of her gender in the Victorian age. Whether in domestic chores or in play or in family relations or in love, the unbending conventions of patriarchy were ever present. As Underhill recounts, for a girl to be exceptionally intelligent in this period was considered a curse. Her natural curiosity was contained, not cultivated; even certain salacious biblical stories were forbidden. Consider that the proxy of Vassar told Underhill that the goal of her college education was to train her to make a good home for a good man! It is little wonder that Underhill describes her own mind at age twenty-five as that "almost of an infant," so overprotected was her life. Underhill's first job interview was conducted in the company of her mother. "I went out into the world without any arts," Underhill recalls in her draft memoir.

When Underhill arrived at Columbia and discovered her life's calling, patriarchy could not be entirely shrugged off. She was surrounded mostly by young men, and the women around her were still too often treated as second-class citizens. Even Boas, who consciously promoted gender equality, practiced a paternalistic form of science in which he "gave" students different cultures to study, while fieldwork was done *for* "Papa Franz." This is why we kept in this book Underhill's long account of Henrietta Schmerler, a fellow graduate student at Columbia University, who was tragically murdered doing fieldwork in Arizona. Underhill's sympathetic version is a mirror reflecting her views on the challenges of being a woman in the field, a heuristic to compare her own failures and successes. Ultimately, these problems of patriarchy underpinned Underhill's approach to life and anthropology, which almost inexorably led her to produce her first novel, *The White Moth*, and her first ethnography, *The Autobiography of a Papago Woman*, both steeped in the tangled questions of gender and power and identity. It is entirely correct to interpret in hindsight Underhill's published works as feminist efforts that "set out to elevate a woman's struggle against patriarchal culture."*

Underhill lived as the perpetual alien, the permanent outcast. She was a stranger in her own home, even as she was at home among strangers. This experience cut both ways. Feeling a stranger to her

---

* Quote from: Lavender, Catherine J. 2006. *Scientists and Storytellers: Feminist Anthropologists and the Construction of the American Southwest*. Albuquerque: University of New Mexico Press. Pg. 103. See also: Colasurdo, Christine. 1997. "Tell Me a Woman's Story": The Question of Gender in the Construction of "Waheenee, Pretty-Shield," and "Papago Woman." *American Indian Quarterly* 21(3):385–407. Pg. 386; Visweswaran, Kamala. 1994. *Fictions of Feminist Ethnography*. Minneapolis: University of Minnesota Press. Pg. 3.

own culture liberated Underhill to break away from Victorian norms. Not fitting in led Underhill to seek refuge in books, stories, and long walks in the woods—all activities that in a sense prefigured her eventual turn to anthropology and a life of the mind. She was comfortable being in the role of the outsider in anthropology because she had felt an outsider from her first memories.* Yet feeling a foreigner at home wounded Underhill, at times filling her with guilt at not becoming, in her self-assessment, the sweet girl she was raised to be. Underhill could never quite fully embrace the life of the perpetual stranger, even as she could never play the role expected of her either. For instance, when Underhill finally decided she could marry, it would seem at last she would accept the role of housewife. But then in less than a decade she divorced—apparently the first Underhill to do so, during a period when divorces were still scandalous. All of this personal turmoil is fundamental in understanding how Underhill could so willingly become a professional stranger among the O'odham, why she was so receptive to questioning culture and listening to the lives of Native American women.

Of course, Underhill's formative years were not all bad. Her childhood summer trips to Europe exposed her to new people and ways of living. Her father encouraged Underhill to learn the languages of the countries they were visiting, a challenge Underhill vigorously accepted. She loved languages deeply, recalling in her draft memoir how as she learned her first words of Latin "worlds opened to me with those liquid sounds." Such a passion would serve Underhill well when she first worked among the O'odham and had to learn an unwritten language from scratch. Further, Underhill's Quaker background gave her an implicit methodology when she first went to the field.† She was raised to feel it was rude to ask strangers intrusive

* Underhill's inborn feelings of social distance were reframed within anthropology's participant-observer methodology: "Ruth Underhill's insights into Chona, the landscape of her narrative, and the ways of the Papago people are those of an outsider, but an outsider trained to observe carefully and interpret cautiously." This is an explanation of why she also felt so at home in anthropology. Bataille, Gretchen M., and Kathleen Mullen Sands. 1984. *American Indian Women: Telling Their Lives.* Lincoln: University of Nebraska Press. Pg. 51.

† See: Griffen, Joyce. 1989. Ruth Murray Underhill. In *Women Anthropologists: Selected Biographies.* U. Gacs, A. Khan, J. McIntyre, and R. Weinberg, eds. Pp. 355–360. Westport, CT: Greenwood Press. Pg. 355.

questions; instead, she sat quietly, patiently waiting. Small talk without direct questions would lead to friendships and comfort, and only then might more serious questions be pursued. "But mostly," Underhill wrote in her draft memoir, "I was silent and receptive and didn't ask many questions at all." Once in her fieldwork with the Tohono O'odham, Underhill asked a weighty question. Only silence followed, which Underhill was tempted to puncture. Instead, she reminisced, "I tried to sit motionless as I had been taught to do long ago in Quaker meetings."

In a sense Underhill's memoir and interviews late in her life were a kind of myth making, a search for all of the first signs of what she would later become. And yet so many of her early experiences did unquestionably prepare her for anthropology. From a young age, for instance, Underhill claimed a love for the sounds and scents of the church, the poetry of religion. In parallel, her later work among Native peoples was for Underhill a sensual experience—one of the senses as much as one of the mind. Her ability to see religion as an emotional encounter allowed her to revel in the aesthetics of Indian religion without judging its validity, as many of her peers would have done. Her open-minded interest, the early hints of scientific neutrality, appeared in Underhill even during her first job as a social worker solving lewd and lascivious cases. "I didn't quite consider whether it was wicked or not," she wrote. "It was life. That's the way people do, so why don't I get acquainted with it?"

Ever further from her family's custody, Underhill gradually became more loosened from the constraints of Victorian expectations and Quaker morality. On her travels, Underhill always wanted to live with the locals, almost as though she hoped to begin life again, to relearn life with a new set of eyes. It is significant that when she returned to New York in the 1910s, she chose to live in the home of a poor Italian family rather than in her parents' comfortable, if not opulent, home close by. Underhill enthusiastically joined the suffrage movement and during World War I, amid her countrymen's sad errand of death, threw herself into the work of the Red Cross. Independence slowly flowered, fed by her work ethic and interminable curiosity. When Underhill was forty-six years old and sat before a professor named Ruth Benedict, she at last realized the question that had plagued the first act of her life: How could she understand the human race, and, by implication, how should she understand herself? With anthropology she began to find some answers. "I was learning with all my heart, with all my attention," Underhill explains. "Every scrap of information was a prized jewel."

At the center of Underhill's life story is the enigma of why it took so long for her to finally cut loose in order to have the kind of life she wanted. "What was the matter?" Underhill the elder asks of her younger self in her draft memoir. "Why did I wait like those larvae that grow to adult size in a chrysalis while other infantile beings are on legs and moving around?" Underhill was locked in a prison of desires. "It was I who wanted things that must never be mentioned . . . I wanted violent love . . . I wanted an exciting life with all kinds of people, and that meant it must be away from home." Eventually, in her final days as she drafted her memoir and recalled her life to interviewers, Underhill came to understand that the hard-shelled chrysalis had solidified around her from her earliest days, restraining her, taming her. And when a shell is your only home, you accept it as the only kind of existence possible. Underhill could not bound out as a fully formed moth ready for flight until enough cracks in the chrysalis appeared. The chrysalis is the perfect metaphor for Underhill's life—perhaps for all our lives—the power of the unseen forces that constrain us and from which we often struggle to break free.

⌒

If there is any single reason why Underhill remains underappreciated as an anthropologist, it is likely because she held a formal faculty position for such a short period of time and so late in life.* This precluded her from being able to train graduate students who would

---

* Other factors include the broader marginalization of nearly all female researchers during this period of American anthropology and, it has been suggested, the fact that ivory tower scholars have deemed Underhill's writing more literary than anthropological. See: Parezo, Nancy J. 1993. Anthropology: The Welcoming Science. In *Hidden Scholars: Women Anthropologists and the Native American Southwest*. N. J. Parezo, ed. Pp. 3–37. Albuquerque: University of New Mexico Press. Pg. 12; Tisdale, Shelby J. 1993. Women on the Periphery of the Ivory Tower. in *Hidden Scholars: Women Anthropologists and the Native American Southwest*. N. J. Parezo, ed. Pp. 311–333. Albuquerque: University of New Mexico Press. Pg. 330; Babcock, Barbara A., and Nancy J. Parezo. 1988. *Daughters of the Desert: Women Anthropologists and the Native American Southwest, 1880–1980*. Albuquerque: University of New Mexico Press.

then advance her research and remember her successes. As Underhill herself acknowledged in an interview, "I didn't achieve status at all because I didn't take a teaching job and have students who would be my charioteers and talk about what I'd done and advertise me to the world."*

While true, this is only part of the story. It is unclear how Underhill could have become the anthropologist she did become if her life had taken another route. If Underhill had taken a more traditional path—from college to graduate school to academic post—she would not have developed into the self-confident poet and sympathetic friend that later gave her a strong foundation for her anthropological work. Underhill was a talented anthropologist *because* she was a world traveler who experienced so much early in life, *because* she worked as a social worker before entering graduate school, *because* she started her formal training so late in life, *because* she worked in applied anthropological contexts for more than a decade. Her upbringing and her ultimate role in the field are what made Ruth M. Underhill the gifted anthropologist she became.

We are not Underhill's students appointed to sing her praises. But as two of the stewards appointed to help care for Underhill's final papers, we see this volume as an important way of rejuvenating a conversation about Underhill's fabled life. It is also a contribution to the vibrant dialogue about anthropology's history and earliest progenitors, particularly in the American Southwest.†

---

* Underhill concedes she was never considered one of anthropology's superstars, although her name has had impressive endurance through the years. In some ways, Underhill is a sort of one-hit wonder. Her first major anthropological book—*The Autobiography of a Papago Woman*—was also her most significant and not fully matched again by later efforts. Indeed, *The Autobiography* is a staple of introductory courses today, the first ethnography many students read, even as they are unlikely to study her other work. However, the reasons why Underhill was not able to gain a stronger academic foothold—her gender, her age—are part of what makes her story so compelling. Also, her views on anthropology from the middle range of scholastic stardom provide an important perspective from which to contemplate the formation of twentieth-century American anthropology.

† This work contributes to the recent wave of critical biographies on early southwestern anthropologists (for example: Bostwick, Todd W. 2006. *Byron Cummings: Dean of Southwest Archaeology*. Tucson: University of Arizona Press; Miller, Darlis A. 2007. *Matilda Coxe Stevenson: Pioneering Anthropologist*. Norman: University of Oklahoma Press; Norcini, Marilyn. 2007. *Edward P. Dozier: The Paradox of the American Indian*

This volume is our amalgamation of three rich resources in the Ruth M. Underhill Collection. The first is her incomplete and unpublished memoir. This undated series of documents, which we believe was written in the 1970s, contains deeply personal reflections on influential events in Underhill's life, especially the impact of her family members, social work, and World War I. Shorter sections cover her graduate work at Columbia during the Great Depression and her extensive world travels. The Underhill memoir is deeply personal and at times painful to read, particularly as we see Underhill's struggle to receive notice, much less appreciation, from her mother. Underhill writes with such keen insight, visceral wit, and ultimately redemptive introspection that we begin to understand how all of these challenges drove her to become a successful anthropologist.

The second resource out of which this volume is built consists of thirty-three transcripts of oral histories, interviews, and public lectures recorded in the late 1970s and early 1980s. The transcripts include an honoring ceremony at which she spoke and a radio interview in 1980, a lecture in 1981, and a 1982 interview by Vivian Juan Saunders, a Tohono O'odham tribal member and then Miss Indian America.* The rest of the interviews—the bulk of the transcripts—were conducted by Joyce Herold, Dave Baysinger, Arminta "Skip" Neal, Kris Haglund, and Steve Rich. Although all of these DMNS staff members contributed, most were conducted by Joyce Herold, who between July 1979 and June 1981 industriously extracted a stockpile of vignettes that covered Underhill's entire life. Underhill herself edited and corrected the transcripts into 1983.

Anthropologist. Tucson: University of Arizona Press). But as a reflective autobiography our edited book works more as a contribution to the memoir genre (for example: Hayden, Julian D., Bill Broyles, and Diane E. Boyer. 2010. *Field Man: Life as a Desert Archaeologist*. Tucson: University of Arizona Press; Judd, Neil Merton. 1968. *Men Met Along the Trail: Adventures in Archaeology*. Norman: University of Oklahoma Press). We decided to publish this work as a memoir because of our deep desire for Underhill's own voice to come through—to publish a humanistic chronicle of Underhill's life, not a theoretical tract deconstructing anthropological history. Furthermore, our edited autobiography does not preclude other scholars from writing a critical biography—indeed, we hope our book will inspire such a project and lead to further mining of Underhill's eighty-five linear feet of documents at DMNS.

* Vivian Juan Saunders would go on to become the first woman to be elected leader of the Tohono O'odham Nation, serving as chairwoman from 2003 to 2007.

Figure 4. Vivian Juan Saunders, Miss Indian America, interviews Ruth, 1982.

The third resource around which this volume is built is the more than three thousand photographs, most of them previously unpublished, in the Underhill collection. The cliché "A picture says a thousand words" holds true here, and a volume such as this would simply not be as absorbing without extensive illustrations, both as visual documentation and to establish context for the prose.

Our work as editors was to combine these mixed sources of materials into a complete whole. Many months of effort were focused on combining the drafted memoir and the interviews, which varied in tone and substance, were frequently repetitious or differed in minute ways, and often needed grammatical adjustments and references to provide the reader more context.* Among these sources, Underhill

---

* We do not feel that whether the original source was from Underhill's draft memoir or from her interviews was important enough to distinguish in this book because the two sources are so complementary. Where there are relevant differences, these are discussed in footnotes. Furthermore, researchers who want to read Underhill's unedited texts can find the originals in the DMNS Bailey Library and Archives.

often told the same story two or three times, but impressively, the stories typically varied only a little. It was as if Underhill had absorbed certain stories so completely into her consciousness she could tell them verbatim over and over, even to her final days. Given Underhill's age when she wrote her memoir and made her recordings, there are surprisingly few gaps and contradictions. Most of the confusion of dates and timing of events are in the 1910s, when Underhill was in her late twenties and early thirties. Where there are conflicts between sources, we have tended to trust documentary evidence or, in its absence, her draft memoir, which was seemingly written when Underhill was in her early nineties and came directly from her typewriter. We have also worked to locate the sources of Underhill's many biblical and classical references—a kind of borrowing from the Western canon of mythology to write the myth of her own life—which will be unfamiliar to most twenty-first century readers. We also sought biographical references to the scholars Underhill discusses—references that provide a virtual who's who of twentieth-century anthropology and also subtly emphasize Underhill's true cross-disciplinary training.

The editing thus often involved threading different versions of the same episodes into one story—taking a phrase here and a phrase there, like quilting, drawing from many patches of cloth to construct a whole piece. In a peculiar parallel, we have done with Underhill's autobiography what she herself did to produce her classic volume, *The Autobiography of a Papago Woman*. Underhill could have been speaking about herself, projecting half a century into the future, when she wrote about Chona, "The story of her past was her constant preoccupation, and snatches of it were narrated at every opportunity. . . . Chona is ninety years old and her memory works with the fitfulness of age, presenting incidents in repetitious confusion." * Like Underhill's strategy to navigate Chona's memories, we found that "the only possible system was to write each one separately, add to it all the amendments which occurred to her . . . until the correct order was

---

* Underhill, Ruth M. 1985. *Papago Woman*. Originally published 1936. Prospect Heights, IL: Waveland Press. Pgs. 32–33 for all quotes in this paragraph. See also: Staub, Michael E. 1994. *Voices of Persuasion: Politics of Representation in 1930s America*. Cambridge: University of Cambridge Press. Pg. 71.

worked out." Underhill insists that if she had simply written down everything Chona said, the result would not have been compelling for the reader. The same goes with Underhill's autobiography.* And yet like Underhill, when she wrote of Chona, we "felt most deeply the objections to distorting" the narrative provided to us. Despite our grammatical, lexical, and organizational quilting work, the ultimate product is Underhill's words.

The amalgamation of these complementary assets—the written memoir, oral histories, and photographs—have allowed us to produce a single volume that we believe tells the story, in Underhill's own voice, of the making of an anthropologist. This volume is just the proverbial scratch on the surface of a life of great profundity. We hope this book invites other scholars and the public to come to the Denver Museum of Nature & Science to plumb the depths of Underhill's life as told through her archive, to gain a better understanding of one woman's journey through the twentieth century and the history of anthropology.

---

* Since not all find Underhill's original argument about this method convincing, perhaps we are mistaken for adopting it. But we would suggest the quality of readability should rival the quality of authenticity in any book—because, after all, books must be read to be understood. And, in any case, no narrative is purely authentic, since all narratives must be constructed. Even "authentic" texts are selective, edited. See: Colasurdo, Christine. 1997. "Tell Me a Woman's Story": The Question of Gender in the Construction of "Waheenee, Pretty-Shield," and "Papago Woman." *American Indian Quarterly* 21(3):385–407. Pg. 398; Sands, Kathleen Mullen. 1997. Collaboration or Colonialism: Text and Process in Native American Women's Autobiographies. *MELUS* 22(4):39–59. Pg. 40; Clifford, James, and George E. Marcus. Editors. 1986. *Writing Culture: The Poetics and Politics of Ethnography.* Berkeley: University of California Press; Hegeman, Susan. 1989. Native American "Texts" and the Problem of Authenticity. *American Quarterly* 41(2):265–283.

PART ONE

~

Becoming
Ruth Underhill

A Zigzag Life

WE WERE EATING ROASTED CATERPILLAR, the succulent, furry kind. The fur, of course, had been singed off the instant the wriggling bodies skewered on a stick had been held over the embers of the outdoor fire. What remained looked like portions of pretzels, though more ridged and slimy. You could swallow it almost without tasting, as I used to do with the raw oysters that were the expensive delicacy of my girlhood.

"Do you like it?" asked the father of the family.

Literally, his words should be translated, "Is it to you good?" for the O'odham Indian language has no exact word for *like*.

"It is good." I nodded vigorously while managing to swallow a bit of pretzel without chewing.

I would have said the same of rat flesh, dog flesh—not my dog, of course—and I don't know what else. For this was my first summer in southern Arizona on an anthropological field trip. It formed a station on a bridge that still felt rather high and uncertain. This bridge connected my girlhood in a conventional suburb of New York City with a life among American Indians where my only permanent home was an old Ford car. The girlhood end of that bridge is, to my young friends of today, almost unbelievable.

"You drove a chestnut horse? And called your boyfriends 'Mister'? And your mother went with you to dances?"

The young people who ask that might be trying to envisage the period of the French and Indian War. But it was only the years around 1900.

Yes, how American life has changed! Then again I changed, and often. For I did not start, like you lucky ones, with a career and a goal in mind, not even the goal of marriage, for nice girls did not know whether they would be asked or not. No, I pushed out blindly like a mole burrowing from instinct. My burrowings took me to strange

27

places, and now, in my last hole, I am trying to remember how I bumbled and tumbled from one spot to another.

This is the story for those friends who wonder how I could even have started the bumbling, for many girls of my era did not. I can't say that dates or even events will be exactly accurate. If a picture is not true, at least it's the way I remember it, and psychologists say there is a truth in that, too.

⁓

Those early worlds look, today, like pure myth and a grotesque myth, at that. Quite frankly, my young friends cannot believe that people lived in such surroundings and had such thoughts. Harder is it for them to conceive that relics of such thoughts and feelings are alive today.

"But you're not a fossil," they sometimes admit, after acquaintance. "Then how did you make the change? How could anyone?"

This personal narrative is meant to explain, as far as any explanation is possible, how I made the change, bumbling from one hole to another—Quaker girl to New York tenements to Spanish vineyards to college classrooms (at the age of forty-six) until I erupted on the surface with a study of Indians.*

⁓

This is not a success story. Not, at least, in the typical sense. Recently I have been reading autobiographies, and they have told me of women born about when I was and in similar circumstances who moved in a straight line to achievement. I did no such thing. My course was a zigzag one, with stops and reversals. Perhaps my life's very failures would be interesting to a nonheroic reader. Yet perhaps the main thing I have to give is a description of my particular times and place. Their like is almost unknown since World War II. Perhaps those interested in looking, either for understanding history or for writing fiction, may be glad to get the flavor of one village on the Hudson, one family of Quaker tradition, one woman who made a life for herself, these being of course just a little different from those of any other village, family, or person.

----

* The Religious Society of Friends, also known as Quakers, is a Protestant Christian movement founded in the seventeenth century. Tides of Quaker migrants from Europe, Underhill's ancestors among them, settled numerous colonies in New England.

Do Good to Others

"BE A SWEET GIRL," is what they told me. "If you are sweet, if you love your family and do good to others, then, at the proper time, He will come, with all the virtues that a husband should have—and, of course, good looks and good manners too. Don't be impatient and seem to want Him, for only vulgar people do that. While you are waiting, you can occupy yourself with good works and with improving your mind."

Something went wrong between me and this future. I did wait. I did improve my mind, but I did not make the status of a sweet girl. Then why not give it up early in the procedure, break from my cell with a hell of a yell, and start the career that, actually, I began only in middle life?

That part, I cannot explain. Around me, I see colleagues who began careers when I did, only they were in their twenties, while I was over forty. Now, when I am retiring, they are at their peak and I note, with a twinge like the nastiest indigestion, that I must accept this. Oh Time, unlock the vault that contains my dormant years! You can't? Then at least tell me why they were dormant. Why did I not give up the attempt at sweet girlishness and get out? Comforters tell me I was born in an age when that was not done, but wasn't I born with a brain? Couldn't I have *seen*?

Time won't even answer that question without some work on my part. On the following pages, I plunge into that work.

❧

"Elsie," I called excitedly. "See if you can kick your fat!" I must have been six at the time. With a neighbor child, I was running down the grassy hill beside our house at the top of the village. It seemed to me an interesting athletic feat to raise my fat little legs high enough to smack my buttocks, but my exhilaration came against a cold, granite barrier.

Figure 5. Portrait of Ruth Underhill (left) and possibly her sister Margaret in front of their childhood home in Ossining-on-the-Hudson, New York, circa 1890.

My parents were sitting on the porch. "Piazza," we called it in those days, with the *z*'s pronounced in the American way, not the Italian.

"Ruth," said Papa, "don't say that!"

"Say what?" I was as dumbfounded as the kitten I have now is when I roar at him to get off the table, where he can see meat just like that which I gave him on the floor a few minutes ago. He does not mistake the roar. He jumps down and sits drooping. I drooped too, for no one ever disregarded Papa's commands. I stood by the piazza steps, pulling down the pink gingham skirt that I had rumpled around my waist. Papa and Mama were both sitting there in rocking chairs, as they did almost every evening. I looked at Mama for some consolation, though of course I knew she would not go against Papa.

Mama's face looked very much as I have once or twice seen my own in the mirror when I happened to part my black hair and my gray eyes looked serious, but I do hope I have never drawn my features into that gently pitying expression that Mama so often turned on me.

"We don't talk like that about our bodies, dear."

Should I ever dare to use the word *fat* again? I sarcastically thought but didn't ask. I was being invaded by a misery and shame so deep that I thought I might never run down that hill again.

"I don't want to play anymore," I told Elsie abruptly. She began to propose other games, but I turned my back on her. When Mama began to pull down my pink dress, I jerked away. I never did run down that hill again.

Papa was not really terrible. We called him "Papa" in those early days, though later the style changed to "Father." He was a tall, slender man. When Mama told me that he weighed 150 pounds, I thought how tremendous that was. In those days, I seem not to have noticed the piercing gray-blue eyes that impressed his clients and, later, impressed me too. What I remember is the short, soft beard that encased his chin as soft fur encases a cat's rump. Kissing him was as pleasant as rubbing against a velvety pincushion. He kissed all us children on holidays or when he came home from trips, and he told jokes at the supper table at which we always laughed much sooner than Mama did.

Father was a power always looming over my life, but in the God manner, distant and inscrutable. Mother told me once, in a sudden confidence, that these were the years when Father was "making his way." For an almost penniless Underhill, just off the farm, that way must already have been a pretty long one.* Now I pictured it a handsome avenue, with stone bridges and leading to a mansion or maybe a great big bank building. I wished I could walk along it a little way with him, but he was much too busy. It was understood

---

* In a few sections of the draft memoir Underhill wrote, she assigned fictitious names to her family members. Underhill becomes "Bostwick," and Murray becomes "Routledge." She also gave false names for herself (Susan), her father (Jonathan), her sisters (Lillian or Celia, and Violet), the house's butler (Tom Riley), and so forth. Our presumption is that Underhill was considering publishing her autobiography anonymously or for some other reason wanted to mask the names of her family members. We do believe that, although the names were fictionalized, these are factual stories, since they perfectly match with the narratives Underhill told at other times; the genealogy is entirely consistent with her own; and these sections with the fictionalized names easily fit with the sections Underhill wrote in which she used her family members' real names. For consistency, here Underhill's fictionalized names have been changed to her family's real names.

Figure 6. Abram Underhill, circa 1880.

that he would take my brother Robert along that avenue as soon as
the son of the family was big enough, but not us girls.

We all knew that Papa ruled the house as God ruled heaven. Dan
Tierney, who looked after the horse and surrey, Nana, who helped
with the sewing, and whatever Swedish girl was in the kitchen—
they practically saluted when they spoke to him. Dan called him
"Your Honor."

Mama spoke of him as "the Dear Man." She made us realize that
there had never been any wisdom or any power like those of the
Dear Man. The half hour before six o'clock when he was due home
from the office was a period of almost religious expectancy, when
we children were all washed, in clean dresses, not playing or even
talking much while we waited. Papa would come swinging up the

steps that led from the sidewalk to the lawn, then from the lawn to the piazza. Papa always walked to his office on Tuesday, Thursday, and Saturday, to the station for the commuter's train for New York City on Monday, Wednesday, and Friday. He did the same up to two weeks before his death at almost ninety years of age.

❧

Every day, always we had breakfast at seven o'clock. We all appeared at the big dining room table. There were four children in my youth whom I'm remembering, I being the oldest, and my pretty sister Margaret, a year and a half younger than I, then the lone male inheritor, Robert, and finally the baby sister, Elizabeth.*

We all sat around the table. We had oatmeal with cream, muffins, cornbread, sausages—oh, I can't remember what else. Father had fried eggs. Mother had her soft-boiled eggs in a little cup where you knocked off the top. She said that was the way they had done it in Scotland, from which her family ultimately came. If you broke your egg and ate it in that way, it was "a messy modern method."

After breakfast, everybody had work to do. Of course, we little girls were supposed to wash the dishes. We always had a Swedish maid, but she had all the heavy work to do. We learned to sing hymns while washing dishes, and I can sing those songs still. Then we made our own beds and dusted. That was proper for young ladies to do. Of course, it was all right for me to learn to make cake. That I ought to do; any young lady ought to. So I spent some time in the kitchen with a great big yellow mixing bowl.

---

* Quite mysteriously, two obscure historical documents suggest that Underhill had an older sister, Helen E. Underhill, born on February 5, 1880 (Birth of Members, Chappaqua Monthly Meeting, Westchester County, New York, from 1719; Nicholson, F. W. 1883. *Alumni Record of Wesleyan University, Middletown, Conn., Volumes 1881–1883*. Third edition. Harford, CT: Press of the Case, Lockwood, & Brainard. Pg. 35). Our hunch is that Helen Underhill died in infancy or childhood and thus would be a difficult memory for the family, her name best left out of conversations. While most genealogy websites do not include Helen as Ruth's sibling, we did find two that give Helen's death well into adulthood, in 1935 or 1974. The only other hint we found—small though it is—is the sentence from Underhill's draft memoir, "Poor Mother! She had borne four females . . ." We had initially assumed this was a typo, but the documents and websites cited above suggest otherwise.

Mother Was an Angel, Part 1

MOTHER WAS AN ANGEL. I had learned that fact, I believe, about the time I was taught how to use a spoon and that you blow your nose on a handkerchief. Then I was told at regular intervals by the seamstress who came twice a year to make our clothes and also by ladies on the street. This was usually after they had remarked that I wasn't a bit like her. Oh, I knew I wasn't. I did not have soft, light brown hair that parted in waves over my forehead or blue eyes like gentians or small hands and feet. Why does God do these things to his creatures! I really needed small hands and feet, what with my lank black hair and big mouth, but it was Margaret who got them.

Margaret, my sister, was only two years younger. Yet somehow the ability to be an angel had come to her magically, as such things did to princesses in fairy tales. When ladies patted Margaret's head and said, "How like your mother," she could smile at them and did not have to think of anything to say. "Angels don't have to," I used to tell myself, after I had jerked my own head away and admitted I was not an angel but only Ruth.

"Not quite like anyone in the family, is she?" a lady once commented about me. In my heart I hoped I was like Father, whose hair was black, too. Or even his sister, the Latin teacher. Mother, it seemed, did not think of that. She only shook her head with her lovely, gentle air and mourned like a dove, "Not like my family, the Murrays."

Naturally I wanted to be an angel. As far as I knew, it was the only career open to a female in a suburban town in the 1890s. Yet I could not have been more than five when it was revealed to me that I was practically impossible material, like the outer cabbage leaves or the tough, dirty ends of carrots that Mother always cut off and threw away.

"Of course, you can be a sweet good girl, Ruth," Mother used to say rather plaintively after some remark of mine had shown me as destined for the garbage can. "Ask God to help you."

Figure 7. Ruth (right) and likely her sister Margaret as children, circa 1890.

Well, I did, every night, kneeling by the white iron bed in my blue-and-white-checked flannel nightgown. Golden-haired Margaret knelt beside me and pushed my foot with her little pink one when I wriggled in a desperate effort to be eloquent. "God, make me a good girl! *Please* make me a good girl!"

It was my impression that, if the prayer were effective, my straight black hair would begin to turn golden, like Margaret's. When I opened my mouth, sweet gurgling words would come from it, as pearls did with that princess in the fairy tale. Instead, there were remarks that nearly turned my elders to stone. That happened one day in kindergarten. We were playing Birdie in the Greenwood. In the course of it, each little girl took a little boy by both hands. They knelt facing each other and sang, "Birdie in the greenwood, builds himself a nest." My partner was fat little Jack Archer, whom I had to pull and push around, as I did with most boys in the class. They never paid attention to what Teacher said. We bent our heads till they touched as Birdie went to sleep, and I said in my usual hearty voice, "Now we ought to kiss, Jack, because that's what big people do when they go to bed and . . ."

"Ruth!"

Teacher was turning to stone. All but her voice, and that ran an ice-cold knife through me. I had been kissing dolls and kittens, but there was a difference I ought to have known about. I could not imagine what it was, but I pushed Jack till he tumbled over. Teacher whispered to Mother about it. I would not play Birdie after that.

Grown-ups were always whispering—Teacher to Mother, Mother to Father. I ceased to pay much attention because, by six, I had learned to read. I had nice books, given me by Grandma Murray, about Bible heroes, but they were funny looking with their large print. I much preferred to prowl among the big books, lying sidewise on the bottom shelf of the parlor bookcase. There was one about the Ancient Mariner; its pictures were wild and exciting as when you first lit the kerosene lamp and it flared up high. I used to say over and over to myself:

> The sun came up upon the left
> Out of the sea came he*

Once Mother heard me, and I thought that would remind her about the big book with gold letters on the cover. Maybe it was a magic book that no one could see but me, because she only said, "Oh, are you making rhymes, dear? That's nice, but you had better say 'east.' Then it will help you remember your geography."

That night, before supper, she whispered to Father. Father looked over his paper at me, his gray eyes very bright over his neat black beard.

"Do you write down the rhymes you make, Ruth?" he asked.

"I-I don't make rhymes."

"Shush," Mother said to Father. "Don't force her."

---

* From Samuel Taylor Coleridge's 1798 poem "Rime of the Ancient Mariner."

Figure 8. Portrait of Anna Murray Underhill, Ruth's mother, circa 1880.

Father went behind the paper again. "I hoped there'd be some special talent. It would make up for . . ." They both stopped talking.

This may sound as though I was unhappy, but I was not. Our house was comfortable. Our dining room always smelled pleasantly of muffins and steak and corn pudding. Outside there was a grape arbor, with big leaves you could make into hats for dolls. You walked through it in the morning, carrying the "vessel" out to the backhouse. (I think "privy" is a modern, intellectual word.) In the afternoon, you sat in the arbor telling fairy stories while a little breeze made the leaves move up and down. In the evening, the whole family sat on the porch. Margaret and I played jack stones on the steps. Father had his paper. Mother held Robert, the baby, and sang to him.

Robert had come when I was seven years old, and from that time our family life changed gears. Now we all waited on the baby, held him when he cried, and even stayed home from school to care for him if

Mother had to be out. Robert cried a lot, even when he got past the red-faced, kicking stage. He would yell for what he wanted and slap us if we got in his way. It seemed plain to me that he would never make the angel class, but that did not matter. He was the first male child.

You could tell by the way Mother spoke of him to visitors how set apart he was and how wonderful. He had been christened Robert Lindley Murray Underhill, after Mother's sire, with the Underhill tacked on. It was understood that he was heir to the grandeur of the Murrays, but also he was going to be brilliant like Father and his sister. I never questioned this idea, for it looked to me as if it came into the world with Robert, trailing in clouds of glory.* Mother took it for granted and often told us about it. Poor Mother! She had borne four females, two who did not live, before she achieved this male child.[†] I guess it was natural that he seemed to her almost holy.

Robert had another claim to supremacy, and that was a poor digestion. I envied that high road to Mother's attention as I am told some women envy other people's diamonds. No, I was not bitter. That would be hard for a healthy child who had plenty of food and fresh air, but when I got tired of asking God to make me a good girl, since that seemed to be something He wasn't considering, I would add a whispered postscript, "And let me be sick for a little while. Anything you say. Just so Mother will be telling Father about *me* at night, instead of always about Robert."

❧

I was eight when Elsie came to live across the street.[‡] Mother had often raised her eyebrows about the house over there, smaller than the others and painted yellow. She raised them higher on a Sunday afternoon when a red-haired girl came out of that house and raced

---

* A reference to William Wordsworth's 1804 poem "Ode: Intimations of Immortality from Recollections of Early Childhood."

† See the previous note about the fourth female being Helen Underhill, about whom almost nothing is known.

‡ Underhill noted a few pages prior that she and Elsie played together when she was six. It is possible that they first played together when Underhill was six, and then Elsie moved across the street when Underhill was eight. Or Underhill has one, or both, ages wrong. Whatever the case may be, it is clear she and Elsie were fast friends during their early elementary school years.

down the street toward the lamppost. She had on a red dress, which was flying up to show her garters. She was leading two others and yelling, "Last one there is a rotten egg!"

"They're Cat-Licks," breathed Margaret. "Mrs. Lowry down the street says so."

"Children," said Mother portentously, "it doesn't matter if they're Catholics, what church people go to. They are trying to be good, and that's all we should think of. But that new family is—is not our kind of people. I had rather you kept away from them."

Those words were echoing in my head like the far heard whisper o'er the sea that scared the Ancient Mariner when Elsie caught up with me next day on the way home from school. Elsie did not go to Miss Cornelia's but to the public school across the tracks. It was surprising to me that its pupils should come out at the same time as we did, for I had imagined it as a sort of workhouse, perhaps with prison rules.

"Want to play jacks this afternoon?" asked Elsie.

No one had ever asked me before. The few girls my age at Miss Cornelia's all lived too far away. I tried to remember whether Mother was at home, whether I could invite . . .

"At my house," said Elsie, "we've got pink ice cream."

"I . . . I . . ."

"In the backyard, there's a big flagstone."

I had never been in the backyard of that house. The unknown was enticing me.

"Will your mother mind?"

Mother was away, I now remembered. At a church committee meeting. Anna, our Swedish "girl," was taking care of Robert. If I came in, he might call for me to tell him stories, but if I went with Elsie right now . . .

"Mother's out," I said, in a social lady tone.

Elsie winked. "Then that's all right. Last one there is a rotten egg!" She raced for her back door and I after her. It was glorious. We played jacks. We ate ice cream. Then we sat with our arms around each other and talked.

That was the turning of a life page for me. Elsie was better than I at jacks, rolling hoops, and croquet, but she was no good at stories, and she would listen when I told them. Really listen. She did not say,

like Robert, "Oh, I don't like that princess. Don't tell about her."
She listened with bulging eyes. (Elsie's eyes were prominent, not
like either a Murray or an Underhill.) She never asked any questions
except, "What next?" She made no comments but, "Oh my! Oh my!"

I used to come home from her house as inspired as I think poets
must have been by their muses. I knew about that by this time.
Mother disapproved. She and Father whispered a lot when we heard
that Elsie's father *drank.* Yet I was not strictly forbidden to play with
her. Perhaps Mother thought that could not be managed. Perhaps
she was too much taken up with Robert and his stomach. Anyhow,
the days bloomed gloriously. I had a friend.

◢

Elsie and I were walking home from school. Elsie didn't go to the
white mansion surrounded by its spacious lawns where Miss Cornelia
reigned over us nice girls. I accepted the fact that Elsie was never
invited to our house. Since I was bright—oh, how I wished God had
not cursed me with that dreadful abnormality!—I was always in a class
with girls older than myself. They talked over my head about boys,
and they had jokes. Not for the world would I have showed them
I did not understand and felt inferior. Still, it was a relief to talk to
Elsie, from whom I need hide nothing.

"And they grow inside of ladies," Elsie instructed.

"Babies do?!"

"Honest they do, and you can see the lady get big. It's awful."

"But where do they come out?"

"We're not supposed to know," said Elsie, in awful tones, "and I
don't yet. But the reason I'm telling you is—your Mother."

"My Mother! She's going to have a baby?"

"Honest. Cross my heart. Don't you see how big she is?"

"Yes, but," I countered desperately, "people get fat."

"Not *there.* I mean it's her stomach, kind of."

I pictured my mother's silhouette. Yes, I had noticed how strangely
her apron stuck out.

"Do the ladies know it?" I faltered.

"My mamma did. She told my papa."

"Could they stop it?"

"They can't stop it," said Elsie, in a voice of doom. "It comes."

The stupendous nature of this fact had not yet been born in me. In my reading, I was accustomed to skipping the parts hard to understand, like Sir Walter Scott's footnotes about Gaelic and some of those conversations between men and women where there was no kissing.*

"But what makes it come?"

"Well," said Elsie, "you have to have a marriage 'tificate."

I fell to pondering. "It's queer that a piece of paper could do all that. How do you suppose . . ."

"It's one of the things we ought not to know," said Elsie. "Not till we get married ourselves."

"But suppose we don't?"

Elsie stared, and now it was my turn to elucidate a mystery. "My aunt told me this. She said all little girls don't get to be mothers."

"But what happens? Do they get," Elsie goggled, "get poisoned or something?"

"They don't get married," I said sepulchrally. Then I dared to add the awful thing that had been revealed to me. "Men don't want them."

"But why not?"

Now we were getting close to a secret of my own, something that Auntie had allowed herself to tell me on a summer afternoon when I had been sent to her house because the doctor was at ours. Yes, the doctor had been coming regularly, and just as regularly, Mother had said, with a remote smile that I always thought the model for the Blessed Damozel, "The others are too little, but I think Ruth had better go to Auntie's."† So Auntie and I had shelled peas, while she told me some wonderful stories about Rome. There was that one about Cornelia and her jewels, and when I murmured ecstatically that I would plan to have sons like that, Auntie had come out with the awful truth.‡

---

* Sir Walter Scott (1771–1832) was a well-known Scottish historical novelist and playwright.

† The Blessed Damozel is the subject of an eponymous 1850 poem by Dante Gabriel Rossetti (1828–1882) in which a deceased, unmarried young woman (Damozel) watches her lover from heaven, yearning for a blissful reunion that will never come.

‡ Cornelia Scipionis Africana (ca. 190 BC–100 BC) is remembered as embodying the ideal of a virtuous woman of ancient Rome. A story, likely apocryphal, has Cornelia answering people who asked her why she dressed so simply by pointing to her sons and saying, "These are my jewels."

"It may be that you are one of the people who will not marry, Ruth," she said, and I thought I had never heard her use my name so caressingly. "It seems to me better to tell you about it, so that you will know how many other things there are that you can do."

"Like go into a convent?" I inquired.

"We are Protestants, dear."

The shame of having no husband was something I felt ill able to bear, and at twelve years old.

"It is better not to think of boys, Ruth dear. They are often nasty. A girl can lead a much cleaner life if she is interested in books and in doing good."

Of course I knew that I must do good. Whipping up an interest in that activity was one of the ordeals of my life; if, in private, the idea had no charm, at least I could recite it in public. "Oh yes, Auntie," I averred. "I will live to do good."

"That's my fine girl," said Auntie. Never before had she patted my head. When she actually did so now, I almost melted with bliss.

"I guess I'd rather not get married," I said firmly.

It seemed I had found a key to life's management. But later that evening, I was rather dashed when I made my proclamation at the supper table.

"Not get married!" Father's grey eyes shot lightning at me from out of the black beard.

"Well, it's, it's . . ." I stumbled.

"The child is too young to know what she's saying," said Mother, in that tone that brought the pang of indigestion. Robert began to chant, "Won't get married! Won't get married! Old maid Ruthie!"

Good gracious! I had not realized that the noble situation described by Auntie really added up to being an old maid. "I guess I didn't know what I was saying," I faltered.

"Well, dear," said Mother, with her ineffable smile, "you wait till Mr. Right comes along. Then we'll see."

"Might be better if not," said Father, with another sharp glance.

Mother never allowed Father to be on the opposite side of a question from her, and immediately she hastened to him. "I want you to know, Ruth—and you too, of course, Margaret darling—that if you do not marry, your family will always be glad to take care of you."

Somehow, my fate seemed to have been decided over my head, for naturally I did not take seriously that inclusion of Margaret. I continued eating my salmon croquettes in a sort of gruesome exaltation. No one would want me, but that was an honorable state. At least I could be pure and good.

I thought Mother was especially sweet when she kissed me goodnight. It was as if she, too, thought I could dedicate my life to this task.

～

A month later, the baby came. For that month, there was a fat woman in the house, Mrs. McBird. Mother spent most of the time in her room, and we hardly ever saw her except when we came in to kiss her good morning and goodnight. Then she gazed at us with swimming eyes that made a lump come in my throat, but those eyes changed to pieces of a cement sidewalk when she saw the badge I was wearing. It was a bit of black tape, fringed at one end and embroidered with the letter *B*.

"Why dear?" said Mother, "Is that something you have at school?"

"N-no."

"You didn't get it because of your lessons?"

Ah, but she could see how homemade it was.

"It's, it's a club."

"And who is in the club, Ruth?"

"Elsie." The eyes were already clouding over. "Elsie and me, and Francine says she wants to, but I have to decide. You see, I have to be president."

"You had better tell Mother what the club is, dear," said an icy voice. "Mother is always interested."

I began to weep. When I embroidered my badge with *B*, I had felt that I was penetrating into life's innermost mysteries. It was like entering that cave in the story where She, the eternal, had her fount of life.* I felt almost as the Daughters of Men must have when the Sons of God came down to them.† But Mother was gazing at me with an expression that made me want to bite the dust.

---

* A reference to the serialized 1886–1887 story *She* by Sir Henry Rider Haggard (1856–1925), in which the heroine "She" is the goddess Ayesha, who discovers eternal life in a mysterious underground cave.

† Genesis 6:1–4.

Figure 9. Ruth's brother, Robert (right), and likely her sister Elizabeth (left) as young children, circa 1895.

"You must tell Mother what *B* stands for, Ruth."

"Baby," I wept. "B-b-baby. We thought . . ."

"Dear," said Mother, in a voice like the prophet saying, "Comfort ye, comfort my people."* She continued, "We don't talk about those things. I would have told you at the right time. Little girls who think about things like that have nasty minds. I wish dear, oh how I wish, that you would not play with Elsie anymore."

"Oh, I won't! I won't, Mother! She's awful!"

---

* Isaiah 40:1.

Suddenly the cave of She had turned into a den of demons. I wanted to be out of it into the beautiful, good sunlight.

"What can I do to help, Mother?" I sobbed.

"You can amuse Robert and maybe read to him. The little boy gets very lonely."

So it was at this time that Robert and I really came to know each other. I found that he actually liked the books I did, like the *Lays of Ancient Rome.** Oh, what fun it was, playing Horatio at the Bridge!†
Of course, Robert was Horatio and I only one of the helpers, but I had expected that, being a girl. Margaret sat and watched us, for she was still delicate and forbidden all violent action. "We are so blessed to have her with us," Mother used to say when warning me of this. Margaret was the crowd beside the Tiber, though really doing nothing but sitting on a cushion brought from the house with blue dimity skirts spread around her. Meanwhile, Robert and I threw the army of Clusium down from the top of the grape arbor when Mrs. McBird came out of the house.

"It's a girl," Mrs. McBird announced.

For a minute, neither of us realized what she was talking about.

"You have a darling baby sister. Named Elizabeth."

"Another girl!" griped Robert.

"Oh, how sweet!" cried Margaret, who always said the right thing.

"Is she pretty?" I asked.

"It's too soon to know that, Miss Ruth, but I'm sure she'll be very lovely, since she is your mother's daughter."

---

* Published in 1842, the *Lays of Ancient Rome* is a collection of four narrative poems by Thomas Babington Macaulay (1800–1859) that describe semimythical heroic episodes in Roman history.

† In the late sixth century BC, Horatio and his forces destroyed the Sublican Bridge over the Tiber River in order to strand King Clusium's Etruscan army on the opposite side, thereby saving Rome.

They Were Murrays

IT WAS EASTER SUNDAY, and Margaret and I were walking to Sunday school. I was twelve now. Mother always put Margaret's hand in mine as we left the door and said, "Now take care of your little sister. You are the oldest." Robert did not have to go to Sunday school, even though he would have been old enough for the infant class. Mother said that a boy must not be forced, or it would break his spirit. She reminded us how Grandmother Murray, a magnificent old lady inhabiting a brownstone house in New York, had never forced her sons. One committed suicide later, I remember, and one died after his company had gone bankrupt. That had not happened yet, however, and we looked upon Murray uncles as kinds of demigods. They were *Murrays*.

Margaret and I felt wonderful in our new dresses of pink challis, dotted with little blue flowers. I had thought of a pink coat to match, but Mother said *we* did not wear such loud things. So we had tan coats and straw hats with wreaths of tiny pink flowers. *We* did not wear big flowers either. The church was half a mile away, down streets where houses with cupolas stood on big lawns, behind rows of elm trees. We never thought of riding to church, even though we had a surrey and a coachman. All coachmen had the day off on Sunday, and people did not think it reverent to rattle up to the house of God on wheels. So there was no danger for two little girls in crossing the elm-shaded streets. The few buggies and carts that were out on business drove slowly, and in this year of 1895, there were no automobiles.

I liked the church with its great arched door, which was dedicated in carved letters "To the Triune God." That word *triune* was wonderful, for I could not imagine what it meant. The books did not tell, even though, by now, I was reading everything in our library, including incomprehensible chapters in the Bible that were marked in the writing of Grandfather Murray, deceased, as "not to be read at family worship." One knew instinctively that such subjects were not to be discussed with Father and Mother, but once I had lowered myself to inquire of Margaret.

"Do you understand how a person can be three in one and one in three?"

"Why, of course," said my golden-haired sister.

"But how? I don't see."

"It just is."

That was the way Margaret answered. When I couldn't seem to read the notes in the school songbook, I made up the notes by ear while Margaret warbled soprano. Was I defective in some way? That fear was beginning to shake its black wings at me while Margaret lightly dismissed any question of the Triune God.

"I should think anybody could see that," she added.

Well, if I was feeble minded, I would keep it to myself for a while. They said you got worse and finally had epileptic fits. Fortunately, this fear came only very occasionally, like heartburn. I hid it, even from myself, as I sometimes hid the dirty handkerchiefs that Mother thought I ought to wash.

Now the carven portal was behind us as we pattered around to the side door where the Sunday school rooms were. I loved this Sunday morning arrival, with all the dressed-up people walking about and with swarms of strange children whom I never saw at any other time. In spite of the superintendent telling us that we were all God's great family, Mother had carefully explained that we must not speak to any unless we had been introduced. "They might not be our kind of people," she explained. So we walked among them, only stealing excited glances, until we reached the big Sunday school room where all the classes sat around tables. Margaret went to Miss La Barre's class, where she always sat cuddled next to the teacher. Miss La Barre sometimes came to our house for Sunday night supper, and then she would pat Margaret's head in a sort of saintly way and tell Mother, "A lovely child." Margaret had got so used to hearing those words that she put on a look just like our dog, Pudgy, when you spoke his name and he thumped his tail on the floor.

I was in Auntie's class. Auntie was Father's sister—only an Underhill, of course, but looked up to in town as a fine woman. She lived with Grandma Underhill in a big white house covered with grapevines and with ground-glass flowers on the double front doors. Mother told us how Auntie had a "Fine Mind" and how, years ago, she had even gone to college, far away somewhere, and there had been a man. Before Auntie finished college, though, Grandma Underhill had gotten sick. Of course, Auntie had come home to take care of her as a daughter should. Nay; not should, but *must*. So she had sent the man away, and now, though she was very intellectual, it was all done through books gotten from the library. She did not need to teach school, I was told, but she did, in the girl's school where all nice families in our town sent their daughters. I was in her Latin class, and it is owing to her that, for me, the Romans still walk as gods, different from all other people on earth. She did not believe in spoiling children, though. I have seen her give Mother a Moses kind of look when Margaret was being praised, and it was Auntie who decreed that my lanky hair must be cut like a boy's because I never kept it tidy.

"Ruth," said Auntie without greeting, "I hope you know all the Ten Commandments today." I had thought maybe we would hear about the resurrection and the angel on the tomb, but Auntie was not one to alter an organized course of study. Just now, we were on our way through the Old Testament, with all the begats and the wandering of those poor Israelites in the desert. *Begat* was another word I didn't understand, but I always tried to work things out before asking questions. Light had come when Elsie, who went to the Cat-Lick church, told me that there they had something called the Magnificat.* I decided that *begat* must be the Protestant equivalent.

"I guess I know them, Auntie," I murmured. In fact, I burned to chant aloud those wonderful rolling words, especially the ones about Jehovah:

> Visiting the iniquities of the *fathers*
> Upon the *children*
> Unto the third and fourth generation of them that hate me
> And showing mercy unto thousands of them that *love* me
> And keep my commandments.†

---

* The Magnificat, also known as the Song (or Canticle) of Mary, is one of the eight most ancient Christian hymns and comes from Luke 1:46–55.

† Exodus 34:5–9.

How gloriously my voice rose on the italicized words and fell on the last line, as I stamped about dusting the parlor. I could almost hear the children of Israel chanting with me, while Moses stood on the lowest ledge of Sinai, like a symphony conductor. (All of us Underhills began the symphony at the age of ten, except, of course, Robert, who must not be forced.) Auntie was not going to pander to my vanity. She turned to Francine, the girl whose mother wore the prettiest clothes in town and actually took her to the theater in New York. Francine stumbled along, twisting her gloves. (Yes, she had light blue gloves and a light blue coat!)

When she bogged down utterly about committing adultery, I said in the silence, "What is adultery?" Auntie bent on me those blazing gray eyes under black eyebrows that were so like Father's. Later, when I no longer cared about the color of my eyes, I learned that I had them, too.

"Adultery," said Auntie, with her lips together, "is a sin."

But what kind of a sin? My mind was flying to sorcery and black witches. A sin! I pressed, "But how'll we know not to do it if we don't know what it is?"

I had gone too far. The other girls snickered. Auntie said in a tone that Moses himself could not have bettered, "I hope my girls will lead such good lives that they will not even need to know about sin."

Again, that pang, remotely resembling dyspepsia. To distract us, Auntie asked me to recite that one about the ox and the ass and the stranger who is within the gates.* Now I stumbled. How did those gates look? Surely not the white picket fences of our town! As I imagined them, made of some strange wood and all studded with brass, we rose to sing.

Then we streamed upstairs into the big church, scented with Easter lilies. Mother was in our pew in her gray satin dress, her white gloves, and the hat with gray ostrich plumes. Father always came late because he talked with other men in the vestibule. He looked magnificent as he ambled down the aisle, with his frock coat and all the closely clipped black hair that was a moustache and a round beard, just the shape of his chin. When he had taken his place at the end of the pew, church could begin.

---

* Deuteronomy 5:14.

I loved church. Rarely did I follow any of the words that were said, for they seemed to belong to some strange magic language like:

> One in faith and doctorin'
> One in charitee

I puzzled over the fact that we really had not one doctor in town but several doctors, including a homeopath. I finally made up my mind that *doctrine* was probably not some ecclesiastical spelling of doctoring. Still, I knew perfectly well that we were not all one, because look at the Cat-Licks. It was better to ignore this language of ritual and to enjoy the smell and sound of church, with people tiptoeing about the carpeted aisles and getting up and sitting down. Mr. Horsey, in front of us, had a mole on the back of his neck, which never showed about his collar until he knelt.

Mr. Horsey, who owned the grocery store, was not interesting, but scattered among the walnut pews were unknown beings, all in their best clothes, about whom I could make up stories. That lady who always sat with her little girl and no husband was a deserted duchess, waiting for the duke to come back from war. What had she said when he left? "My liege, I am ever thine." At his point, I actually cried, and Mother leaned over quickly with a handkerchief. That night I heard her and Father talking a long time in their bedroom, which was next to mine. They always discussed us children there, and sometimes I heard a few words, as on this occasion.

"Very early for religious fervor."

"Not healthy. My family never did that."

"Oh, but we must be very gentle."

I was amazed the next day when Mother asked if I had ever thought of joining the church.

"How do people do that?" I asked, for we young ones were always walked out before communion.

"You're not thinking of doing it, dear?"

"No, I don't guess."

"'I don't think so,' Ruth. Where do you pick up such expressions?"

I couldn't hear any of the words said in the parents' bedroom that night, but the talk was not so long, and next day, both of them seemed quite cheery.

~

The Quaker meeting was in Chappaqua, and we didn't always get over to Chappaqua. It was an eight-mile drive.

We had, of course, as our means of locomotion a surrey and a horse, Dolly. All proper families had at least that much to get around with. If we had shorter distances to go we walked in our black shoes; if we did need to go farther, then we had Dolly. We also had our helper at the house, Dan Tierney—our man from County Cabot, Ireland—who told me many a story about how he met fairies in Ireland in his youth.

When automobiles came in, Dan went to my father and said, "Now, Your Honor, I have taken training in driving a car, and I wish to drive a car. If Your Honor wants to buy a car, I will be only too glad to drive yours, but if you wish to keep on with Dolly, I'm afraid I must give notice."

Dolly was disposed of, and we had a car.

Abram S. Underhill

MY FATHER, ABRAM SUTTON UNDERHILL, was a farm boy. The Underhill farm near Chappaqua was a long forty miles from New York City. It was not even on the Hudson River, the great highway of American civilization where sailing boats were common and people in the river towns often went to the metropolis by steamboat. The farm was near Croton Lake, the city's water supply, and I remember, before the modern waterworks were put in, the sloping grass banks, the elm trees, and the rutty dirt road that led to it.*

Father used to tell us with pride about rising at four in the morning to milk the cows and do the barn chores before breakfast, and I took it as a dictum from on high that the corn must be planted early enough so we could go through it once—that is, weeding—before Yearly Meeting.† That was in June. I can barely remember Grandfather Underhill, a gentle old man with a white beard shaped to his chin. He told me that in planting corn, each hill must have four corn kernels:

> One for the cutworm
> One for the crow
> One for the beetle
> And one to grow

"It's an old Yankee saying," he explained. Perhaps. But the Yankees learned about corn from the Indians. The Algonquians of the

---

* Underhill has the broad geography right, but more specifically a brief biographical note gives Abram Underhill's place of birth as New Castle, New York (about three miles north of Chappaqua), while Croton Lake, New York, is an additional six miles north. See: Nicholson, F. W. 1883. *Alumni Record of Wesleyan University, Middletown, Conn., Volumes 1881–1883.* 3rd ed. Harford, CT: Press of the Case, Lockwood, & Brainard. Pg. 35.

† This is an annual gathering of members of the Religious Society of Friends, the culmination of smaller, more frequent meetings held within a geographical area.

Northeast, I learned later, always planted four kernels in a hill. Their sacred number was four, while that of us whites is three. Father, Son, and Holy Ghost. Three princes or three maidens in all the fairy stories. So more likely Grandpa was following an ancient tradition born out of Indian expertise.

Grandfather was, of course, a Quaker, as all his ancestors had been on both sides for many generations. He and Grandmother used the plain language, the gentle "thee" and the "First Day"—all of which still have for me a warm fireside glow, very different from the "you" and "Sunday" of "the world's people."* I had to be careful with my pronouns, though, for the Underhills spoke the language of the north of England, which says, "Does thee," while the Murrays, Mother's people, used the more literary, "Dost thou." Grandfather was a gentle being, not one of the leading Friends who sat on the high seat, like our cousin James Wood. Grandfather was content with a quiet, industrious life, but not so Eliza, his second wife, who was our grandmother. Her daughter Anna, my maiden aunt, in her last illness looked at Grandma's photograph on the wall and murmured, "That is my mother. She was a cold, hard woman."

Grandma Underhill used the plain language and wore the standard simple dress, but she could have functioned quite well as a Catholic of Inquisition days or perhaps a Calvinist. Father used to tell us about the night when she and Grandfather got into an argument about the personal devil, the one who haunts each individual to tempt and destroy him.

"I don't believe God would allow that," said Grandfather.

"Jesse H. Underhill," challenged Grandmother, "if thee denies a Christian belief like that, I can't stay in this house."

So she put on her Quaker bonnet and went out into the cornfield. Grandfather took a lantern and spent hours searching for her among the rows of corn. I don't know whether he submitted on the subject of the personal devil.

---

* The plain language of the Quakers refers to the use of "thee" and "thy" instead of "you" and "your," a rigorous deference to the literal truth, and biblical turns of phrase. Quakers object to those names for days of the week and months derived from pagan deities, and so Sunday is, in the plain language, the "First Day." See: Densmore, Christopher. 1985. The Society of Friends in Western New York. *Canadian Quaker History Newsletter* 37(July):6–11.

In this atmosphere grew up Abram Sutton Underhill, loved inartic-
ulately by his father, adored by his younger sister, and commissioned
by his mother to "fight the good fight and run with patience the race
set before him." Besides the farmwork, he learned to make and repair
most household equipment, and the taste for such craft work stayed
with him so that my brother and I imbibed a little of it. But Abram
must early have been thinking beyond the farm.

I don't know when Abram met my gentle mother, Anna T. Murray.
I suppose it was at the Friends meeting house at Chappaqua, a little
shingled building on a hillside where the buggies and surreys drew
up on First Day morning. The Murrays were New Yorkers, people
of property who spent the summer at Chappaqua in their big, red,
shingled house, with its cupolas and balconies. I have no picture of
Mother as a girl, for photographs were not usual in those days. Parents might have a miniature made of a pretty daughter, but Quakers
probably thought that to be "vanity." At any rate, Anna had not only
a younger sister but four brothers, and any money spent for vanity
went for the males.

A younger Mother, I imagine, looked a good deal like the pictures
taken in her early married life. Brown hair was parted and crimped
on leather curlers into four rolls, two on each side of her forehead.
Her eyes were a gentle blue. Both Murrays and Underhills spoke with
aversion of brown eyes as a sign of "those foreigners." Her skirts,
gray or dark blue, came to her toes. Above it was not the standard
Quaker uniform with its white kerchief, but a basque (a tight-fitting
bodice) buttoned down the front and with tiny tucks slating in a V
to a waist made tiny by corsets. Her shoes were high and buttoned
and, of course, they and the stockings were black. Even in summer,
white footgear was unknown in Mother's circle.

I have meditated a little about that love affair of the 1870s. Neither Father nor Mother would give us any information other than
smiling hints about buggy rides. I have seen Father's picture as a
slender young man with a blond mustache, and surely his blue-gray
eyes must have flashed sometimes as I saw them do in later life. How
did the Murrays of Murray Hill regard this young farmer from an
upstate college? Of course, their Quaker principles would preclude
their thinking unduly about "this world's goods," and the Underhill
Yankee ancestry was even better than theirs, but . . .

When she and Father married, it must have been an adventure because of the difference between his farm roots and her city roots. Although Father lived forty miles away from New York City, he had never visited it. Mother had lived in New York City and thought that was the only place to live, and that a brownstone front with a front parlor, back parlor, and a dining room in the basement was the only definition of a house. I always thought that, too, as I grew up and saw how people lived. I think those two must have had quite a time adapting themselves, their two very different forms of life and their two kinds of experience. It never showed, though. They were always peaceful and pleasant to each other. I never heard a quarrel. But they must have had a great deal of adaptation to do, praying to the Lord in secret about how on earth to get along with each other.

I never heard a word from my parents or from the Murray relatives about a misalliance, but I remember now how Father quietly avoided contact with my Murray uncles, easygoing gentry who kept losing money on Wall Street. Once I caught just an edge in his voice when Father mentioned lending money to a Murray uncle, the suave, mustached oldest of Mother's clan. Now I pick out tiny colored pieces of that story from the web of recollections. I remember my cousin Effingham lightly informing me, "You know, the Murrays are snobs. We can't help it." For the Murrays of my generation, while remaining nominal Quakers, were as fashionable as any New Yorker. They had the gentleman's attitude that Wall Street was the only possible sphere of action for a young man. One by one, they lost their money there, while Abram Underhill slaved in a lawyer's office and did real estate business in the evenings.* There was no hint of dissension in the benign family atmosphere that brought us all together at Thanksgiving and Christmas. I was told to love my Murray cousins, and I have no doubt they received a like admonition. The quiet sweep of the whole affair must exemplify what is meant by the Victorian attitude, but I remember the acrid tone of some of Father's commands, like the smell of a burnt-out fuse, and Mother's constant adjuration, "We

---

* In addition to being a practicing lawyer, Abram Underhill also reportedly worked in fire insurance and real estate. See: Nicholson, F. W. 1883. *Alumni Record of Wesleyan University, Middletown, Conn., Volumes 1881–1883*. 3rd ed. Harford, CT: Press of the Case, Lockwood, & Brainard. Pg. 35.

must think the best of everybody, dear. We are put in the world to love each other."

Even in childhood, I could not agree with that, and I suspect now that Father could not either. Would that I could have been party to his purpose, for then I would have understood the occasional harshness of his commands, the lack of time to listen to his children's interests. It was during my teens that the smell of the burnt fuse grew so strong. Before that, there had been pleasant anecdotes at the supper table, Sunday walks in the woods, readings of Scott's poetry, and talks on botany and astronomy. Then came an investment in Texas real estate and a gay trip south when Father took Mother with him. It was the first of his long railroad trips in connection with investments, for Abram Underhill was going to be a moneyed man. He once told me he expected to leave his family "at least a quarter of a million dollars." That was the farm boy's scale of success in the days of the great tycoons. But Father thought, not of the Astors and Vanderbilts, but of the Murrays.

The investment failed. Of course, we children were not told about it. We were never told anything, except to be good and love our neighbors as ourselves, but I sensed the crackle of electricity some- where about, only we did not use electricity then.

Perhaps the feeling was like that when a cold is coming on. The aches and shivers are vague and may mean nothing, but they may mean that tomorrow you will be in bed instead of on your feet. Life's emphasis has shifted. I can only guess, at this late date, at the battle that may have been going on between the egos of my parents. In this age, it would have sounded out in arguments and recriminations. "Why didn't you?" "How can you?" In the late 1800s, however, I can believe that no word was spoken on the subject, though even a child could sense that Mother's smile was sparked more by determination than gaiety and that was the date of crisis when Father told us girls sharply that our hair was frowsy and he did not want us downstairs until it was decently combed.

The law business proceeded in spite of bad investments. Father's shingle, under the words "Attorney-at-Law," carried the information "Mortgage Investments."

I can understand now why our Sunday walks were discontinued. Father still felt that work of financial nature should not be done on

Sunday, but he spent time in the little library, with its huge armchair inherited from some great uncle and its jigsaw walnut table with red felt top. In that room were the glass-fronted bookcase filled with plant specimens and I think the huge rolls of manila paper on which the solar system was pictured in chalk. There was not much wall space for books at that early date, but the tall, narrow shelves contained Renan's *Life of Christ* and somebody's book on the Pre-Adamites.* Father was also struggling with the dictates of the old religion.

I believe those years before I was a teenager were a time of intense struggle, because there was little calm and gaiety in the house. There was nothing outwardly wrong or bad tempered. Never did I see a sign of such improper things in the Linden Avenue house, but this was the period when I spent more and more time with my girl playmates. We made fancy underwear. We creamed our faces and looked every night for the wrinkles that would one day appear.

~

My father's father, Jesse H. Underhill, was the heir to a long line of Quaker farmers all the way from Captain John, the exuberant Britisher from Warwickshire. John was a warrior, paid to defend a Quaker colony in Connecticut, and became involved in the Indian wars sparked by the settling of New England. Before his death, though, he succumbed to gentle influences and joined the Society of Friends.†
In fact, he married three successive wives within it.

John's Quaker descendants did not fight in the Revolutionary War, such acts being against their principles, but they did not profit from the fighting done by others either. When the war was over, much

---

* Joseph Ernest Renan's *Life of Jesus* was originally published in 1863. The second book is probably a reference to Isabel Duncan's 1860 volume *Pre-Adamite Man; or, The Story of Our Old Planet and Its Inhabitants, Told by Scripture & Science*, which attempted to reconcile the implications of geological and other data with accounts recorded in scripture.

† Some historians have suggested that such "gentle influences," unfortunately, did not come earlier or extend to America's Native peoples. John Underhill, one historian has suggested, "was the archetype of the 'Indian fighter' . . . his campaigns resulted in merciless slaughters of men, women, and children. Underhill engendered terror in Indian country from 1637 until his death thirty-five years later." See: Hauptman, Laurence M. 1992. John Underhill: A Psychological Portrait of an Indian Fighter, 1597–1672. *Hudson Valley Review* September:101–111. Pg. 101.

confiscated good Tory farmland was offered free to citizens of the republic. Our Underhill ancestor was eligible, even though he had not fought. Still, he refused to take cruel advantage of honest fellow farmers who had only been true to their principles. He insisted on buying land. So the farm in the Hudson River Valley was only a modest one.

Papa was brought up there, and in expansive moments he told us children about getting up at four on cold winter mornings to milk and do the other chores before breakfast. (I remember, by the way, a description of this practice in Edith Wharton's *Ethan Frome*.* The little book was given us at college as a model of narrative writing, but I threw it down halfway through with a howl of disgust. Ethan, before going out to milk at four in the morning, was shaving. Shaving! I lost respect both for Edith and for my English teacher.) Papa used to tell us about what he heard, on the farm, about the spectacular wickedness of New York City some forty miles away. I heard, he used to say with a twinkle, about the bad robber barons, about Wall Street. "Oh darling!" mother would murmur in reply, since her father had lived on the proceeds of Wall Street.

And Father would go on about lawyers. Lawyers, they thought in our neighborhood, were the smartest people in the world and to blame for everything. "Oh darling!" we'd hear again. Mother never understood that kind of a joke. She looked ready to weep until Papa finished triumphantly, "So I thought I'd be one and find out about it."

Father did just that. He had won a scholarship to Wesleyan College and perhaps his father, gentle old "Jesse H.," did not expect him back to Chappaqua. Wesleyan was a Methodist school, and many Quakers looked with horror at the "Methody" singing and shouting, but there were no funds to send Abram to Haverford College, the famous Friends institution in Pennsylvania, and I doubt if anyone could have kept Abram from getting out into the world of intellect. It was Father's chance. He graduated with honors from Wesleyan, with memberships in Psi U fraternity and Phi Beta Kappa.

---

* Underhill's aside is seemingly apocryphal, as Edith Wharton's well-known novel *Ethan Frome* was published in 1911—six years after Underhill graduated from Vassar. Still, the underlying themes here—Underhill's distaste for tales that run counter to basic facts and her skepticism of authority figures—seem genuine.

Then he settled down to read law, as they did in those days, in a lawyer's office. It was in Sing Sing, the nearest village to the farm.* It had churches and lawyers, but no Friends Meeting. Reading law, I understand, took two or three years, so Father supported himself and Mother meantime by selling mortgages on real estate, or were they not married till that probation was over? Father did pass an examination, got a degree from Columbia University, and hung out a shingle. In my childhood, his office was a front room in an old brick building. It was approached by a flight of creaking wooden stairs, and when Mother took me there, we sometimes met solemn people coming down after signing papers.

Mother spoke of the place with awe, but I think her mother and brothers accepted her words with raised eyebrows. A shabby little office in a village? And such dirty people come for mortgages. Foreigners! Grandfather Murray was dead by that time, and the dividends seem to have died with him. Anyway, his sons were going to work, but the work, of course, was on Wall Street. Some of my earliest recollections are what I must call the *reek* of grandeur that surrounded my Murray uncles. It surrounded them like an invisible gas, even as their money percolated away. Quakerism was not really a good preparation for Wall Street.

I think it was Mother's friendship with Jesus that prevented her having any feeling about the raised eyebrows. To us children, she often said that she could see no fault in "the Dear Man," and we must not either. I have wondered if my life could not have been different if I had been able to think of Father as a fallible human being. Imagine asking, "Why did you do that?" and being given a reason! I think that happened between him and my youngest sister after Mother's death, but in the early days of which I am thinking, my mind made no distinction between Father and Jehovah. Both of them thundered, and then you hurried to obey commands. Sometimes they smiled, and then you flourished. Father did more than that. He often made jokes (on permitted subjects), and once in a while, he told stories

---

* As previously noted, "In 1901, the village of Sing Sing changed its name to Ossining because local merchants did not want their goods associated with merchandise from the nearby prison of the same name." Cheli, Guy. 2003. *Sing Sing Prison*. Charleston, SC: Arcadia Publishing. Pg. 15.

about the office. At some of these Mother looked pained, and they became fewer. Of course, if Father found "dagos" and "micks" a little comic, she explained to us, that did not mean he was un-Christian. Still, we must not talk like that. We were too young to do it wisely.

❦

I am almost as old now as Father was when he died, and one of my profound regrets is that I cannot sit down for a salty interchange with him, two experienced old worldlings together.* For now I think I understand him. I have pieced out his history, from the Quaker farm boy with the gentle father, reliable and productive as the corn-fields themselves, and the striding, sharp-spoken mother who always thought everyone should do a little better than they did.

------

* Abram Underhill was eighty-nine or ninety when he died in 1942. Underhill was therefore in her late eighties when writing this portion of her memoirs, which means she wrote them in the late 1960s or early 1970s.

Mother Was an Angel, Part 2

MOTHER ALWAYS SEEMED so far away, living with God, Shakespeare, and the Sunday School Home Department, that I never aspired to wondering how she felt. I do remember one episode when I was about ten, sitting beside her doing some of the endless sewing that was part of female life in those days. Elizabeth, the baby of the family, had been born some months previously, and the talk at home was all about her.

"Mother, it must be exciting to have a row of children," I said, thinking of us four siblings, "and to watch them grow up, exactly like you and Father."

"Darling," said Mother, "it isn't like that."

Indeed, the horrible difference between her gentle and God-serving self and this awkward eldest daughter must have been painful to Mother. At the time, I thought the pain was all mine, but now I wonder.

Margaret, my sister next in age, was her comfort. Margaret was tall and slim, while I was stocky. Margaret had golden hair, while mine was ordinary brown. Margaret "loved her home," as Mother was constantly saying—and Margaret really did love the tight, enveloping atmosphere—while I kept trying to get out of it. Margaret did not like to sew, though I did, because it was a sort of achievement. Yet she was not blamed for the lack, though I was not praised. She was "delicate" and needed to be petted and considered. Oh, how I used to pray to the Lord to make me delicate! The fact that prayer remained unanswered all my life did much to set me against "the Lord" as Mother presented him to us. I don't know to this day whether Margaret implored the Lord. It was my impression that she did not have to. Mother had done it all for her.

❧

Painting flowers and kittens. Of course, I had no desire for any such thing. Flowers were too familiar. Kittens one can dominate, they purr so easily at a touch. I didn't even want to try. I had thought this was a good thing to say to Mother, that it might lead me in behind Mother's glass wall. It did not.

"Won't you try, dear?" pleaded Mother.

She gave the kind, patronizing smile that I came so much to dread as years went on; I think it concealed suffering. I suppose she was thinking, "I must be kind. I must encourage every impulse of this queer creature unless it is definitely evil. Perhaps it will add up to something useful." But is painting flowers and kittens the best result to be hoped for from all these divagations? They should lead, at least, to the revelations of Saint Theresa.*

The flower-and-kitten approach was given up. Sometimes I tried talking about the books I read, asking Mother questions. Her usual answer was, "We are not expected to know the answer on this earth, dear. It will all be clear when we get to heaven." Mother believed that. What faith she must have needed to carry her over the sight of children, at least two out of four, who did not develop as God meant children to do.

Mother could only trust that God would guide my thoughts. Meantime, she gave me all she could; but it was always with that patronizing smile, which concealed both hope and disappointment. I was a monster of ingratitude. So everybody told me, and I have to acknowledge it, but the emotional food with which I was feasted was something I could not digest. I was like that Spanish horse left with the Aztecs. Wanting to do their best for this strange new creature, the Indians fed it on wildfowl, their most delicate food. The horse died of starvation.

Humans are not as helpless as a horse confined in a stable, so I found food of a sort. I found it in books and in walks in the country. I made up long stories to myself that took place in the Arctic or in the Middle Ages. Oh, how selfish and stupid I was! For Mother would have loved to tell me all about her girlhood. She would have

---

* There are several possible saints to which Underhill refers here. Saint Teresa of Ávila (1515–1582) was canonized in 1622 in recognition of her work to reform the Carmelite order. Saint Thérèse of Lisieux (1873–1897) was canonized in 1925 in recognition of her dedication and personal devotion to the teachings of Jesus and the Catholic Church, especially as a very young girl. The context suggests that Underhill is referring to Saint Thérèse of Lisieux.

blossomed in the description of that dignified old New York house, her imposing, bearded father, her handsome brothers. I could still feel her dutiful awe of them when we visited one Murray uncle, whom I thought was a mustached old bore. It was necessary, in talking to him, to realize that the Murrays were the quintessence, not of nobility, but of high-mindedness. Even though it was whispered to me that this uncle borrowed money from Father, I could see that Father himself shied away from the crystalline stratosphere of Murray dinner parties. Father was often unable to attend, and I detected in his pronunciation of the uncle's name a tone that reminded me, distantly, of the smell of dog urine.

Mother dear, I would be glad to talk to you now about your problems, for I think that, even with Father, you had some. That bold blue eye of Father's could light sometimes with an intensity of excitement that might be intellectual or emotional. Once in a while a remark of mine elicited such a look, and suddenly I pictured Father away from home. In his New York office. On the street. Addressing a meeting. Did he think, as I did, about things not communicable to Mother? I know that Father's firm purpose was to have the dignity of a moneyed man, even a millionaire. He never achieved it, for his big investments failed, one after another. I don't know how near to God's way some of those investments were, for he never told us about them or told Mother. My brother assures me that he cut corners, but his respect for respectability and his Quaker training were too powerful to allow actual dishonesty. He hinted to me, after I was grown up, something of the good savor of besting an opponent by "honest trickery." That is what all lawyers are supposed to practice, and these days we admire it. I don't think Mother did. The innocence of her upbringing is, to me, almost incredible. She really believed that one should turn the other cheek and forgive until seventy times seven.*

It has always been my opinion that World War I hastened Mother's death, with all its carnage and horror, and with the armies on both sides calling upon God, the same Jehovah whom we had all been brought up to trust! Mother, in her forties, had a recurrent illness, a defect of the digestive system. It came again in the war years, while I was away with the Red Cross. Patriotism or not, the whole war was

---

* Matthew 18:22.

un-Christian. How could God have allowed it? How to reconcile the death of all those fine boys with the command, "Thou shalt not kill?"* The world was not proceeding

> From precedent to precedent
> To that far off, divine event
> Toward which the whole creation moves.†

Mother loved Tennyson and gave me a copy for my twelfth birthday, but the handsome Tennyson died before a war to end war crashed into his beautiful pictures. God allowed my brother to be too young to fight, but he left the explanation of the fighting until Mother could get to heaven. So she went.

My sisters tell me that, in the last days, doctors told Father that they could keep her alive. They could not say how long, but she would never be her old self again, perhaps not even conscious.

"Of course," said my young brother, "everything must be done."

"No," said Father, "let her go."

In my maturity, I honor Father for that. Few men of his time would have had the wisdom and courage for such a decision. He told me long afterward, "I could not let her become an unconscious vegetable."

❧

I never made up with Mother. People always do that in books. True, this is a book, but when she left us I was away in the process of creating a new life. I do what I can by giving financial help to the sister who followed her way and ended in sorrow and poverty. My brother and sister say it is her own business and do not help. Perhaps they have not my bad conscience. My little sister, at least, was never outside the wall. She concealed her lack of intimacy with God and his way, but she took no other way. She did not hurt Mother.

❧

It sounds grim and dismal, but in time, I became comfortable in withdrawal, as one might in wearing a brace or long underwear. I would have liked ebullience, hugs, petting, and praise. Oh, especially

---

* Exodus 20:13.

† Paraphrased from the 1849 poem "In Memoria A. H. H." by Alfred, Lord Tennyson.

praise! I had some, of course, when I did well in school or looked neat when going out, but it was not the gorgeous burst of adulation that makes the heart flare up. All my life I have yearned for that utterly satisfying experience, at least just once. Of course, I never had it. Why should I? The yearning is perhaps the reason why my storybook heroes always have such a rotten hard time, with misunderstandings and unfairness.

Of course, there were parts of Mother's green park where I could enter without stepping in puddles, and pleasant they were. She and I could sit happily sewing. We sat in Mother's bedroom with its southern window whose view was almost filled by branches of a big sycamore tree. Mother would tell news about all the aunts, uncles, and cousins, their plans and doings. If there was any criticism, it went no further than a bare hint that something was "not practical."

My women friends sometimes mention casually about what their mothers told them on the subject of looking their best for attracting men. I cannot imagine Mother dealing with such a subject. Good looks and popularity were, to her, simply one result of being good. But we poor creatures who have barely sufficient goodness to be tolerated by our fellow men need all the arts we can get, like applying makeup to a basically homely face. Goodness knows, I went out into the world without any arts.

I am appalled when I realize that never in my life did I try to put myself in Mother's place and feel what she must have been feeling. For Mother dwelt in the City of God where

> Right through the streets with silver sound
> The living waters flow
> And on the banks on either hand
> The trees of life do grow.*

I knew very early that I could never inhabit that city. Even when I went on short visits as an adult, I had to be on my very best behavior. I learned early not to talk religion with Mother, for on that subject she was immovable. It amazes me that a religion so gentle as Quakerism could produce such immovable firmness. Mother had the belief that would have taken her to the stake, not triumphant, but smilingly

---

* From the hymn "O Mother Dear, Jerusalem."

secure. The slightest infringement on her articles of faith produced, not a rebuke, but a sad little smile and, "Oh Ruth!"

So I was on my good behavior in her green park, her City of God. I never spoke of religion except with respectful aloofness. That part was safe, and I kept my doubts and longings to myself, but I found that the City of God included also some economic and political territory. I stepped into it once, when I stated that I thought that suicide was a sensible move for anyone with a fatal disease. "Oh Ruth!"

And when I suggested that it would have been a fine thing for Woodrow Wilson if he could have been assassinated in his days of triumph after World War I, that "Oh Ruth" made me draw my mental foot back as though I had stepped in a deep puddle. I wonder if the habit of silence and withdrawal acquired after such missteps influenced my gait for the rest of my life.

❧

I try to picture life as Mother must have seen it, and to me the result is tragic. It must have been tragic to her, too, except for her friendship with Jesus Christ. That friendship cast a gentle glow over even the picture's darkest corners. I cannot believe she knew about the depths of rebellion and disappointment that surged under her. She passed over them, comfortably smiling, like Christ walking on the water.

Her family was New York Quaker, living on Murray Hill, as all Murrays should, and supported by their dividends. In these days it seems impossible that one could live a sheltered life in New York, but I believe she did. Quakers, in those days, kept themselves apart from the world's people, and there were enough in New York to form a contented little community. I doubt if Anna Murray knew any young men who were not Friends. The circle was small and all young people married within it, so she was unacquainted with the search for a mate as conducted in other spheres. Her mother gave her no admonition except to be good and gentle.

Anna Murray did marry a Friend, but he was a country boy met while the family was at their summer house at Chappaqua. I once saw that big, dark, shingled house, with its verandas and cupolas, but it has long since been pulled down. I imagine Anna in her long skirt serving lemonade on one of those verandas to visiting Friends. In rocking chairs sat her mother, in gray silk, and her father, with his brown spade beard. The guests were just as often old people as young, but Anna was taught to enjoy them all equally. The young did not go off alone.

We never could get Father to tell us how he got Mother off alone to propose to her. It was in a buggy, that much we elicited, but were there transports of joy? Did the world change color for her? When asked about it, Mother would only say, "You will know in time, dear."

With her scallops of brown hair, her boned basque, and her long, flounced skirts, Anna Murray became a married woman. She was lifted out of the commodious Quaker nest into a little house in a village with a big sycamore tree and a high stoop. Plucked from her gray-silk-lined nest, Anna Murray was bringing up four children in a village where there were no Friends. How to make a new nest, to line and feather it, was information not supplied by her religion. As for acquaintances, I think Mother expected them to blossom out as church members did in Paul's Epistles. I was a bit shy about approaching new people, and so was she. So we took what came. Mother fared well, on the whole. She could not possibly have made friends with anyone who was even slightly vulgar, nor would such a person have approached her. But don't let me make it sound too tragic. I felt no tragedy at the time. Mother stayed busy with her home Bible study and her Shakespeare Club. She saw to it that her children were properly fed and clothed.

~

As the years pile up on me, I have before me the image of the old lady I must never allow myself to be, one like Grandma Murray. She was a saint, people told me. So the word *saint* thus came to be in my childish mind a *schimpfwort*—a hateful term. True, she never lied, stole, or killed. Still, she hovered over some of my young days like a buzzing wasp, the kind one can dodge but cannot catch.

She was a little woman. In youth, perhaps she was delicate and slender. I have a daguerreotype of her, for I was her oldest namesake and elected to carry on the tradition of Ruth the loyal, the self-sacrificing. The daguerreotype, now dark and cloudy, shows a serious face, with brown hair lapping down in scallops, a gray dress, and folded hands. She wore Quaker dress all her life, and in widowhood it was always black. Quakers, who did not drink, ate plenty of good food, and Grandma got fat. I remember how her little round stomach bulged out under the black pleats. And she smelled. Maybe it was just old age, but there had been no bathtubs in her youth, and the sponge from a basin must have gotten more onerous with time. I remember my revulsion at having to sleep with her or on the sheets she had left, and the kissing, though that was rare.

Perhaps these troubles would not have stirred me so except for the sainthood. On that, all adults were agreed, and my failure to feel and respond to it was a defect as profound and unnatural as the failure to attract "beaus." I knew very well that I should never speak of Grandma with anything but love and reverence, and that burden was heavy enough, but I should also never *feel* otherwise. There, I was almost in a nightmare, for I almost always felt otherwise.

"Ruth, why doesn't thee lay down that book and go for a nice walk?"

"Ruth, has thee cleaned thy bureau drawers?"

"Ruth, thy mother needs help."

Well, I *was* going to help Mother if I could only finish the chapter first, but saintly grandmother was not to be kept waiting.

She did not always live with us, and I believe Father appreciated that fact as much as I did. Once he got the through train on which she was to leave us to make a special stop at Ossining. "I told the ticket man," he said unsmilingly, "that it was for my mother-in-law." Mother turned her head away.

Grandma had once had a house in New Bedford. In old age, she gave the house up and divided her time among her married children. The prospect of it was, to me, like the coming of winter, long, dark days when you waited in discomfort for the return of the sun. In the first place, my sister and I had to give up our play area, the dining room bay window. The space was given to Grandma's rocker and her small table holding the Bible and the printed matter about "Paul's Trips."* What objections I developed to Paul, whom people called "Saint," with his shipwrecks, and his tribulations, and his scoldings of those poor churches! I have not gotten over the idea that Paul and Grandma Murray were a good deal alike, demanding the title of saint while often acting like a sweet-talking old curmudgeon. Oh, for a worldly grandmother, perhaps even one who had sinned! How I could have poured out my doubts and difficulties, for as I grew toward girlhood, they kept piling up. Instead I dared not express them, even to myself.

---

* A reference to the extensive missionary journeys of Paul the Apostle (AD 5–67).

Youth Passing

WE OFTEN WENT TO EUROPE in the summer for two or three weeks. People have been amazed at the apparent wealth of my family. They've asked, "Were you rich?" No, not at all rich. A very modest situation actually.

We didn't think we had to travel grandly. Father didn't think so. There was, at that time, a one-class group of steamers called the North German Lloyd, which took about ten days to cross the Atlantic. When we arrived we would stay in boardinghouses. Father's idea was we should, of course, learn the language of the country, so we went to a place where they would speak German or French. My sisters and brother did not really care much about learning languages. They wanted to make jokes among themselves and play games, but I wanted to learn the language. So at dinner I would always ask that I should sit on the end of the family string, and then I would certainly have somebody of the language to talk to. It often worked out very well. The time I remember was when two very elegant Englishmen were the people next to me. I was about twelve years old, with long, braided hair hanging down, so there was no chance of any dallying. But I waited to hear them speak. How would British English sound? What would the accent be?

After two courses had passed and the third and last course was coming, one of them said, "Tomorrow is Friday, is it not?"

I held my breath.

The other answered, "Quite so, quite so."

That was when I learned the Queen's English and my love of languages.

꙰

One summer we went to Germany. Another, France. Quite often we went to Switzerland, which, Mother said, was a particularly nice, clean country. You didn't have to worry about lice or fleas, like you did in

69

Figure 10. Portrait of Ruth at about twelve years
of age, circa 1895.

France and Italy certainly. Of course, you learned some German in
Switzerland, and we stayed at these rather cheap places there. When
we were going from one village to another, we walked. The Swiss
do that, so Father said, "Why can't we do it? We don't have to take
a carriage, to pay for it. We'll walk." So we did. It really was a good
training for a child.

∾

The Ossining School for Girls was a yellow wooden building—long,
high, and studded with windows. I enjoyed my years at that school.
Even now I can feel a little tremor that is "wild with all regret" at

the remembrance of the big school room with its dark hardwood floor and the grand piano on the platform. We girls—thirty or forty of us—sat on curve-backed double seats with a double desk in front of us containing a hollow for books. Every morning there, we had chapel when the lovely, elderly voice of Miss Fuller intoned softly, "The Lord be with you."

The words of the Lord's Prayer, with that peculiar phrase about leading us not into temptation, never seemed to me like English words with normal meaning, so I did not ask myself what the phrase meant. I did not even feel that I was speaking to the Lord. I was reciting a beautiful and gentle spell that broke my life in two and placed a section of it in the realm of learning. Learning without bounds! It included Greece and its gods, the wild, tapestried history of Europe, the poets with their lovely, rhyming words—"Tears, idle tears, I know not what they mean."* I did not know what my occasional tears meant either. Those words, like the Lord's Prayer, were like bars of music meant to waft one into a dream.

We had American history, but that was too full of dates and the homes of presidents. I never have known them after McKinley. And we had civics. An utter bore! I do wish someone could have made me want to understand the workings of the United States government. But Latin! What a thrill it was to acquire that first simple sentence. *Ranae sunt in aqua.* "The frogs are in the water."

Worlds opened to me with those liquid sounds, and I did not mind the declensions and other technical aspects of grammar that came later. They were like beautifully made, intricate locks giving access to uncountable treasure. I gobbled Caesar and Cornelius Nepos and chanted the hexameters of Virgil. It is hard for one who had enjoyed meter and rhyme to the full to get profound satisfaction out of modern verse.

Of course, there is more about school, for it occupied the years from five to seventeen. Of course, it had its dark side, also its sad history of crushes and quarrels, but I am thinking now of the most poignant memory of all. It had been absent for most of the years of my adult

* "Tears, Idle Tears" is an 1847 lyric poem by Alfred, Lord Tennyson.

life, buried so far that when I heard of Miss Fuller's death I said absently, "Oh, really?" But the other day it came back to me with an intense stroke of memory, cutting like acid through steel. I know exactly how the great memoirist Marcel Proust felt when he was given a madeleine and suddenly felt the doors that hid his past slide open.[*]

How often I had seen it before I was a senior myself! The families in camp chairs on the lawn. The french doors to the schoolroom open and the girls in their white dresses blooming out, one by one, into the June sunshine. We walked very slowly, and the dainty, formal music seemed to throb with expectancy. One phrase moved into something like a wistful cry. I can never think of that music as belonging to richly dressed dancers in the don's pretentious hall. It must be played softly on a grand piano while white shoes move over the grass and young hearts rise and fall with every step and every beat.

"Tears from the depths of some divine despair."[†] Does everyone feel that, at sixteen, a world of wonders is before her? And does everyone feel it almost incredible that with time these wonders dissolve without noticing?

I cannot imagine that music as played for satin-clad dancers in a pretentious hall, as an opera would have it. In my memory, those throbbing, expectant notes tinkle out from a school piano, while white slippers tread the grass. Sunlight and leaf shadows fall on smoothly brushed hair and swirling white skirts. The notes drop like crystal beads, each splashing into a pool of memories and hopes—sending up a delicious spray that makes the mouth tremble and the eyes fill.

Proust takes many a page to tell of the sensations that came as he touched the pastry, the feeling of joyous expectancy, all unexplained until he remembered his aunt's room on a Sunday morning. Then his mind, as if rising by inches, began to float over the scenes of his childhood. He remembered.

In my case, I heard the minuet from *Don Giovanni*.[‡] I must have heard it countless times before, as Proust must have eaten countless

---

[*] See Marcel Proust's novel *In Search of Lost Time* (also titled *Remembrances of Things Past*), published in seven volumes between 1913 and 1927. Underhill is here referring to a famous episode in the first volume, *Swann's Way*, in which a pastry dipped in tea hurls Proust's thoughts back in time to a tender moment in his childhood.

[†] See again "Tears, Idle Tears" by Alfred, Lord Tennyson.

[‡] An opera by Wolfgang Amadeus Mozart, first performed in 1787.

pastries, but this experience came at a time when the past, like a quivering membrane, was lying just below the surface of thought. Any tiny event could puncture that membrane, and, for me, the stab came from a wistful high note in a minuet. As the notes fell from that high point, I was flooded with a happy expectancy, near to tears. For a moment, my feet seemed to be treading on soft grass. I caught the delicate, heady smell of green things in June. I imagined murmurous voices, just beyond my hearing. Only then did I realize it was that music, formal and piercingly sweet, which was our yearly commencement march at the Ossining School for Girls.

~

In my teenage years, although there was nothing I wanted more in life, I was still not a "sweet girl." I knew that I could not achieve such a thing, any more than I could be six feet tall. I struggled to imagine what the sweet state would be like. I suppose it would mean I must love and cherish people who seemed to me fools. I must find joy in doing for others. Well, perhaps that was a possible activity, but it took so much attention and others wanted such funny things, like Grandma Murray always wanting a particular footstool carried to the bay window for her. I would have been glad to do it in the morning and get it off my mind, but you never could tell when she would suddenly heave herself up from where she had been sitting, grope for the footstool, and start lugging it. That was the signal for all grandchildren to jump up and sing in chorus, "Let me!"

Quakers and Darwin

FATHER BEGAN TO THINK that some of the things the Quakers believed in were just not what a person who was onto things would believe. Little by little he changed his beliefs very much indeed.

Though he could never take Darwin. Because Darwin said man is not the owner of the universe. Darwin says the animals have just as much right as we have. They were developed in one way; we were developed in a different way. We and the animals are all along the same line.

At first he didn't even think about Darwin. He was too busy with his business. Finally he began to buy books on the descent of man and so forth.* And then he would tell me that he objected. "I can't take it, Ruth! I can't take it!" Then he would argue all the arguments that are very simple to us now. "I cannot see it," he would say. "Man was created to rule the earth. Here this fellow Darwin says we're not created for that. I cannot believe him."

❧

Father really suffered over trying to make his modern knowledge about astronomy and history fit the Bible, because it had to fit. Even I, at sixteen, understood that much of it could be classed as mythology. In fact, I was in danger of discarding the whole thing had I been concerned enough, but I was absorbed in other matters and not concerned.

Father was. He taught a men's Bible class and kept them on purely practical subjects. They were enthusiastic, but at home Father had

---

* A vague reference here to Charles Darwin's 1871 book *The Descent of Man, and Selection in Relation to Sex*, which expands on his renowned 1859 volume *On the Origin of Species by Means of Natural Selection, or the Preservation of Favoured Races in the Struggle for Life*.

Figure 11. Abram Underhill, Ruth's father, at an older age, circa 1900.

Darwin's books. He would not talk to me much on the subject, being afraid, I think, of corrupting me, but once he groused about the miracles to me.

"It doesn't seem reasonable. It could have been done some other way."

"But Father, you don't have to believe all the Bible."

He glared at me. "It's the word of God."

"Maybe the gospel writers got it wrong."

"But the Old Testament has miracles too."

"Suppose it's all just Jewish mythology."

That brash statement was too much, even for Father. "I don't want to hear such words in this house again," he thundered.

At one point I bought him Frazer's *Folklore in the Old Testament.** He did not read it. Finally, I rescued it from a hidden shelf and took it into my own library.

Mother had no such troubles. My brother and I, the questioners, began very early to ask her about our Bible lessons.

"But Mother, where could heaven be? The earth is round. There isn't any flat place in the sky for it."

"Perhaps some distant star," said Mother, going on with her sewing.

"But Father says the stars don't have good climates. There isn't any place on them for living waters and trees that bear fruit."

Father had not told Mother this, but she was not disturbed. "Then it's in some other sphere that we can't see."

Mother's faith had taken a leap that science-fictioners are only venturing now, but she made it with no effort at all.

"But Mother, that's impossible!"

"With God, dear, nothing is impossible."

Mother was not troubled, either, about the evil in the world.

"These things are sent to try us. We must love others and serve God."

"But some of the others are wicked. They don't deserve to be loved."

"That we can't know, dear, but one day in heaven we shall know."

Then we had the old argument. What age will people be when they are resurrected? Will we be allowed to choose? And will there be no changing?

"Darling, we are not meant to know those things. For now we 'see through a glass darkly.'"†

"That's not fair of God. We could do so much better if we *knew*." Now we had got to the point of blasphemy, just as we did with Father, but Mother did not thunder. "Darling," she calmly retorted, "God is to do his will, and then you will see that these questions do not matter."

But Father was different. One time he admitted to us that he did not believe the world could have been created in 4004 BC, as Bishop Usher had calculated.

---

* Frazer, James G. 1919. *Folklore in the Old Testament: Studies in Comparative Religion, Legend, and Law.* London: Macmillan.

† Corinthians 13:12.

If it had a beginning out of nothing, then it could end in nothing, I had suggested. Father nodded. He himself was wrestling with that awful possibility. To us children, it did not seem awful, for surely we would be long gone before such a catastrophe happened. Still, this new fact affected the possibility of heaven, which *was* of interest to us. "What about the universe?" asked my brother, risking a question that has only lately been voiced by astronomers. "Could that have a beginning and an end too?"

"If it was God's will," Mother cut in.

"But where would heaven be then?"

"God would see to that, dear."

"But Mother!" I began to display some of my new knowledge. "'Universe' means *everything*. From the Latin *unis*. If the universe ended, so would heaven."

"God could make another universe, dear."

Picnics and Dances

SIXTEEN! AT THAT AGE a girl is at her loveliest. Mother used to bend on me one of her angel looks and say, "Standing with reluctant feet, where the brook and river meet."*

I was reluctant all right. My feet had not grown any smaller or my hair less lanky, even though it was now long and worn in a thick braid. God had not relieved me of the awful curse of being bright, and people talked about it in hushed voices. Mother gave me an autograph album on my sixteenth birthday and wrote on the first page, "Be good, sweet child. And let who will be clever."† But how could you even tell what was going to sound clever? If I told a boy at one of the school dances that he was more like Maurice De Bracy than Reginald Front-de-Boeuf, he wasn't flattered a bit.‡ The girls jeered at me for reading off the Latin translation. "Grind! Grind!" snickered Francine, but I hadn't been grinding. I liked Latin, but I learned not to say so.

It was Margaret who ought to have been sixteen first. She hadn't had any awkward age. Her golden hair and her slender hands and feet carried her straight through the teenage years like Venus on her shell.

"Cometh up as a flower," Mother said, looking at her from the window.§ We were in the sewing room and our half-yearly seamstress, Abbie, was trying a new pink dress on me. It just wouldn't seem to fit.

"I guess I'm more like a weed," I said with what I considered a hollow laugh.

---

* See Henry Wadsworth Longfellow's 1842 poem "Maidenhood."

† See Charles Kingsley's 1856 poem "A Farewell."

‡ These are two characters from Sir Walter Scott's 1820 historical novel *Ivanhoe*.

§ Underhill is referring to Rhoda Broughton's controversial 1867 novel *Cometh up as a Flower*, in which the protagonist, a young and brash woman named Nell LaStrange, is torn between conflicting commitments to family and her own passions.

Figure 12. Ruth as a teenager, circa 1900.

"Ruth, darling, where do you get such ideas?" Mother's eyes were on Margaret, but she put her arms around us both, as she so often did.

"My darling girls," said Mother, "I want you to know, you must always know, that I love you both equally."

When Mother said those words, I took them for gospel. Yet, long afterward, I came upon that sentence of Shakespeare's, "Methinks the lady doth protest too much."* Then I knew, but by then I had ceased to care.

---

* See William Shakespeare's (ca. 1600) *The Tragedy of Hamlet, Prince of Denmark*, act III, scene 2.

Mother went out of the room to call Margaret, who was to be fitted with a blue dress, all frills, and Abbie said to me, "Your mother is an angel."

I realized the awful implications. I was about old enough to be an angel myself, and there were no signs at all. I had, indeed, joined the church, and for a time, I had hoped a great deal of God, but he did not make my hair curl or unloosen my tongue.

This sounds as though I was unhappy all the time, but actually those indigestion-like pangs were rare. The sky was so blue in that summer of my sixteenth year. The shadows of elms on the hilly streets of our town were entrancing. I knew that boys from the military school came to spend afternoons on the porches of other girls, but I could not imagine how that was brought about and did not want it. Mother now and then invited a boy to Sunday supper, and she and Father talked to him politely about his lessons. Then he went home, and the next guest would be a different one.

I was much happier when it was not Sunday or a dance night, and I could take a book under the maples or just lie there without one. I had three or four serial stories running in my head, and sometimes I let them unroll during the afternoon as well as at night before sleeping. Margaret and I used to build up these stories together. Now Margaret had a best girlfriend at school, and they told secrets, even about boys. When I was left alone with the stories, they became much more dramatic and went on, sometimes, for three generations. Each had a hero, usually not handsome but oh so brave! There was Count Rupert, oldest of three noble youths in some European place. He was not so loved by his father as the two younger, but he was much finer, as they all found out after he had rescued both his brothers and the princess. Then there was Richard, that engineer in Africa. He jumped down a hole, or something, thus saving the life of the stupid businessman whom Constance, his beloved, was planning to marry. Richard was partially crippled for life, but he went right on working, and as for Constance, she adored him and never looked at the other man again.

Later in life, a psychoanalyst was much intrigued by these tales. He could not decide whether I had been seeing myself in the role of the male hero or whether I was preserving these gentlemen in knightly virginity until one Ruth Underhill could lighten their lives. For knightly they were in the highest degree; when I imagined their kisses, they were something like Auntie's, only longer and with much nicer things said. I was twenty years older when, one day, I burst out laughing at the remembrance of the last night Count Rupert spent with his princess before a battle. He took her hand most tenderly when he said he might not come back. Then, although *he* was the one with a hard day ahead, he told her that she must sleep. I pictured her lying upon a great walnut settle, with her green velvet gown trailing, while he sat by her all night and held her hand. I simply yearned over that scene.

"The child is dreamy," I heard Mother say in the bedroom, and I guess she meant me. However, Father was not so emphatic about the necessity for sweetness as Mother. He used to give me some sharp looks when I answered a question about Latin. Of course, Robert was really the one who must know Latin and go to Harvard. Still, Father liked Latin, and when he had time he would discuss it, even with a girl. He seldom had time, though.

Once, I remember, when Mother had been explaining to me what would be the nice way to behave, she sighed and remarked, "You may never know, Ruth, how strange it is to have children not at all like yourself."

"Well," I said, "I guess they take half from their father."

Mother was in a sort of dream such as she rarely permitted herself. "You expect your life to be just like your own mother's life, with good and respectful children, all glad to obey you."

"But Mother, we do obey you," I tried.

"And then they have characters from a family you never knew."

Oh, the poor Underhills! Mother had nearly said an un-Christian thing about them, and she clamped her mouth shut. "Now, Ruth, let's talk about your summer dresses."

I wouldn't need much, I thought privately. I wasn't going anywhere or doing anything. Then, just before school commencement, there came the picnic.

~

Probably no one knew the agony that wrenched me every time that word *picnic* was mentioned, for it had not yet been decided whether each girl was to invite a boy. Never in the world should I have the courage to do that, and really I did not know any boys. I should have to stay home, and already I was making tentative moves toward that end.

"I don't really like to go on the water, Mother," I ventured, "and they have such queer food."

"Ruth, aren't you well?"

Not being well was a sure passport to Mother's most tender solicitude, and if only I had not been so well trained about lying, I would have grasped it.

"Oh, I'm all right."

"I think the picnic will be very nice, dear, even if the girls are older."

I dared not mention the subject of boys, for Mother assumed that they would flock to me as they did to Margaret. I lived in a welter of unhappiness to which there seemed no outlet until the news of redemption came. A class of boys from the military school was to be invited in a body. I believe that Miss Damon, the teacher who was to chaperone us, made this decision, and only later I wondered if it had not been just for the sake of the less popular girls.

We were to row over the river and land on that wooded point where all our town had picnics. We girls were bringing sandwiches and cake. We would make coffee over a campfire and sing. Apparently most of the other girls had their boys chosen, blanket invitation or no. Still, there were some "sad birds" who were no one's property. Of course, they could not hold a candle to Frank Holden or Duncan Hodge, who was a dreadful cutup. Apparently all the girls had some experience with him. Anyway, if there were leftover boys as well as leftover girls, the whole thing would look better. I was moderately cheerful as I tucked my starched pique skirts into a rowboat, where Francine sat practically on my lap and covered my stiff remarks with her chatter. Duncan Hodge was rowing. It appeared that he had been Francine's boy up to almost yesterday. Now she had this new one, Rory, who was at the other pair of oars, and they all joked about it.

Landing and getting the picnic ready was a blessed period because I could work. Miss Damon, the chaperone, actually thanked me for it, not knowing that I could have cried to her, like people in peril on the sea, for this temporary rescue. Then we ate the food and drank the coffee and piled up the dishes. The moon was out and a lot of stars, so that the pine trees on the point were gray lumps against water that ran like quicksilver. Francine was gone, and now I noticed that Rory was gone too. Everybody was scrambling up and moving, and I was wondering how I would get over by Miss Damon and what I would say.

"Like to take a walk?"

It was Duncan by my side, not one of the sad birds at all. He even had his hand on my elbow.

"Let's walk in the dark, shall we?"

I had never heard the words "shall we" in such a coaxing tone. My heart fluttered as I assented, fluttered as in the books.

"Do you like the dark?"

"Yes." The flutter would not let me say more.

"Going to slip? I'll hold you."

I am afraid I felt rather stiff in Duncan's arms. The flutter had now become like ten thousand eagle wings filling the sky.

"Let's sit down."

He found a seat on the rocks. He spread his coat for me, just like Sir Walter Raleigh or maybe one of the Knights of the Round Table.

"Ruth, you're a queer girl."

"I'm not." The words sounded like a croak.

"Awful queer." He was pressing close to me. "You keep still most of the time and then all at once you do something wild, or you think it anyway. I see it in your eyes."

There was a long pause, and I wondered why sitting close to Father never felt like this.

"Are you wild?"

"I—well, maybe."

"I thought so. Let's try."

Then suddenly his lips were on mine. This was a boy's kiss. A man's. I was ready to let out a sigh of pure relief, but the kiss did not stop. Duncan had hold of my tongue and was trying to suck it down his throat. Surely the knights of King Arthur never did anything like this! I wriggled. Then I wriggled harder. Ouch! Stop! I had jumped away, slipping on the wet rocks until my skirt came up to my waist.

"You don't like kissing?"

"But that—isn't . . ."

"Golly, Ruth, I wouldn't have thought you were like that."

"You—I wish we were in love, Duncan."

"In love! When you won't even kiss! Let me out of here!"

Duncan got up and I after him. On the way back, I was not squired by a knight who guided my steps. I scrambled along as best I could with Duncan ambling ahead. He was chewing gum. I was glad to hide myself among the girls at the campfire, the leftover girls and the sad birds. Miss Damon did most of the talking. Then we sang songs, and we went home. I was so shaken that, for days, I made no stories and thought of nothing, not daring to think of anything. It was almost a week later that Francine inquired at school, "How do you like that Duncan fellow?"

"I don't believe I like him."

"Mutual," said Francine, gaily. "He says you're the most stuck-up prig he ever saw."

Girls are cruel. The sword went through my heart, and just then, I would have taken Duncan, tongue swallowing and all. However, my mental sacrifice was unnecessary, for Duncan never spoke to me again.

~

There were dances that winter at the military school, and Margaret and I went. All the girls went. I heard Mother tell Auntie that the superintendent's wife selected very carefully, so that the boys should meet only nice girls. Margaret and I were nice girls, we knew that already, but when we went to the dances, in our long white gloves and our flowered net dresses, somehow the boys did not flock around us, at least not around me. They finally did around Margaret, even though she was too young.

Margaret was in her pretty blue party dress. Mine was pink, and I think, now, that I must have looked a little like those hams that they exhibit at the butchers.

At first I didn't mind sitting in the row of camp chairs along the wall while people danced. The superintendent's wife came to talk to me, then the woman secretary did, and finally one of the grown-up men teachers. I hoped he would talk about the Romans, but it seemed he taught chemistry, which we didn't have at Miss Cornelia's. Anyway, he did not come again.

It took a while before I realized that no other girl sat in that row of camp chairs, not for more than one dance. Then began the terrible agony that some girls know, the agony of deciding where to hide yourself, what to be doing, so that people will not realize you are a wallflower. Of course, the other girls knew, even Margaret, but girls have a code about such things. No one mentioned the fact to me. They simply gathered away from me to do their whispering and their talking about boys. I saw them in the corners at school and on the playground, and I knew I must not approach and try to enter the mysteries. I pictured them as votaries of Apollo, fluttering around his white marble temple. Naturally, the uninitiated kept away. I had read about that.

There were six dances a year at the military school. For every one of them, Margaret and I put on our party dresses, blue and pink, and our long white gloves. We were driven in a cab to the school. It was always exciting to get out of its black depths at the big stone doorway, to see the lights, hear the voices and the rustle of silk. I always felt wonderful at that first entrance, like the turning of a great illuminated page in a wonderful book. Then dance cards were put in our hands, and boys came to sign their names. There was a red-haired boy from the country whom everybody laughed at, and he always came to me. Then there might be a male teacher and perhaps one of the smaller boys. At least you could sit out with him and pretend it was a joke. After those three names were on my card, I had to plan for the terrible blank expanses. There was the powder room, but no girl dared stay there very long because the others would see her. If it was summer, I could sneak outdoors; in winter, perhaps, to the library. Once, though, I found the superintendent there, with his shoes and coat off. He glared at me, or I thought he did. I fled like the money changers out of the temple.*

Movement was the best solution. If you kept on the go between powder room, ballroom (yes, we called it that), and refreshment room, you might perhaps give the impression of being temporarily at loose ends. Some boy on his way to another girl might even stop for a word with you. The girls, of course, never stopped. They and I both accepted the fact that the struggle to "have boys" and be popular was to the death. There was no place in it for mercy or even for sharing. How dare a girl introduce her snared partner to me when it might mean that she, herself, might be unescorted for a few minutes!

---

* Matthew 21:12.

Vassar and Europe

IT SEEMED TO HAVE BEEN ALWAYS DECIDED, as far as I can see, that I would go to college. The family had apparently known for a long time that I was never going to get a man. My sisters had told me that, and I just accepted the fact that if men didn't want to be got, then, that was the way it was! I'd do something else.

But when the time came, my father had decided that for me to go to college was an expensive thing and there was a question of whether he ought to bother to send a daughter. He would send his son to college, of course, but as for a daughter? Well, he was a Phi Beta Kappa, and this was a means to persuade him. "Well, if you get Phi Beta Kappa," said he, "I suppose it'll be all right." I was careful to get Phi Beta Kappa.*

Vassar College was in the backyard, as it were, right up the Hudson from where I was. It was almost a part of the home country. It seemed natural that if I would go to any college it would be Vassar. It is in a beautiful situation on the Hudson with a wonderful view and great open country behind it, ideal for walking out in the woods and skating on the pond.

Those four years at Vassar were pleasant, comfortable ones. I made friends in college, several good, firm friends; people who liked the same things I liked and whose families must have been established in just about the way that mine was, just about that much comfort and that much feeling for respectability, which I imagine to a great high degree. One friend, Katherine French, became a medical doctor in the end. Ernestine Patterson's father became governor of Indiana. Grace Abbott lived in New York and had the normal family life. The proxy of Vassar used to tell us that the aim of Vassar was to help you make a comfortable home for some good man.

---

* See: Phi Beta Kappa, Vassar College. 1905. *Constitution and Catalogue of Members.* Pg. 14.

I didn't spend too much time thinking about outside things. I didn't take much part in the sports, because I find that my reflexes are slow. The sport I liked was walking, so a good many of us girls would start out together sometimes on the weekend and go for long walks way back in the countryside. It was very ancient country at that time. There wasn't very much of any other kind of social life.

I specialized in languages. Then I did not know anthropology even existed. But I'd always liked languages very much, and I could already speak a little of French, German, and Italian. I took courses in them and kept on with my Latin and began with Greek. I had already started on Greek because my mother's brother, Uncle Augustus, was a professor of Greek.* It was his idea that, of course, young ladies ought to know Greek; it was silly if they didn't. I was very fond of it; it seemed to me a beautiful language and a beautiful people, and I was very much interested. I enjoyed the whole thing very much. I enjoyed studying. That's something I used to find somewhat difficult to explain, because it was the fashion at Ossining not to enjoy study, to think that study was a horrible thing forced upon you and that you were in prison while you were doing it. I found out I could tolerate it very easily, and it wasn't any trouble to understand the lessons. They were not hard to do.

~

How pleased Mother was when I achieved my first real suitor! I was the right age, seventeen, and he was the right kind of "aspirant" for my hand, a Philadelphia Quaker, and heir to a prosperous factory. I did not achieve him at home, of course, for at home I always felt quenched by Margaret's more approved approach to the males. I was visiting a school friend, Emily Allen, of a good Quaker family from New Jersey. I don't remember being rowdy, but at Emily's I let myself go in games and jokes. Mr. J. Stogdell Stokes was sometimes there in the evening. Before I knew it, he was writing me letters, then coming to call at Ossining, then coming to New York to take me (with Mother) to dinner and the theater.

---

* Augustus Taber Murray (1866–1940) was a prominent professor of classics at Stanford. See: Ohnsorg, Roger W. 2011. *Robert Lindley Murray: The Reluctant U.S. Tennis Champion.* Bloomington, IN: Trafford. Pgs. 111–112.

It was pleasant, but I don't remember being touched in the slightest. J. Stogdell was just plain stodgy. I accepted his attentions without even thinking about marriage. Girls were supposed to get "attentions," and I was glad not to be left out, but there were plenty of things I wanted to do, including college and writing. J. Stodgy did not figure in them. Maybe he would later, for my reading of Scott and Dickens had assured me that once a man had fixed his affections, he kept at it for years.

I went to college, and J. Stogdell came to call in the manner of those days at Vassar. That is, he sent in his card, which went to the chaperone, or whatever she was called, Mrs. Kendrick. She looked up the name to see whether it had been authorized by my parents, and after that it went to me. I told him once that I had seen his arrival from my window, and he asked, in a spirit of scientific inquiry, why I had kept him waiting so long. I really hated to explain about Mrs. Kendrick, but I think he approved. Anyway, his visits kept up during the four college years, and my more convivial classmates used to tease me about the "one man."

The break came when college was over. I was all aflame with adventure and social interest. I was really going to see the world, play in the dirt and hear cursing, maybe even come in contact with *sin*.* I told him about it in glowing terms as we walked along a street in Ossining. Ossining was an awkward place to get to from Philadelphia, and he must have made an effort to come to me right after graduation. Would Stog have proposed to me when we got where we could sit down? I never knew, because I launched immediately into a description of my future. He listened without a word, and before we reached our house, he said goodbye. I never saw him again.†

---

* In an earlier draft, Underhill indicates here that she told Stogdell she was going to be a social worker. However, according to the rest of her narrative, she did not decide she was going to be a social worker until some years later, after the European sojourn following college.

† John Stogdell Stokes went on to become a Philadelphia civic leader and owner of Stokes and Smith, a food packaging machinery firm. Between 1933 and 1947 he served as president of the Philadelphia Art Museum, successfully growing the museum even through the depths of the Great Depression. A 1930 portrait of Mrs. J. Stodgell Stokes by Diego Rivera is in the museum's collections. See: The Philadelphia Museum. 1951. *Life*, September 3: 73; www.philamuseum.org (accessed March 15, 2013); http://articles.philly.com/2007-11-20/news/25225382_1_conscientious-objector-seed-packets-backyard-garden (accessed March 15, 2013).

Long, long afterward, I remember telling myself, "Well, I could have been a respectable married lady like these others." But I said it without regret.

～

After Vassar, back home I could hear Mother and Father again having their long talks in their bedroom at night. Low tones in conversations that lasted hours. I supposed that they were wondering about this problem child they had. What would they do with Ruth?

Finally it was proposed to me by Mother, but she came with Father's permission: "If you wish to spend a little time in Europe now that you have graduated, perhaps it would be a very educational thing for you."

"I'd love to spend time in Europe." I didn't hesitate. "When can I go?"

"We'll have to see. You'll have to go with somebody responsible, a chaperone."

There was a good deal of talk and consideration. Finally the head of the settlement where I had stayed for a while was Miss Bradford, who was about sixty years old and a social worker. Social work people were commanding in that time, because those poor people had to be helped: it was believed they didn't know how to support themselves and be decent citizens, and therefore they needed to be commanded! It turned out that Miss Bradford was planning to go to Italy that summer. So it was arranged between them that I was to have a letter of credit in my own right and take it with me and I was to go with Miss Bradford to Italy.

We went on one of those cheap lines, the Atlantic Transport, where there was no first class, no second, everybody was lumped in together, and it took about ten days to cross the Atlantic. You did not meet any people of any great millionaire type. I had a very pleasant time crossing the Atlantic, though. One always flirts with the first mate, and if you can't get him, then the second mate! I had the second, I believe. I was not really beautiful enough for the first.

Finally we arrived in Italy and got to Rome. Miss Bradford wouldn't spend much money on a hotel. We went to a pension, and it turned out that it was a place for retired English ladies who made a great point of spending their old age in Rome because it was cultured and didn't cost as much as England did, and they met people of their own sort there. There were six or eight retired English ladies in this pension, nobody else.

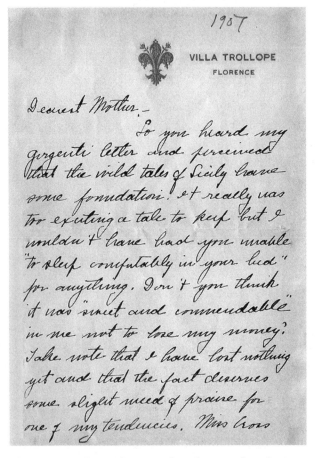

Figure 13. A letter from Ruth to her mother during her European travels, dated 1907.

In the evening I would go religiously to the art galleries and things that have to be seen before you dare talk about Rome. I would wander around the streets alone with a catalog and go to the museums. Then I would come home, and we would have English muffins because that's what the ladies liked. We did not have Italian spaghetti or anything of that sort and of course, no wine, just maybe tea before we went to bed.

Pretty soon it dawned on me: this isn't what I came for! I said to Miss Bradford, "What about finding an Italian family where we could stay and really get to know the people?" "Oh, my dear, Italians? Oh no, I couldn't live with Italians, certainly not!" My way of thinking now was very surprising; I hadn't thought in this way all through college. I'd been given rules at college. I obeyed them and thought what I was told to think. I had not done any rebellious thinking of this sort, but I decided I would!

The next day, when I was at a museum, I talked to a very pleasant young Italian signorina. She was well-mannered and nicely dressed. We talked together and finally she explained to me that I was one of the first Americans she had really done much talking with, because they all spoke such queer English. I tried to teach her, and we became intimate. After a few days she finally confessed to me that her family was really very poor, although they lived in a very nice house, a flat.

"We are taking boarders at present because . . ." she hesitated, "Do you do that in America, people who need money take in boarders?"

"What? Could I live at *your* house?" I replied.

"Si, signorina, with great pleasure."

We fixed it up immediately that I would go and stay with her family. When I came home and told Miss Bradford, she arose in wrath.

"But my dear," she exclaimed, "I expected to stay in Italy only for four weeks. The four weeks are almost up. You must be ready in another week."

"No, Miss Bradford," I said steadily, "I'm going to stay."

"What!"

"Yes, I'm going to stay."

Well, she found that a little bit difficult to take. Finally she relented. After all, I was over twenty-one, and perhaps that would do.

～

Miss Bradford departed, and I left that pension immediately and went to my Italian family. I soon got to jabbering Italian really fast. They taught me "intellectual" Italian. They not only talked about Dante and other authors, but they could quote a whole lot of Italian authors and quote poetry, and then I could quote English poetry to them. We had a beautiful time.

After about six months in Italy I met a middle-aged American lady with gray hair who apparently was quite an adventuress, of a proper sort I mean. A lady who liked adventure—not the other kind! Her name was Mrs. Cornell. She and I became wonderful friends immediately, because she would talk about anything. I could ask her, "Is there a red light district in Rome?" "Oh yes, my dear, of course there is, haven't you been there? Well, I'll take you sometime." Things like that.

After a time, Mrs. Cornell said, "I'm leaving, my dear, it's getting to be winter now. Of course winter is fun in Rome, but I rather like a more picturesque environment. I am going to the Tyrol." I followed her there to western Austria, and then on to Munich, and then on to England.*

In England I met the Merstens, they called themselves, though it was Meyerstein to begin with. There was a little prejudice against Jewish people in England then. I hoped to stay with them.

"Could I possibly pay some board, be your boarder for a little while?" I asked.

"Oh no, we don't take people like that!" they laughed. The Merstens had a lot of money. "We don't take people as boarders! But we'd be glad to have you visit us."

I enjoyed myself, but I didn't want to stay in England and make it my home. Their lives were just a sort of theater, these wonderful people who thought they owned the earth. I saw the young Britons go out of Oxford and apply for some sort of foreign office position. They would go to those strange places and then come back and tell us about the peculiar things they had to eat and the funny things that servants said to them and the strange way the people acted over there, "always under us, of course," they said. "We had to settle their silly quarrels for them." So I would listen to that with great interest and just think, "When they wake up and find out what the world is like, this can't last."

～

My parents were very good about my time away in Europe. I think I was just so queer that they didn't know what to do with me. They thought maybe if I stayed in Europe a while and got to know a little bit more about life, I would settle down—that they'd better just let me know what life is all about.

And before I knew it two years had blown past. Maybe I had learned a little about life. I was ready to go home.

---

* During this period Underhill took courses at the London School of Economics and the University of Munich. See: Ware, Susan, ed. 2004. *Notable American Women*. Cambridge, MA: Harvard University Press. Pg. 651; Lavender, Catherine J. 2006. *Scientists and Storytellers: Feminist Anthropologists and the Construction of the American Southwest*. Albuquerque: University of New Mexico Press. Pg. 104.

The Society

WHEN I RETURNED HOME, however, I was thrown right back into my old predicament. I had no future. That was when I decided I must have a real job. I couldn't fuss around anymore. I'd better not stay at home and be an old maid.

I looked over the possibilities. That was when the advertisement of the Massachusetts Society for the Prevention of Cruelty to Children made itself known to me.* There was an advertisement in the paper for people who had a college education and some sociology. Of course, I'd had no sociology. I'd done nothing but languages and literature, but I gave it a chance.

Mother and I were talking about it, I remember, in the library. Mother sitting quietly with us sewing.

"Mother, it boils down to teaching or nursing, doesn't it?"

"What boils down?" said Mother. "There is nothing else for a girl to do. I'm surprised that you want to leave home in any case." And I knew right then that the figure of Mr. J. Stogdell Stokes was in the background of her mind. But he was lost to me, gone forever.

"Well," I said, "I don't like either of them, Mother. What am I going to do?"†

"If you live quietly at home, dear, I think we're all glad to have you, and I suppose something may eventuate." So I knew she was thinking

---

* In some interview segments, Underhill indicates that she had her first social work job in New York. However, most evidence suggests that she worked in Boston first. See, e.g.: Underhill, Ruth M. 1985. *Papago Woman.* Originally published 1936. Prospect Heights, IL: Waveland Press. Pg. ix; Griffen, Joyce. 1989. Ruth Murray Underhill. In *Women Anthropologists: Selected Biographies.* U. Gacs, A. Khan, J. McIntyre, and R. Weinberg, eds. Pp. 355–360. Westport, CT: Greenwood Press. Pg. 356.

† In an interview, Underhill explained that both marriage and teaching to her "looked tame." Eicher, Daiane. 1984. Ruth Underhill, Noted Writer, Dies. *The Denver Post.* 16 August: 6A.

it will only be a year we'll have this girl on our hands; very soon she'll have a man to take care of her. I somehow always had not been the least impressed by Mr. J. Stogdell Stokes. He hadn't rung one bell in my mind. I knew all about how a wonderful chivalrous gentleman probably does come along sometime in your life, and you give him the first kiss you have ever given a male, and then life turns out beautifully, but this hadn't happened to me, and I didn't feel it was going to happen.

"What about social work, Mother? I think girls do that sometimes."

"Oh, not nice girls, dear."

"Some of the girls at college had sisters who did it," I retorted.

"I don't believe that anybody of your age ought to go into the slums among people whose behavior we cannot understand at all. Now, I don't want you to think about it."

&

But I did think about it, and I thought very hard. Somehow I convinced Mother, and soon we were traveling together to Boston.

We found there was a nice, big colonial house at the top of Beacon Street, where the society had its headquarters. We met the head man, Mr. Carston. He told us that several women employed there were older than I; each had a specialty. One of them looked after the delinquent girls. Another one looked after marriage troubles. I mentioned to Mr. Carston that I spoke Italian. "Oh," he said, "we have very great difficulty with young Italian girls who don't know how to behave in this society and who let men get the better of them without realizing, because they are used to being protected and kept at home. They don't understand what will happen to them. So you can work on the cases of Italian girls who've been raped." Though I don't think he said "rape" before Mother. He said, "Who've been in trouble." Mother didn't realize what I was getting into!

Getting the job really was a revelation. I'm very much shocked now when I realize that the job was given to a young person—I was twenty-five years or so old—like me. Today that would be a very wise and well-trained age, but in my day, I had the psychology of almost an infant. I believed that the good people were all good, that they all worshiped God, went to church or to Friends Meetings, that telling lies and giving bribes and so forth did not occur among any of the people whom I knew.

Mr. Carston then said to Mother, "We're very sorry that we don't always meet the relatives of our workers. We really ought to do it." Mother thought that was nice. So she said, "I guess Ruth will be in a very interesting and useful place then. That's what a woman ought to do—help the world and not think about money, just dedicate herself to helping others." My good Quaker mother went home much pleased.

In contrast, my father would have nothing to do with social work. He thought, "Those people on the bottom, why are they there? Let them stay there. If they want to go up, it's their business. Let *them* go up. *You* don't have to pull them up. You mind your own business." He had no interest whatsoever in helping the poor. Not one bit!

~

I would get a little piece of paper on my desk every morning when I went to the office, giving the address of some house where there was a girl in trouble. Then I would go to that house and talk to the mother. The father would usually be away, of course. And I'd talk to the girl. She would not admit that she'd been raped. She would say, "He never done nothing to me. No, he never done nothing to me. Never done nothing." I suddenly began to see huge vistas of trouble that I had not seen before.

First you had to find the facts. Generally, you could take the girl to the juvenile court and complain there. There was a very sympathetic elder judge who sat in juvenile court all the time. I had to learn court procedure. Sometimes I was able to take the man—the rapist—to court and get him put in jail. I got very intimate with the Boston police, and I would talk with them about their cases, and we'd have a beautiful time. New England has or at least had a rule called "lewd and lascivious cohabitation."* If you catch people at that, they can be arrested. So we called it "L & L," and I would talk to the police and say, "Now, Captain, was she actually doing L & L?" "Oh, yes, sure they were." We'd go on and discuss the whole matter—everything exciting and interesting to me. I didn't quite consider whether it was

---

* Of note, a Massachusetts judge found in a 1981 case that statute G. L. c. 272, Section 16 (lewd and lascivious cohabitation, a felony), although still law, is now "never, or substantially never, made the subject of prosecution." See: Lawrence Fort v. Louise L. Fort (and a companion case), 12 Mass. App. Ct. 411.

wicked or not. It was life. That's the way people do, so why don't I get acquainted with it?

The girl would sometimes confess to me, but then she wouldn't talk to the judge. That caused lots of trouble. She'd talk to me and tell me using all sorts of queer words. I don't remember what the sex words were in Italian, but very vulgar and physical words. I would sometimes be able to get her into a home where she could be educated a little more. If there was a baby, there was a very nice home; it was right near our place on Beacon Street. It was run by a dignified and kindly woman.

It just happened that the girls always liked me. I acted younger than most of the workers, and I'd say, "What did you do, anyway? Come on, let's hear about it." The girls often got very friendly with me, so that much pleased Mr. Carston. They raised my salary at the end of the year. I began to think, now, I'm really going; I'm in.

~

It happened that my brother and I were the two strange members of the family. He and I always made pacts together excluding the two girls—"The Girls," my two sisters were called, as I wasn't a girl, I was just Ruth! He and I made truces together when we were in Boston. He was in Harvard getting his last work before the degree.* We saw each other now and then.

That first Thanksgiving, before I'd really gotten into anything much, Mother told us both to come home for Thanksgiving dinner. Both of us said, "Oh no, we're not going home! Why would we, just for one day, take all the trouble to go down to New York and up to Ossining? The house and the turkey and everything, we know so well about it, we don't want it!" We both refused to go home.

----

* In 1916, Robert L. M. Underhill graduated with his PhD from Harvard. Robert Underhill's own "strangeness," at least from his family's perspective, is perhaps hinted at in his passion for the then little-known sport of mountain climbing. By the 1930s, while a philosophy professor at Harvard, Underhill was "the acknowledged dean of American climbers" (Waterman, Laura, and Guy Waterman. 2000. *A Kind of Madness: Mountain Adventures Tall and True.* Seattle: Mountaineers Books. Pg. 13). In the "Big Love" section below, Ruth Underhill notes in passing that she too was a mountain climber, though of what degree or seriousness is unknown. In her notes for her draft memoir, Underhill writes, "Then the mountains. Here was realization. How gorgeous! Climbing, achieving, but I couldn't go further because no money."

Figure 14. Ruth (right) and one of her sisters, circa 1910.

Mother came to Boston instead, and brought The Girls, and left Father alone on Thanksgiving Day. He was grim about it, but he just said, "I will not let myself be led around by those two crazy youngsters! It's my business to put them down, not theirs to confront me!" So Father stayed home for Thanksgiving dinner with his own family.

I was successful in Boston. I was just floating along having a wonderful time. It never occurred to me this wouldn't last. I wouldn't be a young girl to whom everybody gives things all of the time. I thought this was the way the world is and if I don't like a job, I don't have to take it; I'll wait for the next. I was offered two or three extra jobs while I was in Boston. They were all executive jobs, but I did not want to be an executive assistant. I wanted to be a worker who had real intimate dealings with people. The person who sits in the chair with big arms and plans for the others to have interesting experiences, I didn't want that. I wanted to be the one who had the experiences. Let the executive assistant have the pay if she liked it.

❧

I should have stayed there forever, you know, because I was having a gorgeous time. I was seeing so many Italians in such queer places. I was seeing it, and I was just thrilled with it. I saw the possibility of a lot of writing, but I thought, "Oh, I can do that on the side. My real work is going to be with courts and Italians and rape. That's something serious. That's not just writing fool stuff." I was quite impressed with that.

I was enjoying everything very greatly, but I fell in love. It should have happened before, but it happened now. Because of him I had to flee Boston for New York. All these possibilities were opening for me in Boston, but I dropped them just as though they didn't exist.

"But Miss Underhill, you have a great future here," Mr. Carston said. "You might even be head of this whole institution."

"Oh yes," I said, "but I could be head of something else. I'm not impressed." How crazy it is to think about now! How really crazy. Still, I went to New York.

The Big Love

I WROTE A POEM.

> Yes, once I loved but that is overpast.
> Though pain is sweet, it cannot always be.
> I have outlived hope's wearying agony
> For hope can torture, but it cannot last.

This time, it really was love, and it nearly killed me. Yes, literally—love and tuberculosis.

It began so gaily, like six o'clock of a summer morning. In Boston I had a basement flat on an alley, and above me there was a young man. Yes, he could quote Shakespeare (though he did not respect him overmuch). Yes, he could talk about books, and he had the right manners. In fact, there was nothing the matter with him at all, and how we enjoyed each other!

He was a drama critic, who initiated me into the modern plays. I wandered with him in European literature. We capped each other's bon mots. I was ready at any minute. Of course, though, it had to be marriage. I laughed lightly at his stories of unmarried affairs. They concerned, of course, a different type of woman, different caste I mean. So I accepted his tentative advances as one would watch the sun come higher on a lovely picnic morning. I did not want it to move too fast, for every moment of the preparations was so pleasant.

His vacation was due, and mine could be managed. Said he, "I have a friend who will lend me a shack on an island in Maine. You bring your books, and I'll bring my typewriter. We'll work and invite our souls." We both liked writing, and we liked the ocean. We would go swimming. We'd live on lobsters and have a lovely time.

It would be like my sojourns in mountain huts, I thought, with perfectly unknown men. As experienced mountain climbers, we had all been quite impersonal, and I was glad my, oh yes, that my love had such a civilized point of view.

"Will you get the arrangements on the boat?" he asked. I was glad to be used but marveled a little at his laziness in not being ready to telephone for a couple of cabins.

The shack was wonderful, empty and creaking, so that we used our blankets and borrowed camp chairs. The communion went on gaily in the sea air, though he seemed a little less brilliant than usual. Then there came a night! That was when he nearly dashed the kerosene lamp on the floor, and I slept outdoors.

"But what did you *think* I meant?" he asked next day, "proposing this trip *à deux?*"

"But, but, I've been on camping trips before."

"With no sex?"

"The men were married."

I shall not finish this story in detail. We tried to make up. He said he respected me and, yes, admired me. Not for my sex attitude, which was silly, but for my brain. Only I must see that a pig like me would never have appealed to him as a wife. Thanks for the gay interlude.

The aftermath of that lasted a long time. I left Boston and plunged into a less rewarding job in New York.* I remember one midnight—I was still working toward midnight—when I sat alone on a bench in the subway. "Why do people kill themselves for lost love?" I thought. No physical act is necessary. One just dies.

A doctor, later, found traces of tuberculosis in my lungs. I don't know when I could have had it except in those dreadful months.

⁓

I got on the train and went to New York and found a place where the social service workers congregated and could maybe get a job. Finally, I met a young woman who reminded me of a big hatchet.

---

* In her interviews Underhill inconsistently states that she left Boston because her true love had moved to New York and she followed him. However, given the story's overall tenor, it seems to us more likely that she left Boston to escape her love.

She was tall and blonde and had a fierce sharp voice and sharp blue eyes. I explained to her that I would like a job in social work. She was with the Charity Organization Society.

"Miss Underhill!" she said. "Are you a good soldier?"

"I don't think so," I answered. "I'm a pacifist."

"Well, if you are with us you will have to be a soldier and take orders. You will have to see that what must be done is done and properly done. Are you prepared for that, Miss Underhill?"

"Oh yes, yes," I said. It seemed I might as well say yes as no! So I was accepted as a social worker in the Charity Organization Society.* But it was a very inferior position, not nearly as good as I'd had in Boston and with people who didn't know me at all.

I was given the Italian cases. Italians, faults and all, are lovable people. They like to smile and to welcome a guest, even if they then spend hours pouring out vituperation on some neighbor or employer. *Social work* is a term of reproach in some people's mouths, but to me it was satisfying work and a satisfying social exchange.

I would go to visit an Italian family and spend half the day trying to get them to tell me what they did, what all the children and the wife and the husband did, how they spent their time, how they spent their money. Then I would try to tell them how they *should* spend their time and their money. They always listened most politely and pleasantly. Then they said, "Thank you so much, signorina, for coming to see us," and I went home and reported it, and it was noted down in the monthly report that that family had been visited and perhaps they had been given a certain amount of aid.

I would report, "I think this family"—Lubinelia, for example—"they are a very decent, hardworking family. The older daughter is away from home. She does send money." I never investigated where the older daughter was. Usually she was a prostitute. Then I would report, "The father, of course, I think he drinks. I never saw him do it, but I think he drinks."

---

* In 1916, Underhill was also employed as a "field worker" for a mental health survey on Long Island. Rosanoff, Aaron J. 1917. *Survey of Mental Disorders in Nassau County, New York.* Publication No. 9. New York: National Committee for Mental Hygiene. Pg. 5.

I was really stymied because how could I decide whether that family should have aid or not? It was left to me to decide. I think this really was a dreadful way to conduct business, but there were no really well-trained social workers that I knew of, at the time, of my age. All the people I knew at home, my family and my friends, were all among the "good" people. They never cheated; they never told very bad lies. (They did say they weren't at home sometimes when they were, but that, Mother told me, was allowable.) But I began to find that there was not the simple distinction between good people and bad people that I had supposed existed.

~

I decided I could not live at home again. First, I got a flat with another very nice girl and we lived together quite a while and had a pleasant time before I discovered she was homosexual. I never heard of such a thing! But she explained to me that it was perfectly normal. Well, if it was perfectly normal, all right, but I had never heard of it. She wasn't at all attracted by me. I was nothing that would be interesting to her. She told me about her love affairs, and I listened with my heart palpitating, my jaws hanging! That was something new.

Later, I decided I would really live with Italians. I found a family in an old wooden house, in a sandy yard in the Bronx. I could share a room and bed with their sixteen-year-old daughter. How her toenails used to scratch!

But I had a home. Coming up the rickety wooden stairs every night, I could smell frying oil. How luscious is that smell to me even to this day! There at the door would be Giovanna, with her spotted calico skirt and her big, bare feet.

"Venga, venga! Si mangia." Come, come! Come eat.

The table in the kitchen had an oilcloth with holes through which the wood showed. We had homemade macaroni with tomato sauce and sometimes meatballs. There were wooden chairs around the table for the father, Mario, the ten-year-old son, Giorgio, then Lucia, the daughter (you know it's pronounced Lu-chee-a, and how I hate to have that lovely long syllable changed and shortened), then for Giovanna and me. There was homemade white wine and a loaf of twisted bread about two feet long. I learned to twist the macaroni on my fork, but it was all right to bite off the extra strings that hung from your mouth.

"Eat, eat, signorina!" Giovanna would say. "Qui non mangia muore." He who does not eat dies.

I ate and I laughed as we all did, often till late evening. There was no television then, of course, no armchairs to go and sit in. We all told funny stories, and I remember the wonderful earthiness of some of Mario's lovable people. Years had taught them, I suppose, that it's easier to live that way. I am sad that they cannot be told to some of my "respectable" friends. I mean, of course, that they could not then. Now Hemingway has far surpassed them.

The mornings were sometimes cold, since all heat came from the kitchen stove, but how glorious the breakfasts were! Another two-foot length of bread and strong black coffee in cups as thick as stoneware. You did not put milk in the coffee. You put water-clear anisette, the cordial made from anise seed. We joked over that, too, then everybody but Giovanna went clattering down the wooden stairs to work or school. Giovanna made pasta out of Italian flour and hung the strings to dry in the backyard. Mother saw them once and asked about flies.

Darling Mother felt that she must come and see how I was living. I cannot imagine how she found the place, but I remember her, in her gray silk dress, coming up the wooden stairs with barefoot Giovanna at the top.

"Venga, venga, Signora," she called, and inside she produced coffee and anisette.

"There's nothing wrong, Mother," I insisted as she looked around the bare room, decorated with just one holy picture and a calendar.

❧

Based on my experiences with the Italians, I did write some little stories. They were published in a magazine called the *Smart Set*, which at one time had quite a reputation. I had twelve stories in the *Smart Set*, and all the Italians were pictured in there, their innocent belief in America as the great free world, and what happened to them when they got here. * I got them published, but I didn't get very much pay for them.

---

* *Smart Set: A Magazine of Cleverness* was a literary magazine founded in 1900 by William d'Alton Mann; it ceased publication in 1930 due to Depression-era economic woes. Strangely, despite the precision of Underhill's recollection here, we have been unable to find any articles by her in the magazine. It is possible she used a pseudonym. Some have suggested that during this period she also wrote for the *New York Times*,

I also later wrote a piece about a very modern woman. It was called "Seraphine and the Great Worth While." Seraphine was the young lady who was a seeker after the light. She kept having ideas about what could be done for the world, and then she'd try them, and they would turn out very badly indeed. That was taken by the *New York Evening Post*.

I made quite a little name for myself, and in fact later I published a novel. I had met a man who was very much taken with me and knew a publisher. He took it to the publisher and got it put in, and I didn't have to do any work at all about it. It was called *The White Moth*, about a woman striving in the man's world of business.* It didn't sell much. But it was out.

~

I believe that one of the other adventures I had during this time was when I refused a real kiss. I had been brought up to think that you never kissed until the right man came; you saved that sacred activity. I was asked by various men I met in social work if there was a little kiss, and of course I said, "Oh no, of course not." Apparently it was said with such belief and fervor that they didn't try anymore; they went to get a woman who was a little more intelligent on the subject!

New York Evening Post, and *Women's Companion*. Underhill's published stories in the 1910s and 1920s that we could trace include: "Ancient Long Island" (December 11, 1915, *The Survey*); "The New Emilia" (December 1917, *The Delineator*); "Red Eyetalian Vendetta" (February 9, 1918, *Every Week*); "Cheeses from Torre" (May 4, 1918, *Snappy Stories*); "No Cripples Any More" (September 1918, *Munsey's Magazine*); "Victory in Olive-Gray" (July 1919, *The Atlantic Monthly*); "The Hounds of Spring Fiction" (June 1920, *The Bookman*); "The Goldfish Bowl" (August 1920, *Ladies Home Journal*); "A Voyage Towards Reality" (August 1920, *The Bookman*); and "Atalanta-June" (March 1921, *Everybody's Magazine*). Of note, readers looking for early Underhill publications should be careful not to mistake her for her contemporary, a different Ruth Underhill of Nassau County, New York, who was also a published writer in addition to being a champion golfer. See, e.g.: On the Ladies' Links. 1900. *Golf Illustrated* 5(56):18.

* Lavender has described how this novel exposes "Underhill's internalized rejection of conventional women's roles," laying bare her feminist aspirations. Lavender, Catherine J. 2006. *Scientists and Storytellers: Feminist Anthropologists and the Construction of the American Southwest*. Albuquerque: University of New Mexico Press. Pg. 105. See: Underhill, Ruth. 1920. *The White Moth*. New York: Moffat, Yard.

Seraphine and the Great Worth While

By Ruth Underhill

The Undesired Art.

"Let us, Clarissa," said Seraphine impressively, "begin to use our brains!"

"Good heavens!" said I, frightened, "they're not going to suspend publishing the newspapers, are they? I thought it was only the magazines."

"Oh, I didn't mean about public matters," said Seraphine hastily. "After just enrolling as party members it would hardly be nice. I meant only at home."

I became extremely uneasy. "Remember," I said, taking Seraphine's hat off the hot water faucet, so I could put the kettle on for dinner, "we are ladies."

"That's just it," Seraphine agreed, taking from the dumbwaiter our grocer's order, which consisted of six cold storage eggs and half a pound of nut butter. "I was beginning to think ladies would never have a chance. There's always been such frightful 'avoritism toward men. They've always been the ones to make all the money."

"A background of culture is not marketable," I magnificently, putting a few meagre teaspoonfuls of rice into the double boiler.

"I believe," said Seraphine, with terrible purposefulness, "that it is. I wish you to think, Clarissa, what accomplishments or what virtues we learned in our childhood that are worth money. I want money. We *need* money."

It could not be denied, but I was a little shocked. "I don't believe you ought to say that. Isn't it considered awfully bolshevik?"

"Not," said Seraphine, "if you state that you want to use brains to get write and office jobs are seen to be the dullest in the world, we're beginning to see our mistake. Or that's what I'm going to say when I write an article after I've 'worked' six months.

"Cooking is taking its place where it belongs. And I'm going to be ahead of my time and seize my chance. I go after a job to-morrow!"

"Do you think the New York housewives will be ahead of their time, too? Like a sort of general daylight saving of the intellect?"

"Women," said Seraphine, firmly, "are always in the van. They'll be only too glad to get the job really done by some one they can receive as an equal, and not have just anybody slopping around the kitchen all the time."

The boiled rice was cold the next night when Seraphine came home. In silence she came into the living room, set the rice pot on the *Atlantic Monthly* and her plate on the *Saturday Evening Post*, and began to eat.

"Is cooking an art?" I inquired sympathetically.

"It is," said Seraphine. "Like blank verse dramas."

"Well, of course," I agreed, "they're awfully nice, but one doesn't actually need them in the home."

"Neither does one need a good cook," said Seraphine. "One doesn't need anything she isn't willing to pay for."

"What," said I, "about the need of people to cook the millions' food? Are they eating it uncooked?"

"They'd just as lief," said Seraphine darkly, "so they had some one to order around. My dear, I entirely forgot, when I said cooking was an art, that nobody really *wants* art. Art can be done without; what people really want is the unskilled workers. They can go out to restaurants for food; what they want at home is somebody to order around."

Seraphine gazed grimly on the advertisement column. "If that's their idea of what's the most necessary thing in a house," said Seraphine truculently, "I know what'll happen to them for eternity!"

I was extremely shocked. "Damning such a lot of people—!" I hesitated.

But Seraphine was unperturbed. "They will go on advertising."

Figure 15. "Seraphine and the Great Worth While," published in the *New York Evening Post* in 1919.

But finally there was a very beautiful young Italian man who was from one of the lower classes. He was not educated, but he did come to affairs at the settlement where I went in the evening, and he seemed to be very nice and well brought up.

One night, when I was leading the singing of some patriotic song, he came and put one arm around me. Well, of course, I immediately moved away. He said, "Just a little, *un bacio?*" I knew that meant a kiss. "Oh no," I said, "certainly not." He came a little further and said, "Bacio, signorina?" Well, I just wasn't going to provide a bacio. I said, "I think my stay this evening is over, I must leave now," which I thought was a very polite, proper way to get out of things.

I got my coat and left the door of the settlement, and as I was walking down the street he came after me! He had a knife in his hand! He called out, "A kiss or I'll give you this knife!" Well, of course he didn't mean it, but how I was terrified! I ran as fast as I could to where I could get a cab and leaped into it for home.

⁓

I joined the women's movement then in New York. Emmeline Pankhurst, the suffrage activist, came over here, and she began exciting the New York women.* Most of them had thought, "Well, things ought to be better than they are, but we are not going to do much about it." Mrs. Pankhurst just got them going, and I listened to her and I was thrilled, too. We had a march about the woman's right to vote up Fifth Avenue in which I was a marshal and walked on one side with a red flag telling the women to keep in step or something like that.

The Charity Organization Society did not feel that those activities were right. When they learned about my participation in the march they fired me. I thought, "Oh, it will be easy. I'll get something else. Nothing about that." But it was not.

Soon after that job was over, I was having dinner with a lot of Greenwich Village people.

"Well, fellows," I told them, "I'm in a bad way. I lost my job."

"Oh, you mustn't worry about jobs," they said. "Everybody loses them."

---

* Emmeline Pankhurst (1858–1928) was a British political activist and one of the suffrage movement's chief advocates. Underhill quite likely saw Pankhurst during the latter's lecture tour of North America, which began in New York in January 1916 (see: Purvis, June. 2002. *Pankhurst: A Biography*. London: Routledge. Pg. 284). So-called "suffrage parades" began in New York in 1910 and continued until 1917, when the state granted women the vote. These demonstrations, "seen as radical at first, . . . eventually acquired enough respectability to attract socialites as participants in the parades down Fifth Avenue in New York City." (Crocco, Margaret Smith. 1995. The Road to the Vote: Women, Suffrage, and the Public Sphere. *Social Education* 59(5):257-264. http://publications .socialstudies.org/se/5905/590501.html). Notably, both of Underhill's sisters, Margaret and Elizabeth, seemed to have been involved in the suffrage movement, as both appear on a 1917 petition (see: www.westchesterarchives.com/ht/images/items/comms/ osstown/suffrage/suffragettetrans.pdf [accessed March 26, 2013]).

"No, I never lost a job before, and I was respectably brought up, and I think you ought to keep jobs." I was very much down.

"I tell you what," one of the boys said, "we'll walk up Fifth Avenue."

"Yes."

"And go into every single drinking place we come to, and then we'll see if that doesn't cure you."

So we did that, but it just put me very fast asleep! I staggered home being pushed by several comrades. My friends were sort of worried that I would turn into a drunkard. But I said, "I will never do this again." I just had a horrid time. A disgusting time. I wouldn't repeat it for anything.

World War I

WAR WAS DECLARED, and I can remember feeling elated. So did all young Americans. There had been several generations of peace, and we sang old Civil War songs as a joke. Now, the martial music and the saluting gave us a feeling like the trumpet calls of Revelation.* I can remember singing "The Marseillaise" loudly in the office hall and everybody clapped. We wanted war.

I applied immediately for Red Cross social work and was frantic when the appointment did not come. Finally, I went to Father's law partner in New York to help me through. Father was practicing in New York three days a week by then. "Well," the partner said, "your father cannot hope to influence *everybody*." I realized why the appointment had not come, and I went home and said to Father that he could not stop me. Never did I consider what either parent was feeling. I doubt if many young people off to Europe did.

꜌

All I can give about World War I is disconnected flashes—like a preview at the movies—only it's an afterview! A flood has gone under the bridge and through the sewers since then.

The first flash, petty though it is, is my pleasure in the Red Cross uniform. It was gray whipcord with four button-down pockets. Oh, the pleasure of not having to carry a handbag! I carried all my money and papers in one breast pocket and never had to worry about its whereabouts or safety, and then, I didn't have to worry about whether I was well dressed. I was not a pretty girl. I had no innate style, for Quaker upbringing does not encourage that sort of thing. So I was constantly troubled about whether I was wearing the right thing

---

* Revelation 8:2.

Figure 16. Ruth in her American Red Cross uniform, circa 1917.

and how much worse I looked than the other girls. So the uniform suited me. The picture of myself in it has a calmly self-confident air.

I do remember the zigzag voyage in a convoy. We Red Cross people were a unit, with a clerkly young man at the head. I remember feeling no great reverence for him, but I had reverence for the project and obeyed him meekly. He forbade me, with fire in his eye, to let my wristwatch show on deck at night. The luminous dial might betray us to a German submarine. We had a lifeboat drill every day, but none of the convoy could sound whistle or foghorn. I remember how, on the return trip, we approached Liverpool, and suddenly our ship's whistle turned loose. Some people fainted.

Lots of boys were going, and I talked to them on the ship. They didn't know why they were going, they just wanted to go. They got tired of staying home in the slums or out on the farm, and they were going to Europe to fight! What for? Well, they didn't really know. Whom were they fighting? They didn't know.

Another glimpse concerns Fred. He was one of the married men I grew a friendship with, and one who, as usual, would have had me if there were not a wife. One did not bother with such things in the face of war, and we were in love, but it was proper love. I don't believe he even asked me to do *it*. We just sat in steamer chairs (for we were officers and entitled to them) and poured out our souls. It was the most complete intimacy I have ever known. When we got to Marseilles and were kept diddling around for weeks, we spent every minute together, seeing art galleries, eating in delicious little restaurants. Then one morning, the call came, and by evening, the unit was distributed over Europe. I did not hear from Fred again, nor expect to. It was after I got home that a comrade wrote to tell me he was one of the dead in France.

After a while I got work that meant something to me. Perhaps I should not be too acrid about those first days. My country, on almost a notice, had had to collect thousands of people and send them off on an errand well meant but not yet planned. People were chosen in great batches, for their enthusiasm, their political pull, their training as far as it could be hurriedly ascertained. I came to meet some very fine workers as I went along.

I went to Italy. I was in a railway carriage with another woman when an American soldier poked his head out of another carriage that was passing. We exchanged gay hails and he grinned, "And you gals don't speak a word of Eye-talian, I suppose!"

"I do too!" I shouted at him. "That's why I'm here." Later, I learned that he had been quite justified in his supposition. Scarcely any of our Red Cross people spoke Italian. What did that matter? We had come from God's country to help, and we helped as enthusiastically as a committee clearing the stadium for a football game. Every American was a friend, to be hailed and even hugged. We went arm in arm through the streets of Rome and Florence (the boys never learned to say "Firenze"). We ate pasta; we drank red wine; we rushed happily into every typing or office job handed down to us.

My job was establishing orphanages for the children of killed Italian soldiers. Italy seemed to have no arrangements for that contingency, at least not in the west-central region of Abruzzi, where I was stationed with a little group of people. When we got there, it turned out that a man who had been the leader of an orchestra was the only American in that area, and so he had been given the job of looking after the poor Italians. Of course, he knew less than nothing about what you would do, and his wife knew less than he did. So we all appeared on this entirely vacant landscape. I was appointed the leader. If you knew how little I knew at that time, you'd wonder how they could have appointed me. But it turned out that the man who was one in our group felt that he must be the leader because he was male. There was quite a little fuss about that.

We fixed up the little hotel there as a place that would receive Italian orphans. I worked to get helpers, to clean and do the service, and was able to employ noble young ladies to take care of a nursery. We did have Italian children, and they were cared for a little bit.

Job aside, what a delicious place is Aquila degli Abruzzi! What I remember of it chiefly is the public square, with its row of fountains where the water poured out from stone lion heads and women of the town came to do their washing. I lived at the Albergo del Sol, in a bare little room without water or heat. In fact, there was no heat in Abruzzi that winter except in the kitchens, where people could huddle around the charcoal stove.

There was not much food, either. At first our mainstay was goat's milk cheese. The hotel proprietor or his helper cooked the big white cheeses, like an egg enlarged to the tenth degree, by holding them on a skewer over a little charcoal fire. How hopefully I tried, later, to do that in America but never succeeded. When the cheese gave out, there were chestnuts only. I had always thought of chestnuts as a luxury, but the mountain slopes around Abruzzi were rich in chestnut trees. On some days, nuts were our only food. There was always wine, though. It was made in the neighborhood and brought to Abruzzi by cart, but the vintner kept losing his horses to death or to the army. He found he had to reduce bulk, so he distilled the wine. A very little of that with your meals was enough.

꒰

There were a few flaws in the golden bowl. On one occasion I was in a group of people who had once published something. We were assigned the job of writing some publicity on the Italian project for American publications. Our uniformed head was a jovial colonel who had been city editor on some small-town newspaper. It soon became obvious that you got nowhere with the colonel unless you were a very compliant young female. I, of course, was not. In fact, if I had been chosen, I should not have known how to respond. A skinny girl who had published one magazine story was elected, and we all paid her a sort of homage. After all, she was second in command of a national Red Cross unit.

It dawned on me, finally, that the colonel expected to make literary hay out of his stay in Italy. He did not speak the language, and I saw a ray of hope when he began asking me to translate. He got hold of a current novel called *L'uomo Finito*, which I translated as *The Man Who Was Played Out*. *The Finished Man* sounded pretty awkward. The colonel liked my title and first chapter and explained to me that he would pay me (I don't know from what funds) for translating the whole book. Was my name to be on it? No. I refused in a real author's rage.

I left the unit soon after that and the only other thing I remember about the colonel is his comment on the Red Cross hospital material. Carloads of bandages and other supplies were sent from America, and I heard, after I got home, how the women of small towns banded together to take them, solacing fear for their sons with patriotism. Some of those carloads may have reached their goal. In the small towns where I was, they stood unheeded in the freight yards unless beggars looted them.

"Shouldn't we let the people at home know?" I attacked the colonel. "If these things are not wanted?"

"Pooh, pooh!" said the colonel. And he spoke the wartime slogan that had brought distraction to many a mourner and many a slacker. "Don't you know they have to 'give till it hurts'?"

꒰

My sainted mother wrote to me, "We wonder if you are comfortable. We think of you so often, sleeping in those strange foreign places. Anyway, but perhaps the Red Cross provides tents or barracks for you. I'm knitting you a good pair of bed socks."

The bed socks weren't useful. When the sun retires from sunny Italy, the resulting gloom is something at which no Harlem flat can even faintly guess. But I didn't tell Mother that unless she had used at least a whole sheep for each sock, they wouldn't have much effect. I always eluded Mother's question as to whether I was comfortable.

I told the American Red Cross, when I answered their questions as to my maternal grandmother's Christian name and whether I drank water between meals, that my health was good and that I was a specialist in camping. War, I considered, after a prolonged inspection of the sporting goods shops, was a particularly businesslike kind of camping—leather cases for things, you know, and little aluminum utensils on a folding table. But in fact my sleeping adventures in Italy are less like those of a nice efficient camper than like those of a fairy tale prince.

I wrote Mother back that I was tired of sleeping in palaces. The palace life is, truth be told, a distinct trial, one of those unexpected hardships of war that you face all unprepared. You see, the family and the Ladies Committee and the Red Cross chapter at home made me a certain provision of woolen socks and bathrobes and blankets, but these were intended to be used under the familiar starry sky or in a nice wooden barrack. I know by experience that one can camp quite comfortably under the cold starry sky, so I innocently told the examining physician that I was quite hardy. I had never guessed then at the damp desolation of marble halls and the awfulness of high gilt ceilings. It takes a brave woman to sleep in a palace.

~

I like having served my country overseas, but I wish I could have been in New York when the armistice was signed, because there must have been *some* shouting there.

November 1918, I was in Milan—a cold, misty place with wide, silent streets where soldiers marched in the morning, where the occupant of a passing cab was generally an officer with his little olive green trunk on the seat beside him, where there were signs under the store entrances that you may take shelter there from air raids, where it was the anniversary of the terrible retreat from Caporetto.*

---

* Underhill refers here to the Battle of Caporetto, in which the Italians retreated in defeat from Kobarid, Slovenia, in October and November 1917, during World War I. Ernest Hemingway recounted the battle in his 1929 book *A Farewell to Arms*.

We had known that something was coming. We had known because for a fortnight the Italian offensive had been on. All that day I had walked about the streets. They were full, a mass of slowly moving people. Not tight packed, everyone had space enough; not in a hurry; not pushing, nor shouting.

"Why don't they shout?" I cried to the woman at my side. "Why don't they laugh? I ought to see victory in their faces!"

"Pensando ai morti," she said. They are thinking of the dead.

They strolled all that day, the shopkeepers with their wives and all their families of babies; the rumpled gray green soldiers home on furlough; the girls, more independent than of old, with cheap new dresses bought with their earnings; the tired, distinguished old men bearded like ancient Roman senators. They strolled arm in arm, as Italians do. They talked in low voices or were silent, waiting. Then the papers were called.

"Our troops have occupied Trento and disembarked at Trieste. The tricolor waves over the Tower of Buonconsiglio and the Castle of San Giusto."* Signed, Diaz.

If one could find words for what that meant! Trento and Trieste were a dream, two cities far apart, whose names were linked together, only as a watchword: two legendary names that meant the very height of Italian aspiration. It could not be true. Men stood dazed, with that war bulletin in their shaking hands, while the tears ran down their cheeks. Why, if Trento and Trieste had been taken, one now and one three months from now! If we had had now only the vague hope that we were approaching one of them, it would have been enough. The people stood, packed in a sort of stupor, silent in all the streets.

That was hardly a holiday. It was too solemn, too terrible. The stupendousness of that good news made us reel until tears were the only expression of which we were capable. We stood in the streets all day, all night, while voices shouted intermittently over and again that bulletin, "Our troops have occupied Trento and disembarked at Trieste," before we began to believe.

While we stood in the streets, waves of motion began to wash over the crowd. We had to move, if only to feel ourselves still alive after

---

* The Tower of Buonconsiglio is in Trento, northern Italy; the Castle of San Giusto is in Trieste, northeastern Italy.

that tremendous blow. We began to surge back and forth through the porticos and through the streets. It was dark. A cold white mist clung about the streets, and through that the great mass of people swayed to and fro, silent, clutching each other, laughing under their breath, frightened and half-delirious.

In the dark I heard a Cockney voice next to me. I whirled—I could not help it—and grasped the sleeve of a dirty khaki uniform. "Ally," I said, "I've got to shout. Haven't you?"

"Rather," said the English aviator, "how will you have it?"

"Next time they call the bulletin: rah, rah, rah!"

"Can't understand the bally thing, but I suppose it's a proper bulletin."

We did it. I choked a little with emotion on the first yells, but then everybody began to help us. They were not wild yells. They burst out as people gasp now and then under the stress of emotion.

"Evviva Trieste!" Long life Trieste!

It was with that news that the week of holidays began. The cold white mist still hung about the city, and no new lamps were lighted. We rose in the morning. We got our meals. We made some semblance of going about life as usual, but Milan lived in a dream. The Austrian armistice, which our wildest hopes had told us might follow slowly on the taking of Trieste, came within a day.*

Americans, I suppose, don't know what it is to have an age-old enemy. Most Americans cannot thoroughly understand what it means to be oppressed. I read the terms of the armistice in a café, where one breakfasts on black coffee in a tall glass and little bran biscuits. Incredible, amazing terms. As my eye traveled down clause after clause of complete surrender, I began to smile a fierce smile. "Oh, at last! We've got them at last!" I had not known I could smile like that about a conquered foe. I dropped the paper and looked around the café. They were all smiling. Those middle-aged shabby men with their few cents' worth of coffee on a cold marble table, they too had the look of a fighter with a bayonet in his hands. Oh, forgive us. That one day, and after those years!

---

* On November 3, 1918, Trieste fell to the Allied forces; Austria-Hungary concluded an armistice on the same day.

The banners glimmered in the mist all that week, the first banners that had been out since the terrible retreat of the year before. For Italy had taken the war in silence, no bravura of flags, no processions, no dancing, no daredevil merriment. Against the old black buildings the emerald green of the Italian flag flashed out like a shout, and we began to understand that the news was true. All that week the slow, dense crowds swayed through the streets. There was little noise. They talk about the music of Italy, but there was little music. It was a women's and an old men's celebration, for the strong men had all gone. There was no singing. Here and there a band of boys trotted through the crowd, with one drum and a fife and a banner too big for them, and when they passed, women with shaky voices and tears running down their cheeks managed to join in the refrain of Garibaldi's hymn, "Forth out of Italy, out of Italy, O foreigner!" *

We never left the streets. It was as though we could not get enough of looking at each other, of realizing that these were citizens of a victorious nation, and then we began to find words. "It's victory! It's victory. This means the end." Four girls, swinging down the street together, saw my Red Cross uniform. "American? God bless America!" and they crowded up to kiss me before they swam on.

❧

The war had ended, but I was offered a job translating Italian labor laws into English. They had quite a new outfit of the labor laws in Italian. I accepted and was employed by the Rockefeller Foundation. Rome was where I stayed, which is a lovely place. Perfectly delicious. Everybody was happy then. The war was over. Italy had had war enough, poor thing.

---

* Giuseppe Garibaldi (1807–1882) was an Italian politician and general, considered one of the modern country's founding fathers. Although Underhill's wording here seems improvised, it gets to the heart of the "Hymn of Garibaldi," which was widely considered "the true expression of Italian yearnings." See: Young, James C. 1917. Anthems of Our Allies. *Pittsburgh Press*, May 21.

A Marriage Begins and Ends

HE WAS A MEXICAN, delicately pretty as a pussycat. On leaving my hotel room in Mexico City, he asked, "Must I go?" I said, "No, stay." He was like no man I had ever known or ever wanted, just something in a foreign land, out of a fairy tale. He did know how to make love, as I had calculated, and he said he knew how to be careful. Nevertheless, when I got back to New York, I was pregnant.*

I regret that part of it. It seems to me that going into that strange, wild darkness, one should have the purpose of bringing back a child, and I feel sure that the complete loss of self that a mother must experience comes to a woman in no other way. I have not had it. I fear I have never been completely, suicidally unselfish, and at this point, I had no pity for the unborn. I did not want a child by Carlos. I was bathed in horror and ready to die, but a woman friend helped me get an abortion.

After that, I was out of the glass case. You see, I *took* freedom. Nobody gave it to me. I just *took* it!

I sometimes kissed men, sometimes accepted them for a night. Usually the pleasure was very mild. The only one who really stirred me, "made the earth move," as Hemingway has it, was Fred, a sign painter.† I liked his descriptions of taking a ladder from the top of a thirty-story building and standing up against the sky to splash out the call for someone's whiskey. We had fun in restaurants to which

---

* It is unclear exactly when this trip to Mexico occurred. However, one suggestive piece of evidence is a report of a Quaker meeting that notes, "Ruth M. Underhill brought a most vivid picture from her recent visit to various mission fields, describing our work in Jamaica, Cuba, and Mexico" (Minutes of Nebraska Yearly Meeting of Friends, Thirteenth Annual Assembly. 1920. Pg. 17). If this transpired around 1920, it also fits Underhill's conclusion at the end of this section about now being ready for marriage.

† From Underhill's notes for her draft memoir, it is unclear but possible that Fred's last name was Salter. For the quote, see: chapter 13 of Ernest Hemingway's 1941 book *For Whom the Bell Tolls*.

Figure 17. Ruth in the years just before her marriage, circa 1915.

I would never have gone. Our temporary absorption in each other was delightful. Usually I did not criticize him, but once when he kept saying "specie" instead of "species," I corrected him.

"How do you know that, dear?" he asked in childlike wonder.

Then I realized that I had been using on him my social worker technique. For with my "cases" I left my world and dwelt completely, for a time, in theirs. I have been, in that way, an Italian factory worker, an Irish laundress. I could understand such a girl's fears and hatreds, why she could not do the normal, reasonable thing the "office" recommended. I was comfortable and happy in this other life, as the girls were with me, and as I was with Fred. Of course, though, it was only for a few hours a day. In the evening, I snapped with relief onto another level. So I snapped finally away from Fred. He gave me too many hours' work a day.

"Cato," the college professor, was in my world, but he couldn't be bothered with me long. Hubert, the middle-aged lawyer, would have acceded to a permanent, part-time arrangement, but none of these was very satisfactory. I decided to marry, and immediately he was there. Handsome. Good mannered. Able to quote, though not Shakespeare. A little like my lost love, though he was a paperback copy. And he was willing to marry, so we did.

~

Yes, I guess then I decided I could marry. If it was a nice enough man, marriage would be possible. It was just this kind of other love that I felt was not real love at all, was just a physical excitement, and I didn't want it.

I had good relationships with many men at this time, but none wanted to sleep with me, nor I with them.[*] I wasn't afraid of anybody in those days, my Greenwich Village Period. That's when I was really learning things my mother never taught me. Around this time, I was part of a crowd that included Robert Lowie, the anthropologist.[†] It may be that he began telling me about Indians, that's about the first I'd ever heard of them. He liked Greenwich Village, and everybody liked him, so he would be at the dances.

Then there was poet and playwright Edna St. Vincent Millay, the great goddess of free love; she was there.[‡] Of course, I didn't see much of her because she would have no woman near her except as a handmaiden. She was getting all the boys. I remember one young man who had come from the South, where they'd been rather more proper than they were in Greenwich Village. He took me to dinner, but only to ask me about Edna. "You see," he said, "I'm told she's

---

[*] Although in notes for her memoir, Underhill sketchily wrote, "I lived in Greenwich Village, took some men, and lost my virginity. It didn't matter then. I wasn't saving [it] for anybody."

[†] Robert Lowie (1883–1957) was born in Vienna but lived in New York from the age of ten. He began graduate work in anthropology at Columbia University in 1904 and obtained his PhD in 1907. He worked at the American Museum of Natural History until 1917 and then left for the University of California at Berkeley, where he worked until 1950. Lowie was a strong adherent to the historical particularism practiced by his mentor, Franz Boas. See: Bohannon, Paul, and Mark Glazer, eds. 1973. *High Points in Anthropology.* New York: Alfred A. Knopf.

[‡] Edna St. Vincent Millay (1892–1950) was a playwright and poet, known, too, for her public love affairs and feminist activism. See: Milford, Nancy. 2001. *Savage Beauty: The Life of Edna St. Vincent Millay.* New York: Random House.

had a thousand lovers, and I'm going . . . to be the thousand and first!" You'd think I would have gotten changed by that, but I didn't. I still thought that if they wanted me, they've got to have marriage.

Finally, I met the man who became my husband. I met him in Greenwich Village, and we got very friendly. He was a very charming, nice man. I had always said to myself, "He's got to use good English. I'm not going to marry any of these people who say, 'He wrapped it good.'" It drives me mad to hear people say that! I met a man who was of English descent, and he spoke good English. I also liked that he was an engineer, different from anything I had then known. His name was Charles Cecil Crawford. I had thought about that before the marriage, too. I don't want to marry anybody who has a hard name. All of these things don't speak of deep love, you see. I would not marry anybody with a name I didn't like.

My father had a big farmhouse out in Westchester County. Cecil had talked about it. He thought he'd rather like to go and live in that area. I said, "I'm going to the farmhouse. I'm just going to devote myself to writing there. I'm through with social work. I have not done any good." He said, "We might team up. What would you think?" I wasn't in love. I just thought he was nice. And he wasn't in love either. We thought we would try it. So we did, and I finally married him. Not grandly at all, very modestly, by a registrar.

He came and lived in the house with me. I believe I counted up eight years of that. It was very pleasant, but little by little, it turned out that the marriage wouldn't work. In the first place, he would be no kind of a father for children; he was too irresponsible. He didn't want children anyway. He wanted to have a nice time in the world.

He expected to give me orders and that I would take them happily and that we would also have a good many joyous times together. But it didn't work out like that. I didn't take orders, and sometimes I told him what I thought he ought to do—well, that's impossible! It is possible today, but then it was not possible for a woman to tell her man what he ought to do.

He liked engineering, but the work stopped in the area, and there wasn't anything he could get. Pretty soon we didn't have any money. Oh, he was a charming, good-looking gentleman, but he was the kind who would come home one night and say, "Well, Ruth, something rather comic happened today. I gave up my job. I told him to take his job and stick it up his ass." That sounded all very cavalier, but he said it with such a charming smile. "What, Cecil?" I stuttered. "How about the coal bill?" He could only say, "The coal bill is pretty well doomed. We haven't any money."

Cecil was not much at farming, but he did some. We had a cow, which both of us tried to milk. I milked that cow for one winter, and my hands wouldn't straighten out for a long time afterward. It was really lots of fun until Cecil began to stray a little. Of course, I ought not to have minded it. I'd known when I married him this was not great love, but I had thought it was a very pleasant and faithful arrangement, at least. Little by little it got so that Cecil and all the people who came for the weekends would sometimes be out all night when I was not invited. I began to think, this isn't much fun! Also, I finally had to go back to New York and get some kind of a social work job to pay the coal bill, while Cecil stayed out in the country.

I was back at the farmhouse after a time, but I began to see it wasn't going to work. We had a great big bedroom with two beds, and Cecil's bed was empty all night. I thought about that and said, "Now, how long, how many times is this going to happen? Is this the kind of marriage I've got for myself?" I pondered a lot about that.

I finally asked Cecil, "How do you feel about quitting this arrangement?"

"Oh, I don't think we need quit," he said. "Can't we both be rather loosely organized?" There was nothing else to do for the time, so I let it go like that.

A very interesting looking young woman came up to spend the weekends, as other people did, and I saw that Cecil was really very much taken with her. Finally, one night that he didn't come back, I thought, he and that woman must have gone somewhere. The next day I asked him again how he would feel about divorce. He said, "I don't think we need do that. We can be comfortable this way." But I felt pretty much worked up. I went to the woman. We were all grown up.

"Now, are you really in love with Cecil?" I asked the woman.

"My dear, for me the sun rises and sets in him," she said.

I thought, well, there's some place where he can go then. "He is not a steady worker," I told her. "If you married him, would you be willing to support him?"

"Why, of course. I love him."

"All right, then. He's safe. I'm not leaving him to starve. He's got somebody who likes him. Just take him, and I'll go back to New York."

~

What did we used to say? Yes, "kaput," it was all kaput.

We got a divorce. It was all very simple for me, but ask me not about my poor family. It was hard on them. There had been no divorces in that family from the time that the first Underhill came to America. My sisters thought it was awful.

For the divorce my friends all assisted and had a good time. One of my friends went to a hotel with him one evening, and the witness who would testify to misconduct came in, paid by somebody. That went off easily. No trouble about the divorce a bit. Both of us wanted it, you see.

I didn't go to court when the case was tried. But I had good friends from Greenwich Village, and they all went in a body and talked about my virtues. The court knew that very often these things are just a routine, so it wasn't hard to get the divorce at all, although they had that law, you can't have a divorce unless it is for sexual divergence on the part of the partner.

~

As I read over this account of myself, a question smites me in the face. What on earth was the matter with me? Why, for so long, did I accept suppression and domination so that I appear to myself like an insect crawling around in a glass case with no attempt to escape? Was I a crypto-lesbian? someone has asked me. Had I loved a woman would the glass case have opened?

Well, I have always felt at ease with women. That, I thought, was because I was brought up with them and was not afraid, but surely a lesbian would have felt real yearning toward some woman at some time, or she for me. That did not happen. I have known lesbians in the course of this third-class journey I call my life, and I have also known medicine men, Hindus, Buddhists. Sometimes they were especially interesting because they were a little different. Two lesbians I knew confided their love affairs to me, about someone else. I regarded those confidences as I did others I received about men, for people of both sexes confided in me. I looked wise, apparently, and uninvolved.

Figure 18. A camping trip that Ruth noted was to celebrate her "unmarriage," likely a reference to her amiable divorce from Cecil Crawford, perhaps pictured here, circa 1929.

What was the matter? I don't seem to myself to have had less health, energy, even brains, than girls who burst out early and made themselves a career or a marriage. Why did I wait like those larvae that grow to adult size in a chrysalis while other infantile beings are on legs and moving around? Those larval years are a grief to me now when I realize I am only a youngster in anthropology in spite of my years.

I can lay part of it to a taming that began almost in prenatal days. Neither I nor my sisters ever dreamed of contradicting our parents. Brother did, but he was a male. The two girls lived happily without contradiction because their interests lay in approved fields. It was I who wanted things that must never be mentioned. I wanted violent love, but with marriage, of course. I wanted an exciting life with all kinds of people, and that meant it must be away from home, where nothing was exciting. "Margaret," Mother kept saying about my golden-haired sister, "Margaret loves her home." That was counted to her for virtue. I didn't love home, and the whole family knew it.

Yet for years and years, it did not occur to me to leave. If I had felt real hate, I suppose that would have ejected me, like air in the bowels, but home was usually tolerable. There were mild friends and mild parties. Sometimes there was a cozy warmth around the dinner table, when Father quoted Shakespeare and one of us capped him. Mother was sweetly companionable when she talked with me about clothes and food. In her favorite storybook, *Cranford*, a whole village lived in that way.* So the chrysalis where I had been placed at birth solidified around me.

Of course, I wanted to marry. Of course, I dreamed of it, and during the dream I shook my head at funny, ineligible men, who made tentative approaches to me. Could I take notice of a man who did not recognize a Shakespeare quotation? Who would not discuss books with me? And if he did read, could I put up with sloppy clothes and bad manners? Such creatures may have crawled on the outside of my glass case, and I on the inside could not feel them. In fact, they usually looked distorted through the glass. Occasionally, they got distorted to grandeur, at least at some point. Then I had a bad time. But I shan't take time on the people with whom I fell partly in love. I expect I looked distorted to them too, for, as a rule, they slid off the glass hastily. Once, I thought I had a broken heart, but I forgot it.

What was the matter that I could never get one who would do, even my husband?

I think my early training in Puritanism and romantic idealism put together built an invisible wall around me. It was like those you read of in science fiction who automatically repel anyone approaching beyond a certain distance. I was all ready for a male to say, "I adore you. Will you marry me?" In such a case, I would have thrown myself into his arms and, I suppose, lived successfully ever after. However, the male must be of my class both socially and intellectually, and the males who did put the question to me, not all beautifully, came nowhere near my requirements. I just thought they were funny and waited for the *real man*. He came in the forms of Hiram and Pliny, who wanted nothing but some nights in bed, and how that horrified,

* Underhill is here referring to Elizabeth Gaskell's 1851 novel *Cranford*, which has very little in the way of plot but reads like a series of vignettes about mostly female characters from the fictitious small, rural town.

terrified, and crushed me!* Hiram nearly sent me into tuberculosis. To Pliny, I succumbed, having decided it was my only hope. I liked Pliny, and we remained friends until his death, but he had a wife. Other women, with him, were only temporary.

As for the other men, I never dreamed of anything but a temporary exploration. I didn't even enjoy the act very much except with one, Fred, the house painter. He was utterly impossible from every point of view, but he had charm. So for one night, I let myself go. I will never forget that one, though in public I was ashamed to be seen with him.

There must have been eligible men in my purlieus all this time. Why did none want me except for a night when it seemed to me all other women were wanted? It must have been the invisible wall. Puritanism and romance were gone from it now, but I was composing stories and verse. I was thinking about writing. I was not thinking at all about men's personalities and how they could be pleased. If I pleased one, it was by chance. He heard some witty remark of mine. He caught me in an unguarded moment when I almost seemed a sweet girl. He was soon disillusioned. I seem to remember how those I knew dropped away and married other people.

It got lonely, and my writing didn't go. That was when I suddenly took Cecil and married him. I kept telling myself I was happy, but we had spats, and, oh, what cutting things he could say. Once I wrote:

Oh glorious day when my love is away
Do thou continue and never end.
Oh lonely hours, your healing powers
Are bringing me back my friend.

---

* We are uncertain which "Hiram" Underhill is referring to, but it seems unlikely that she is referring to Hiram Bingham (1875–1956), the well-known archaeologist and politician at Yale University. Although they were rough contemporaries whose professional circles may have overlapped, the pairing seems unlikely, and the Underhill archives contain no further details on the identity of "Hiram." It seems probable Underhill here is referring to Pliny Earle Goddard (1869–1928), a linguistic anthropologist whose interest in Native Americans stemmed from concern for their daily problems rather than scientific research for its own sake. He served as curator of ethnology at the American Museum of Natural History from 1909 (and began service as a lecturer at Columbia University in 1915) until his death. See: Boas, Franz. 1928. Pliny Earle Goddard. *Science* 68(1755):149–150; Kroeber, Alfred L. 1929. Pliny Earle Goddard. *American Anthropologist* 31(1):1–8.

When I tried to explain in verse how the image of Cecil, the real good in him, came to me with this telescopic, analyzing view, I couldn't get it into verse, and when he came back, things were as bad as ever. Finally, divorce. It should have felt bad, but it was only a colossal relief; a weight was gone.

∼

The glass case did not hinder me with married men. I am sure I must have seemed to them almost mythically pure, for it never occurred to me that friendship with one of them could include even a hint of sex. I treated a married man like a woman, which meant free discussion, free companionship on jaunts, even personal revelations. Such relationships did seem to have a little more life in them than those with girls, but I thought it was because the men had wider experience. How many were there? I can count six or eight. One confessed his marriage with tears and explained that we must not meet again. One mentioned that I was formidable. One said he wished he had met me sooner.

None disturbed me until that rather shambling New England engineer I nicknamed Socrates. He was frank about wanting me instead of his wife. I was frank about saying that I would work to support him if he got divorced and, therefore, lost his job. I guess it was love. When people talk about the rapture of receiving love letters, I remember how my heart used to turn over at one of Soc's careful postcards. "Arrived safely. All well." Socrates lost, not his job, but his nerve. From our camping trip, which was almost a honeymoon (but not physically), he went back to his wife. Years later, when my heart had stopped its turnovers, his wife died. He married a gushing woman who, people had told me, was "after" him. Then he died, and there was a little money for me in his will.

∼

My divorce had been a dramatic one, but it was over. I was on the suburban train, going back to the country house I had shared with him. Of course, he was not there now. For months he had been living in another suburb close to her, and friends had reported seeing them whirling about in a new convertible. And, by Jiminy, I began to think, "How am I going to live now? Where? With whom? Why?

Because there are a good many years ahead." I doubt if I had ever thought before. I had prided myself on quick, emotional decisions. That would be exciting. That would be dull. That—yes, I'll confess it—that would keep me near some man.

Now the man element was out, and how relieved I was. I had the same light-feeling experience later after a minor operation. Now what to do? Live in the house? Try to meet the bills he and I had found so difficult? Take boarders? Not good enough.

Social work? Climb up those same dirty stairs, talk to the same dirty, whining people who had been on relief for years, like their parents and grandparents? (Wait now, I know all cases aren't like that, but enough of them were in my day, so that I quailed at the idea.) Publicity? Oh, such chatter about nothing. Writing? Even if I could be successful with my little essays, what would that mean to one who had just been sojourning in hell? Since my brain seemed to have been dealing with fact for the very first time, I thought, "I will get something more in my head. I will go to a university and get a PhD."

PART TWO

Becoming an
Anthropologist

Columbia, Part 1

I TRAMPED UP DINGY STAIRS and along dingy halls. Columbia University's were far from the neatness of Vassar's, and the people tramping with me, mostly males, looked flustered and untidy. England's University of Cambridge, when I visited it later on, looked just as bad. But I drank in the dinginess like a whiff of beer. It was a stimulant. It was something I had a right to. Here, at last, I would not have to be a sweet girl or a gay sex partner.

I am no longer quite sure which departments I visited before anthropology. I think they were sociology, philosophy, and economics. What I said to them in substance was: "I find that social work is not doing what I thought it did. I wonder if what you teach would really help me to understand these people. I want to understand the human race. How did it get into the state it is in?"

Perhaps I put my question in more academic terms. At least the people who answered me were completely academic. They spoke sentences out of a prospectus. They told me about studies I could make as to why some little group of people moved an inch this way or that way. Must I give up trying to learn something and go back to living in the country? I was planning that when I met Ruth Benedict.* People who

---

* Like Underhill, Ruth Fulton Benedict (1887–1948) attended Vassar (BA 1909) and spent two years traveling in Europe before entering the anthropology department at Columbia University comparatively late in life, in her case at the age of thirty. Like Underhill, Benedict predominately studied Native Americans in the Southwest. Benedict's 1931 book *Patterns of Culture* was wildly successful and influential. Her 1946 book *The Chrysthanthemum and the Sword* provided an early application of anthropological concepts to modern societies, in this case Japan's. It, too, was hugely popular. These publications and others made her a key figure in the culture and personality school that dominated Americanist anthropology in the early to middle twentieth century. See Lee, Dorothy. 1949. Ruth Fulton Benedict (1887–1948). *The Journal of American Folklore* 62(246):345–347; Caffrey, Margaret M. 1989. *Ruth Benedict: Stranger in This Land*. Austin: University of Texas Press; Mead, Margaret. 1975. *Ruth Benedict: A Humanist in Anthropology*. New York: Columbia University Press.

have written about her so often do not mention that she was beautiful.*
I have always liked beautiful people. White hair, with a few shades of
gray swept back from her forehead. Brilliant eyes that looked at you,
not at your eyes, but at your mouth, since Ruth was somewhat deaf.

"You want to know about the human race?" She accepted my question naturally, with a nod. "Well, come here. That is what we teach."

Revelation! That little dark-walled office looking out on a stony
courtyard glowed like the heart of a jewel. Here was a person who,
as used to be said of the Greek chorus, you could speak to and who
would answer you again. That was how I found Benedict and Franz
Boas.† They just opened a door out of which light streamed on me.

I was not sure that I had ever spoken simply to a person about
what I really thought and been answered straight. My decision was
immediate. There was no money, but of that I scarcely thought. I
would get a job somehow, even if it meant washing dishes in a hotel,
working in a factory. Actually, Ruth lent me some money, but really
Father came to the rescue. How glad he must have been to think of
my doing something respectable. My brother was to attend Columbia
law school that year and must live in town. Father arranged—I don't
know what inspired him to do this for us—that Rob and I should
share a flat. So we had a walk-up with two bedrooms, a sitting room,
and a kitchen on 121st Street. I don't remember anything about that
flat except how wonderful it was to walk over to Columbia every
morning. With what joy I sniffed the dust of those dingy halls! How
wonderful it was to be greeted at my entrance of Schermerhorn Hall

---

* See, e.g.: Mead, Margaret. 1949. Ruth Benedict, 1887–1948. *American Anthropologist* 51(3):457–468.

† Franz Boas (1858–1942) was a pioneering German-American scientist who is often
regarded today as the father of American anthropology. Appointed at Columbia University in 1896, Boas had a profound impact on several generations of students, particularly
in his advocacy for a humanistically infused science based on in-depth fieldwork, even
though, as Underhill repeatedly notes, he provided little guidance in fieldwork methods.
Boas emphasized the search for "facts," and he developed the concepts of cultural
relativism and historical particularism while attacking racist and typological thinking
wherever they occurred. See: Benedict, Ruth. 1943. Franz Boas. *Science* 97(2507):60–62;
Bohannon, Paul, and Mark Glazer, eds. 1973. *High Points in Anthropology*. New York:
Alfred A. Knopf. Pp. 81–84; Lewis, Herbert S. 2001. The Passion of Franz Boas.
American Anthropologist 103(2):447–467; Darnell, Regna. 2000. Reenvisioning Boas
and Boasian Anthropology. *American Anthropologist* 102(4):896–910; Cole, Douglas.
1999. *Franz Boas: The Early Years, 1858–1906*. Seattle: University of Washington Press.

by the sight of blackboards and chairs with armrests. I knew how to behave in such surroundings. They could not require anything that I would find impossible.

The classes were very small. When people tell me about going to classes now with a hundred or more people and a loudspeaker, I'm sorry for them indeed, because we didn't have more than eight people or so under Boas. There were some very nicely costumed young men in good business suits, and they were taking this, not because they were thrilled with anthropology, but because they hoped to get jobs as professors. But they just hoped to be important in that new line. There were four or five of those young fellows and one or two women, and me. That was all.

They didn't all go on to a PhD. A few did. I remember first of all Edward A. Kennard, who really was a good student and interested.[*] Then, Burt and Ethel Aginsky, who were bright young people and appeared to have money.[†] Nobody else in that class had money. We all made up our minds that Burt was a bootlegger, and that was how he got it. I used to have a great whispering time after class, and we got so friendly that on Sundays we used to hire riding horses and ride in Central Park.

Perhaps few people would know the name of Elsie Clews Parsons except for those opulent two volumes on Pueblo ceremonies, but she was the Egeria, the patron saint of our little group at Columbia.[‡]

---

[*] Edward Allan Kennard (1907–1989) received his PhD from Columbia University for a dissertation on Mandan grammar under Boas. He made significant contributions to the study of Hopi linguistics, including his 1944 *Field Mouse Goes to War/Tusan Homichi Tuwvota: A Bilingual Hopi Tale.* He also made contributions in Dakota and Navajo linguistics and in applied and medical anthropology while working for the Office of Indian Affairs and other government agencies. See Fowler, Don D. 1989. Edward Allan Kennard. *Anthropology News* 30(6):38; Everson, Gloria. 2011. Edward Kennard, the Federal Writer's Project, and Public Archaeology. *SAA Archaeological Record* 11(3):34–37.

[†] Burt Aginsky (1905–2000) studied at Columbia University under Boas and Benedict and received his PhD in 1934. He and his wife, Ethel, are best known for their research on the Pomo Indians of California, which resulted in their 1967 book *Deep Valley.* Burt taught at the City College of New York from 1946 to 1965. See: Zumwalt, Rosemary Levy. 2000. Bernard W. "Burt" Aginsky. *Anthropology News* 41(7):37.

[‡] Parsons, Reichard, and Underhill have together been credited with being "at the forefront in adding women's voices, along with their own observations," to the anthropological text (Lamphere, Louise. 1995. The Legacy of Elsie Clews Parsons. In *Women Writing Culture.* Ruth Behar and Deborah A. Gordon, eds. Pp. 85–103. Berkeley:

She was a society lady, of means. No one ever knew the funds she provided for Boas to make expeditions or send his students on them. I suspect that she supplied money for publishing my thesis, because in those days you did not get your real PhD until your thesis had been published by an official publisher. Lots of the people did not manage it for years, or if they did manage it, they collected the money themselves. Of course, I had no money, so I didn't collect any, but one day I went to the library and asked about my thesis, and they said, "Oh, it's been published."* I decided Elsie must have been the goddess who did that.†

Jules Henry was a Frenchman, a very mercurial and nervous type.‡ Henry was young, with black hair and brilliant black eyes. He later wrote a well-known book called *Culture Against Man*.§ Boas told him that he must not use his real last name, since it was too obviously Jewish and perhaps would prevent a good circulation. None of us liked Henry. He pushed and he walked ahead of everybody. He interrupted everybody and made it appear that he alone in the whole class had read a book. None of us really were nice to him. Boas gave

University of California Press. Pg. 93). For the two volumes mentioned see: Parsons, Elsie Clews. 1996. *Pueblo Indian Religion*. Originally published 1939. Lincoln: University of Nebraska Press. For more on Parsons, see: Deacon, Desley. 1997. *Elsie Clews Parsons: Inventing Modern Life*. Chicago: University of Chicago Press.

* *Social Organization of the Papago Indians* was first published by Columbia University Press in 1937.

† Independently wealthy Parsons in fact supported a large number of southwestern anthropologists, not just Underhill, including Ruth Benedict, Franz Boas, Ruth Bunzel, Esther Goldfrank, Berard Haile, Dorothy Keur, Morris Opler, Gladys Reichard, Charles Wagley, and Leslie White. See: Hieb, Louis A. 1993. Elsie Clews Parsons in the Southwest. In *Hidden Scholars: Women Anthropologists and the Native American Southwest*. N. J. Parezo, ed. Pp. 63–75. Albuquerque: University of New Mexico Press. Pg. 68; Lavender, Catherine J., and Nancy J. Parezo. 2008. Ruth Murray Underhill: Ethnohistorian and Ethnographer for the Native Peoples. In *Their Own Frontier: Women Intellectuals Re-Visioning the American West*. S. A. Leckie and N. J. Parezo, eds. Pp. 335–372. Lincoln: University of Nebraska Press. Pg. 348.

‡ Jules Henry (1904–1967) earned his PhD at Columbia University in 1935 for his study among the Kaingang of the Amazon rain forest in Brazil, which he published as *Jungle People* in 1941. He held various positions with the US Department of Agriculture and Department of Labor, as well as a teaching post at the University of Chicago. For more on Henry, see: Gould, Harold A. 1971. Jules Henry, 1904–1969. *American Anthropologist* 73(3):788–797.

§ Henry, Jules. 1963. *Culture Against Man*. New York: Random House.

him the best field site—to South America, although he did not even speak Spanish. Poor boy, he was as young as anybody in the class. I don't suppose he knew that we objected to being interrupted every time we opened our mouths and being pushed back when he entered a door. It was the way he lived.

My first years at Columbia, I spent almost every waking moment in class or in the library. How glorious to enter an immense library where books on those subjects could be found and devoured! Some people in class had already had courses in anthropology and could ask questions using technical words. It was long before I was able to see that, though the questions sounded technical, the questioners were sometimes callow young people who had seen less of the human race than I had. I soon began to feel a great sense of home in that shabby old corridor in the shabby classroom with all the stains on the wainscoting and the dirty floor.

❧

Ruth Benedict taught American Indians. I have my notebooks from that course, and when I looked over them for hints in my own lecturing, I was amazed at how scrappy they were. Sometimes even inaccurate, but Ruth was a person above inaccuracy. You forgot it. You decided that she would have corrected herself if she had taken a moment to think. Anyway, you could get the stuff from books. What mattered was that slow, quiet voice putting you into the mood of people born different from you and with a different worldview. After a few facts on some tribe, Ruth might pause, the brilliant eyes would look into space, and perhaps you would wonder if she was ever going to continue. Then would come some interpretation, some connection of ideas you could never have thought of. But of course! Now in your mind, those Indians were human. They were poets, philosophers; they were living through the tragedies of life as vividly as any character in Sophocles.

I remember one amiable young man laughing about these pauses. "I thought I was in the presence of a death's head," he chortled. "The eyes never looked at you, but the voice came like something out of a tomb."

"My dear man, she's deaf!"

"Oh! But she's queer anyway."

To me, that young man was fit for treason, stratagems, and spoils, for Ruth was making me think. I don't believe I had ever really thought in my life—about impersonal problems and without emotion. Don't ask me why! It's a horrible question to be asked at the age of forty. I assume I had been so occupied with myself that no impersonal problem could get standing room in my mind. Now a world of problems was open. I might have become a fish in an aquarium, swimming among waving seaweeds and flashing bodies. Each one needed study, and now and then I could not help dipping into a book on philosophy or even poetry, to follow a silvery body that had slashed by. I was making connections between ideas for myself.

In those first months, I scarcely noticed who was in the class. The boys—they were mostly boys—have told me later how they used to speculate about that well-dressed older woman. Then they heard me say, "Damn," a common Greenwich locution, and I came into focus. They were nice boys, and there was a pleasant young couple. We slid easily into the relationship of brothers and sisters.

I don't think I knew whether they were boys or girls, for sex was out of my life just now. We talked anthropology. We joked about the beloved subjects, as children might about their grandfather. This was when I produced my verses on linguistics:

> Will you tell me why do
> Prefixes in Maidu
> Think it better form for them
> To change the vowel to fit the stem?
> It's so amazingly polite
> I hardly feel I've got it right
> It's so unlike what I do.
> No, I don't dote a
> Whole lot on Dakota.
> Take a look at Chinook
> Saw you ever such a language in your life.
> Grammatically, they put it that he
> Gave to him it, the man, the child, the knife.

I did not hold back, even expressing my opinion to Boas that one of his opinions about Dakota grammar was a weird academic contraption. Apropos of Dakota, it finally got too much for us, what with grammatical complications and Boas's German accent. The linguistics class got together and hired Ella Deloria, a Dakota woman, a protégée of Boas and a very nice lady, to pronounce the words for us and interpret what "Papa Franz" had said.*

⌇

Ruth Benedict lived in a different atmosphere. I can say with Keats:

> Yet had I never breathed that air serene
> Until—†

Until I had the relief and delight of entering her little dark office bursting with one of my ideas. She would turn from her meditation, generally on some book of philosophy, and bend on my lips those dark eyes, brimming behind the spectacles.

"Yes. Yes. I think that is a line which might be followed. Have you read . . ."

She was opening more doors. I never ventured into that little dark-walled office without emerging all agog to move through them and on.

With Ruth's guidance I would follow some book I had never heard of, perhaps in a foreign language. I could thank my dawdling years of travel and Italian charity work because at least I could proceed where she pointed. I remember a callow youth of later years who described one such interview with the eyes fixed on his lips—he did not know why. He was working on the Ojibwe, and Ruth asked him dreamily, "The Ojibwe do not kill the father. Can you fit that in?" The youth found such words plain grisly. He fled that room as if he had been

---

* Ella Deloria (1888 or 1889–1971) was Yankton Sioux and an expert in Dakota and Lakota linguistics and mythology, though without a formal advanced degree. She worked with Boas in the 1910s while an undergraduate student at Columbia University and again in the late 1920s, though her work never came to full fruition because of family, financial, and other difficulties, including an ongoing debate with Boas as to the accuracy of previously recorded Sioux myths that he wanted her to evaluate. She published several popular books, including *Speaking of Indians*, published in 1944. See: Prater, John. 1995. Ella Deloria: Varied Intercourse *Wicazo Sa Review* 11(2):40–46; Medicine, Bea. 1980. Ella C. Deloria: The Emic Voice. *MELUS* 7(4):23–30.

† See John Keats's 1817 poem "On First Looking into Chapman's Homer."

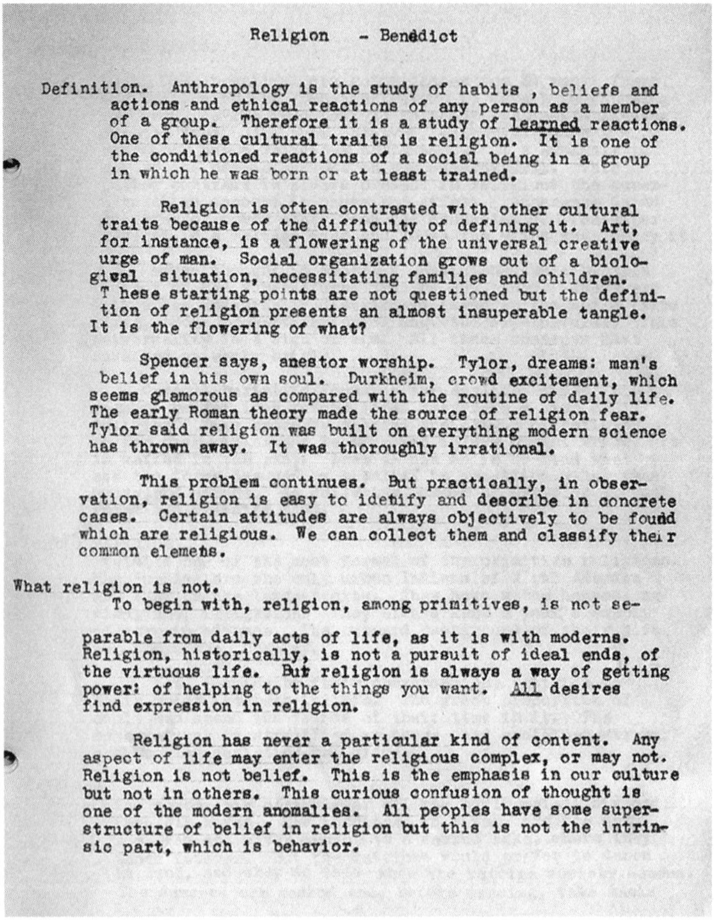

Religion   - Benèdict

Definition. Anthropology is the study of habits , beliefs and
actions and ethical reactions of any person as a member
of a group. Therefore it is a study of learned reactions.
One of these cultural traits is religion. It is one of
the conditioned reactions of a social being in a group
in which he was born or at least trained.

      Religion is often contrasted with other cultural
traits because of the difficulty of defining it. Art,
for instance, is a flowering of the universal creative
urge of man. Social organization grows out of a biolo-
gival situation, necessitating families and children.
T hese starting points are not questioned but the definition of religion presents an almost insuperable tangle.
It is the flowering of what?

      Spencer says, ancestor worship. Tylor, dreams: man's
belief in his own soul. Durkheim, crowd excitement, which
seems glamorous as compared with the routine of daily life.
The early Roman theory made the source of religion fear.
Tylor said religion was built on everything modern science
has thrown away. It was thoroughly irrational.

      This problem continues. But practically, in obser-
vation, religion is easy to idetify and describe in concrete
cases. Certain attitudes are always objectively to be found
which are religious. We can collect them and classify their
common elemens.

What religion is not.
      To begin with, religion, among primitives, is not se-

parable from daily acts of life, as it is with moderns.
Religion, historically, is not a pursuit of ideal ends, of
the virtuous life. But religion is always a way of getting
power: of helping to the things you want. All desires
find expression in religion.

      Religion has never a particular kind of content. Any
aspect of life may enter the religious complex, or may not.
Religion is not belief. This is the emphasis in our culture
but not in others. This curious confusion of thought is
one of the modern anomalies. All peoples have some super-
structure of belief in religion but this is not the intrin-
sic part, which is behavior.

Figure 19. Course notes from Ruth Benedict's religion class
at Columbia University, circa 1931.

faced by Hecate herself.* Ruth meant that some Eskimo, Ojibwe
neighbors, have no way of caring for the ailing old and so think it
a filial duty to put them out of misery. The Ojibwe are more likely
to have relatives and a camp where the ancient can be cared for. She
had not supposed that she need explain all that to a fellow seeker of
knowledge, but the youth went away and wrote a pamphlet, stating
that she was the weirdest human being he had ever met.

---

* Hecate is an ancient Greek goddess associated with crossroads, witchcraft, and
poisonous plants, among other things.

I used to go to Ruth when I was just confounded with things that Boas had said. I couldn't make sense of them. I would say, "What on earth does this mean, Dr. Benedict?" Then, with her very quiet voice, she would begin and explain, and pretty soon I knew what it meant. She had a beautifully clear mind.

For me, all interviews with Ruth were intellectual joy. Even yet, years after her death, I cannot feel a new idea creeping into mind without the accompanying puff of sadness that says, "Oh, I wish I could ask Ruth about that!"

~

There was a time when I thought I couldn't stick with it. This digestion of facts was hard, and Boas showed no mercy. If you did not know the facts, then you were not on the way to being an anthropologist. So you had better know them. What long hours I spent in the Columbia library among those unyielding iron stacks! They towered above the little desk where I sat in the gloom, sometimes till midnight and beyond. This was material with which I was unacquainted. I must do hours of work to catch up with even the high school graduates who had read something about early Indians or Australians. But what a world was opening!

In the middle of that first year, I told myself that I could not take this. I would go to some other university with a more popular lecturer. Mother would have loved to have me at Stanford, where my uncle taught Greek.* Luckily, I got over that.

I recommend everyone who can manage to take up a subject of study at the age of forty. It will double your lifespan. I was learning what other people learned at eighteen or even earlier, but those youngsters, perhaps, were bored. I was learning with all my heart, with all my attention. Every scrap of information was a prized jewel. I feared only that something would slip. That I could not keep all my prize. So I reread books. So I reached out for more and more. I was amazed at my young classmates who grumbled at the routine. The routine was glorious! It meant new bone and muscle for my mind, but could I ever acquire enough? I looked with absorption at that young man with black hair and a prominent chin who had read about Australian aborigines and adduced them an answer to every

---

* See previous note on Augustus Taber Murray, a professor of classics at Stanford.

question. I read about them too, but I did not dare adduce them. Perhaps there were other primitives who behaved quite differently.

So I was a mouse in the class. A humble, middle-aged mouse! I listened and engorged and wanted more.

~

I had a humble position as student teacher at Columbia, and anthropology was swirling through my mind like Shelley's west wind, dispersing old ideas like ghosts.* At Father's diffident invitation I came home for a weekend, and with me I had the manuscript of Ruth Benedict's *Patterns of Culture*.† It was bringing whole vistas of life into focus for me, and its material was perfectly respectable. At some statement of Father's about inferior people, I asked if he would not like to read it.

His smile made me feel like an ant underfoot. "I'll read it after it's published."

I am sure he thought it would never be published. It was probably some insane laborious literary effort by a female and I had picked it up from nowhere.

~

In that aquarium, I believe there was an appearance called Margaret Mead.‡ She was young but already an important person. She had just returned from her trip to Samoa, and the important people were joking with her and asking if she had all the bugs out yet. Margaret went to Samoa to see about the young women, about coming of age.§ She wanted to know how young people developed and whether they didn't become rather hostile, as American young people often do. With each island where she studied it was a bit different, but she would find that the young people were to follow a certain path, and

---

* See Percy Bysshe Shelley's 1820 poem "Ode to the West Wind."

† Benedict, Ruth. 1934. *Patterns of Culture*. New York: Houghton Mifflin.

‡ See: Banner, Lois W. 2004. *Intertwined Lives: Margaret Mead, Ruth Benedict, and Their Circle*. New York: Vintage; Lutkehaus, Nancy C. 2008. *Margaret Mead: The Making of an American Icon*. Princeton, NJ: Princeton University Press; Lapsley, Hilary. 2001. *Margaret Mead and Ruth Benedict: The Kinship of Women*. Amherst: University of Massachusetts Press.

§ See: Mead, Margaret. 1928. *Coming of Age in Samoa: A Psychological Study of Primitive Youth for Western Civilization*. New York: William Morrow.

they did. They were not hostile. She was doing excellent work at that time. All of us were very excited to hear her tell the real facts about people. What did they have for breakfast? What do their houses look like? What did they say to her? She had all of that factual material that many anthropologists, I suppose, have, but they don't think it worthwhile to put it down. It wasn't required in those times. The public didn't want that. They wanted theory.

Sometimes Margaret came to class and sat in the back, occasionally asking a very technical question. All of us turned round and listened respectfully while Boas answered. Margaret lived with her husband in a flat downtown. It seemed to be furnished mostly with camp chairs and sleeping bags. A great many of the students of anthropology used to come to listen to them talk in the evenings. They sat adoringly on the floor and asked her questions. I went sometimes, but I found that what she said was mostly fact, and that it wasn't anything that I felt I needed.*

I expect Margaret decided on sight of me that I would not fit the group. I was too old and came from too different a milieu. Once she asked me, "Do you like dialectic?" Thinking of Marx, I answered, "No, I find it boring." I did not get invited downtown, and soon Margaret was away on another trip.

Margaret demanded a good deal of reverence on the part of her hearers. They had to be pretty quiet and accept what she said. I was already beginning to develop my ideas, so I didn't like to voice them in Margaret's presence. I would get contradicted. Therefore, I didn't quite agree always with what she thought, so she and I didn't have any very intimate relationship. But I had great respect for her and what she was doing, even though I didn't have much real connection with her.

❧

Gladys Reichard was a glorious person.† She was a professor at Barnard when I was at Columbia. Lanky, tough, hard-hitting, loud-voiced,

---

* Elsewhere in interviews, Underhill contradictorily indicates that she was never invited to Mead's flat.

† See: Lamphere, Louise. 1992. Gladys Reichard Among the Navajo. *Frontiers: A Journal of Women Studies* 12(3):78–115; Lamphere, Louise. 1993. Gladys Reichard Among the Navajo. In *Hidden Scholars: Women Anthropologists and the Native American Southwest*. N. J. Parezo, ed. Pp. 157–188. Albuquerque: University of New Mexico Press; Lamphere, Louise. 2004. Unofficial Histories: A Vision of Anthropology from the Margins. *American Anthropologist* 106(1):126–139.

and hearty Gladys was as honest and upright as the hero of the boys' stories I read in my childhood. She had a job as a farm girl, then had been to what Ruth called "a rough Pennsylvania college"—Swarthmore College—and finally got a scholarship to Columbia. She strode around the halls of Barnard, making jokes in Pennsylvania Dutch. Like "don't me et" (come before dinner). She and Boas had got together like two kernels in a nut. It was she who started calling him "Papa Franz" and he, dignified and unapproachable as he looked, simply loved it. Dr. Boas loved her for her German and her integrity. Also, her simple idea of humor chimed with his. His German scholar's attitude never enjoyed the subtle and irreverent humor that pleased the rest of us. I remember one joke over which he and Gladys laughed again and again. He had been explaining to the class how the Eskimo dog harness was attached without metal. He could not remember the English word *toggle*, but someone suggested, "Oh, like the frog of a pajama." This delighted both Papa Franz and Gladys, and they chuckled all the year about a pajama toggle. Of course, they talked German together, and of course, Gladys could get the sounds Papa Franz made when the rest of us might not. Papa Franz gave Gladys every scholastic plum until she got her PhD and then had her appointed to teach anthropology at Barnard. I think it was some time before she got the title of professor.*

Gladys had the top floor of the Boas house, and I think it was a joy to Papa Franz to have her come home at night with some jokes or some question about linguistics. Gladys went to study the Coeur d'Alene in Idaho and had a grand time with their phonetics and grammar. She wrote a darned good book about their myths, too.

The Navajo were her love. She often told me about how Papa Franz sent her out to them her first year at Columbia. She knew nothing about Indians, but Pliny Goddard, a pundit at the American Museum of Natural History, was going out in his car and had a broken arm. Gladys went to drive for him and do secretarial work.† That settled

---

* Underhill is perhaps referring to the fact that Reichard first became an instructor at Barnard in 1923 but did not become a full professor until 1951, just four years before her death. See: Smith, Marian W. 1956. Gladys Armanda Reichard. *American Anthropologist* 58(5):913–916. Pg. 914.

† Reichard accompanied Goddard, a married man with a family, to the Navajo Reservation in 1923, 1924, and 1925, during which time they reportedly had an affair

her with the Navajo forever, the Coeur d'Alene being only a brief interlude. Gladys was good with Indians. She was so darn simple and straightforward that, in spite of her loud voice and brusque manners, they took her to their hearts. She would eat what they ate, sleep where they slept, and write it all down for Papa Franz. When I reached Columbia, she had been doing this for several years, and she was already the adopted granddaughter of a prominent Navajo chapter. She had learned to weave and had a big loom in her flat.

Gladys decided I would do. We were soon behaving like two schoolgirls, lunching and gossiping together on far sillier topics than I ever took up with Dr. Benedict, and what a debt I owe to Gladys. I was so blind about this enormous subject of anthropology, not knowing even the best books to read. Its caverns and canyons stretched so endlessly in all directions, through linguistics, archaeology, and physical anthropology, and the men who occupied those caverns all had specialties to be revered or laughed at. In later years, students have sat breathless while I told them incidents about famous anthropologists. I knew how they felt.

Gladys had an assistant who was paid $1,000 a year and took the girl once a week to the American Museum of Natural History. I looked on this assistant almost like the other flashing forms around me until June approached and Gladys mentioned, "She will be going, and I am thinking of taking one of the men in your class."

That was when inspiration came to me, also boldness. "Do you think *I* would have a chance?"

"You! But you're going to Stanford."

"Not if you'll have me."

So my name appeared in Columbia as a member of the teaching staff.* I was on the cursus honorum.† From that time, I never looked back. Anthropology was for me and I for it.

---

that caused significant tension at Columbia among Goddard, Reichard, Boas, and Mrs. Goddard. See: Lamphere, Louise. 1993. Gladys Reichard Among the Navajo. In *Hidden Scholars: Women Anthropologists and the Native American Southwest*. N. J. Parezo, ed. Pp. 157–181. Albuquerque: University of New Mexico Press. Pg. 163.

* This is a reference to Underhill's formal position as an assistant at Barnard College, under the supervision of Reichard. See: Ware, Susan, ed. 2004. *Notable American Women*. Cambridge, MA: Harvard University Press. Pg. 651.

† A sequential series of offices typically offered to senatorial men in ancient Rome.

Papa Franz

THIS LITTLE MAN WITH HIS funny-looking cheek entered the room, bobbed his head of gray hair, and said, "Good morning." Then he started right away to talk in a thick German accent; his mouth was pulled out of shape by the cut on his face. Gossip said it was from a duel, but actually it was from an operation of some kind. He spoke far too fast, and he assumed that we knew great long technical words.

This was my first class, the introductory course taught by Dr. Franz Boas.* To listen to Boas was really difficult. I felt at first like Sisyphus pushing a stone up a mountain. Yet how wonderful to hear new facts that I had never known or guessed at! Really I didn't mind the difficulty. I had expected that a new subject would be difficult. However, some of my compeers, especially the young men of the class, had felt that they should be catered to. That was the way teaching had been done in America up to then. But Boas did no catering. Many people took a violent objection to him straightaway because we couldn't understand what he said, even when he wasn't reeling off book titles.

Boas made no concessions, though he was kind and polite. When expounding a problem, he often began, "I asked myself why this should be . . ." Then suddenly we of the class would wonder why we had never asked ourselves such things. I scribbled frantically in my notebook and still had to rush to books to make sure what had been said in that German accent—and who were Bastian and Gobineau

---

* The literature on Boas is extensive, but see: Cole, Douglas. 1999. *Franz Boas: The Early Years, 1858–1906*. Seattle: University of Washington Press; Darnell, Regna. 2000. Reenvisioning Boas and Boasian Anthropology. *American Anthropologist* 102(4):896–910; Hinsley, Curtis M., and Bill Holm. 1976. A Cannibal in the National Museum: The Early Career of Franz Boas in America. *American Anthropologist* 78(2):306–316; Jacknis, Ira. 2002. The First Boasian: Alfred Kroeber and Franz Boas, 1896–1905. *American Anthropologist* 104(2):520–532; Lewis, Herbert S. 2001. The Passion of Franz Boas. *American Anthropologist* 103(2):447–467.

and Breuil, mentioned so casually without a reference?* When he'd name some German author we had never heard of, we'd all rush over to the library. "Have you got this book?" "Yes, but only one copy," they'd typically reply. "It's not very popular." Then we'd have to share the old book that was new to us. Some of them were in German. Fortunately, I could read German, but lots of the others couldn't, so I became very popular to translate the German.

I had never heard of Boas before I went to Columbia, but actually he was already pretty famous. He was first a specialist in physics and had studied the color of seawater. But he fell in love with the Eskimo and finally changed his whole goal in life from physical matters to social ones. He was among the first to begin teaching anthropology in the United States and also was a curator at the American Museum of Natural History. Boas was really putting it over in the country. Whenever he spoke, all of us sat there quite breathless to hear about anthropology.

I'd hoped Boas would consider my background of working with Italian Americans to be of significance in anthropology, and perhaps he did, but I think he initially had great suspicions of me. He thought, "She's a middle-aged woman with nothing to do. She just wants to get something new to think about." Really, he had that attitude all my first year. I was so interested and needed to know so much that I would sometimes question him even when I knew he didn't think much of me. Yet he would very conscientiously answer all my questions, and slowly his attitude changed.

I have been told that the students of Boas had a cult for him as for an old-time prophet. They were supposed to accept his dicta as though they came from the Bible itself. That was not the case with me. I was old enough to disagree with what The Professor said. You see, it was not Boas's opinions about diffusion or the revision of American Indian languages that evoked my respect. It was his utter

----

* Adolph Bastian (1826–1905) was a German polymath who contributed to the initial development of ethnology. Joseph Arthur Comte de Gobineau (1816–1882) was a French aristocrat best known for his publication, between 1853 and 1855, of *Essays in the Inequality of the Races*, which provided scientific justification for Social Darwinism and other now-debunked theories promulgated in the nineteenth century. Henri Édouard Prosper Abbé Breuil (1877–1961) was a French archaeologist best known for his contributions to the study of the Paleolithic in Europe.

integrity. In my own mind, I thought of him as one of the men whom Horace meant by those lines:

> He who is upright of life and free from sin
> Needs not the javelins nor the bow of the Moor
> Nor his quiver heavy with poisoned arrows.*

Boas was devoted to the ideal of the scholar—the servant of learning. He went on the basis that science is holy and should have precedence over everything, that a professor has the right to speak in any way he wishes, that nobody should interrupt him. Students should listen with bated breath and never criticize. Of that I approved.

I really envied Boas tremendously because he knew so much and was so well respected that he could say about a person, "He is a fool." I've never said that about anybody in my life and was taught not to and, in fact, I wouldn't dare do it even now! But Boas knew enough and was so respected that he could. Of course Boas did have to defend himself—mainly for being a Jew and thinking the Indians were human. He talked about the Indians as though their plans were just as good as our plans. And he said this publicly. That got him into lots of trouble. He had a good deal to fight against.

～

Papa Franz was a priest in the temple of learning. To his mind, the scholar worked for the whole world of scholarship. Whatever he discovered was to be given to that world, free. The idea that a discovery should be kept secret until it could be published over his name was revolting, impossible! I confess that I, too, had supposed that to be the rule of the scholar's world; I found out to the contrary when I became a salaried member of that world.

When he met a theory based on armchair thinking instead of work-in-the-field facts, Boas was as stern as a headmaster. There had been too many of those in the early days of anthropology, with people talking learnedly about inferior races and the necessary stages of civilization. Many a bright young theorist had the foundations knocked from under them as Papa Franz poked a finger at their flimsy structure. Some never forgave him.

---

* See Horace Quintus Horatius Flaccus's 23 BC poem "Odes."

To Boas, right was right and wrong was wrong. If someone misquoted or made a statement without due authority, that offender should be chastised. He had no personal feeling in the matter. The culprit might be someone of whom he was fond, for example as I am sure Leslie Spier was, but if that culprit made a misstatement or misquotation, Boas let the hammer of judgment fall on him, though he expected that this would not interfere in the least with friendship.[*] Truth is truth, and why should the statement of it make any difference? Sometimes I, too, fell under the weight of that colossal hammer. I was one of the sufferers, for I loved theories. In the rush of new ideas where I was being whirled around, I would collect something I'd read, something I'd heard, and something I hoped, then rush to headquarters with it, to be greeted with that deadly four-word sentence, "What are your facts?" He did not intend a cruel death to that inspiration, though that is what happened.

I did not have many facts, but his comment sent me out to get them. Sometimes the inspiration was proved fruitful, and then what a pleasant smile I got. "Yes!" Boas would exclaim. "I think that could be stated." But other times I woke up to realize that I had none, and the shift of balance I felt on that awakening has been vivid to me ever since. It left me with a permanent need for having facts, and sometimes I have administered to a student the same violent slash that Papa Franz gave me.

~

I have said that my kind of humor found no channel in Papa Franz's mind. I once handed a paper to him in which I feared I had made unfounded suggestions. So I typed at the end a passage from the Psalms, "Who can understand his errors, cleanse thou me from secret faults, keep back thy servant also from presumptuous sins."[†] He did not seem amused. Perhaps Boas had never read the King James version of the Bible.

---

[*] Leslie Spier (1893–1961) earned his PhD under Boas at Columbia University and made significant contributions to the archaeology of the American Southwest and the ethnography of Native American groups across the western United States. See: Basehart, Harry W., and W. W. Hill. 1965. Leslie Spier, 1893–1961. *American Anthropologist* 67(5):1258–1277; Campbell, John Martin. 2009. The Founder: Remembering Leslie Spier. *Journal of Anthropological Research* 65(1):1–4.

[†] Psalms 19:12–13.

Coming of Age in Arizona

FOR ME, THE SUMMER OF 1931 was the coming of age in a new life. How long it was since I had looked into the future with joy and confidence! The surprise of it was almost heartbreaking, and more so since I had expected nothing.

I knew that assignments for work were to be given out, but I expected nothing. I knew that money was scarce in that year of the Depression. The grants would go to established scholars like Mead. My heart did thump a little when Gladys told me that Ralph Linton was taking a group of first-year graduates to the Comanche and suggested that I apply.* I did, and the answer was no. Three of the boys in the class were to go. I was used to being the left-out female.

"Papa Franz wants to know if you're going with Linton," Gladys shouted.

"Of course not."

"Why didn't you tell me?"

That was because I was not used to telling anyone my disappointments. I was planning to earn a little money during the summer and perhaps take some courses.

"Well, you've lost some time in waiting," Gladys scolded. "Go see Papa Franz right now." I felt a stirring all through me like that of water as it is just coming to boil, the tiny bubbles along the rim of the pan, scarcely recognizable. The small movement at the bottom

---

* Ralph Linton (1893–1953), like Underhill and Reichard, was of Quaker roots and grew into a well respected though at times controversial archaeologist and ethnographer. During the 1930s he was associated with the training expeditions of the Laboratory of Anthropology in Oklahoma with the Comanche Indians. Linton held positions at the Field Museum in Chicago, University of Wisconsin at Madison, Columbia University (he was appointed to Boas's post upon his retirement), and, finally, Yale University. See: Gillin, John. 1954. Ralph Linton, 1893–1953. *American Anthropologist* 56(2):274–280.

Figure 20. Ruth, likely during her graduate school days, circa 1935.

of the pan. Is it? Will it continue? I know nothing more moving than that delicate beginning of upheaval, prophetic of so much strength.

I saw Papa Franz. He sent me to Dr. Benedict. I was told that only $500 was available for a beginner like me.* It would not take me across the world, to any of the darling problems we had all dreamed of.

---

* Underhill's dissertation fieldwork would also be financed by small annual contributions from her father and fellowships from the Columbia Humanities Council. Griffen, Joyce. 1989. Ruth Murray Underhill. In *Women Anthropologists: Selected Biographies*. U. Gacs, A. Khan, J. McIntyre, and R. Weinberg, eds. Pp. 355–360. Westport, CT: Greenwood Press. Pg. 357.

"But," said Ruth, with her quiet look of a seer, "there is one Indian tribe which has had no recent study. The Papago, a quiet agricultural group." Seeing my stunned expression, she added, "Oh! You would find them too uninteresting?"

"No, no, no!" The scarcely recognizable bubbles were seething within me. I had never heard of the Papago, or Tohono O'odham, as they're now called. I did not know where they were, but this meant my first touch of anthropological tools. I would glimpse some live human beings from this new point of view that had nothing to do with reform.

"There is a party going?"

"No. Dr. Boas thinks you might go alone."

I? Alone? My bubbles were hissing, snapping, boiling over. I could not make out the sense of Ruth's words.

"Could you manage on that amount?"

"What amount?"

"Five hundred dollars."

In these days when even undergraduates get grants of several thousands, that statement sounds comic, but this was the Depression and, to me, $500 seemed like a chime of bells, a shower of gold.*

"Of course. Where, where are the Papago?"

"In southern Arizona. A small tribe. In a very hot country."

❧

I really had no experience with, no exposure to Indians. In my youth Mother used to read us "Hiawatha," which I liked only because of the story's rhythm.† I knew that Buffalo Bill with his Indians performed at Madison Square Garden. Also, the Quakers were always interested in Indians. I remember once, when I was twelve or so, sitting in the business meeting and hearing the expenses for the year read out. One was for education of Indians, $32. I punched the girl next to me and joked, without knowing what anything in the world cost, "That ought to do it!" That was all I ever heard about Indians until I was college age.

---

* Five hundred dollars in 1931 is the equivalent of $7,500 in 2012 (www.westegg .com/inflation/infl.cgi [accessed March 4, 2013]).

† See Henry Wadsworth Longfellow's 1855 poem "The Song of Hiawatha."

Henrietta

I KNOW HENRIETTA'S STORY from the witnesses I met at the trial of her killer. I will not say "murderer." That boy was neither a wild Apache nor a civilized American. He did not know into what an impasse life had led him, so he cut his way out. I never knew him, so I must begin with Henrietta.

↬

We all knew that Henrietta Schmerler came from a strict Jewish family in Brooklyn.* She was not used to gay and informal young people, and perhaps, for her, there was a glass wall. Her loud laughter, her overcordial moves toward acquaintances, caused us to withdraw, even the Jews in the class. I know that she sat at the feet of Margaret Mead, literally and figuratively, and perhaps Margaret did not even know it. Margaret had investigated sex in Samoa. No one had done the like with American Indians, and why should not Henrietta? She asked sex questions of all us older women, and I think we answered brusquely, telling her to go to the books. Instead she went to the Apache.

I did not know Henrietta well. She was an earnest, determined girl from a very different background. Where I had been enjoying the militant informality of Greenwich Village, she had lived as the protected daughter of an Orthodox Jewish family. She knew nothing

---

* Underhill's account hews quite closely to others while adding insights to both the tragic events and Underhill's own views on the struggles of gender and fieldwork and the cultural prodding that goes into the ethnographic endeavor. See: Parezo, Nancy J. 1993. Conclusion. In *Hidden Scholars: Women Anthropologists and the Native American Southwest*. N. J. Parezo, ed. Pp. 334–367. Albuquerque: University of New Mexico Press. Pp. 361–362; Wood, Nathalie F. S. 1986. Past is Present: "Adventure" in Anthropology. *Anthropology News* 27(6):3; and the resulting letters to the editors in *Anthropology News* of November 1986, January 1987, and May 1987. There are also multiple newspaper accounts, such as: U.S. Orders Report on Murder of Coed. 1931. *Washington Post*, 28 July: 3.

of nightclubs, of jocular flirtation, to be taken only as an evening's entertainment. She knew nothing of my attitude, which regarded everything in the world as joking material as long as the joke was clever and, if possible, erudite as well.

So I exchanged very few words with her. I understood that she was a devoted disciple of Margaret Mead, who had just come back from the South Seas with her husband, Reo Fortune. Together, they held court in a downtown apartment where the innocent, middle-class young could hear about the sex mores of primitive people and about how Reo had mingled with them clad only in a loincloth. To adults, this would have been merely an addition to knowledge, as I am sure Margaret and Reo meant it to be, but Margaret was young, far younger than I. Her study of primitives had not included the young of a Brooklyn congregation, bound by taboos quite as strong as those of Samoans but different.

I should not speak of these South Sea sessions, for I did not often attend them. Margaret and Gladys Reichard, my enthusiastic helper in the new world, had somehow got smeared with repellant. Was there some bitterness connected with the warm regard Boas had for both of them? He had found positions for both when employment of women was rare in anthropology, and there was plenty of talk about the use of Gladys as a lecturer and Margaret as a museum worker when most people thought the positions should have been reversed. Margaret was a true intellectual, a maker and investigator of theories. Gladys was a lusty day-by-day worker who enjoyed people as comrades. Her language, with its Pennsylvania Dutch overtones, was somewhat crude and simple, but a good friend she was. What a companion. I, swimming uncertainly in new waters, was touched to the heart by her generosity to me. If a friendship with Margaret would seem to her like "whoring after strange gods," I was willing to forego it.*

Henrietta saw enough of Margaret to glimpse a stupendous new world, swirling with customs and problems hitherto unguessed. I am sure that she made up her mind to be a revealer of such problems, just as Margaret had been. So our first winter, not of discontent, but of initiation and revelation, came to an end. The next thing in prospect was fieldwork for the summer. At present I note with a shock and, I admit, some pangs of envy that young anthropologists seem to hold

---

* Deuteronomy 31:16.

up a finger and attract thousands of dollars, never mere hundreds, for the study of a detail in parts of the earth never heard of before World War II. Research has been registered in the official mind as a necessity. It rings the bell of the cash register as reform used to do in other days.

In the early 1930s, research was an extra, scarcely to be included in a normal budget. Obtaining money for it meant scheming, fighting, and influence. The first was unknown to Boas, but the other two were sanctioned and even encouraged by his innocent integrity. He wanted fieldwork for every one of his beginners who was serious about anthropology. This included both Henrietta and me.

Ruth Benedict had a workable idea. An old Apache couple was already known to some Columbia ethnologists. Let Henrietta go and stay in their wickiup, which would make a nice adventure. She could, supposedly, be learning basketry while getting a line on Apache home life, and perhaps she could do a little with the language, although they spoke English. So Henrietta got her bit of travel money, though Boas refused to give her complete directions. If people do not know what to do, he said grimly, they should not go. It was the dictum of a scholar dealing with scholars, but his benevolence had put Henrietta in a class where she did not belong.

My story had been told. I shall be endlessly grateful to Boas for regarding me as an adult who could be sent out alone and trusted to get results. Henrietta was at least fifteen years younger than I, awhirl with curiosity and ambition.

The decision came partly from his conviction that there were two classes of people who did not get justice in American society and particularly in the academic world. These were Jews and women. He was right. Since that time there has been such change that the two classes seem almost to head the list of favored ones. Yet in those days, I knew of many Jews and women who felt themselves shut out from opportunity. Yet one can understand how Papa Franz sometimes tipped the scale a little, particularly for Jews, his own people. So he acceded to Henrietta's request that she should have a field trip, young and inexperienced as she was.

~

She started west when the rest of us did, the boys to join Linton to tackle the Comanche, and I, to the Tohono O'odham. A young man, a fellow student I'll call Robert, was my passenger in the old Ford until we got to Oklahoma, and Ruth had asked if I would help Henrietta save money by taking her too.

"Don't do it," said Robert. "That girl is trouble."

Ruth Benedict sighed. "The others won't take her either."

I suppose we all feared that intensity, that straining toward a goal, which would ignore all rules and rights. So she arrived alone on the Apache reservation, and the rest of the story I know only from hearsay because Henrietta was killed in the middle of the summer. The details I heard from witnesses at the trial of her Apache killer.

It was in the middle of the following winter that the Department of Anthropology at Columbia had a communication from the Arizona police.* The Apache who had killed a Columbia student was about to be tried. A representative of the department would be subpoenaed for the prosecution. I can understand what a spear wound this was for our Papa Franz. He felt that the killing was not the fault of the ignorant Indian boy or of the ignorant white girl. It was his fault, the consequence of his overkindness to one who needed help. Probably he would not have let another student of Henrietta's age go alone on her first field trip, but Henrietta was both a Jew and a woman. He had slipped. Gladys told me that he was almost in a nervous collapse, and so was Ruth, who shared the responsibility.

"But someone from the department has to go to that trial," said Gladys. "Would you?"†

---

* Schmerler was killed in July 1931, charges were brought in November 1931, and the criminal case began in March 1932. Presumably, then, the department would have been contacted sometime around the end of 1931 or early 1932. See: Girl Student Slain in Arizona Canyon. 1931. *New York Times*, 24 July: 1; Solves Mystery of Apache Killing. 1931. *The Sun*, 3 November: 14; Jury Finds Indian Guilty. 1932. *Los Angeles Times*, 22 March: 1.

† Lapsley has written that Franz Boas wanted to serve as a witness during the trial but fell ill as March 1932 approached. Ruth Benedict was to go in his stead, but not wanting to make the trip, she conspired with the department secretary to get Boas to think of sending Underhill. Lapsley further describes a surprising lack of outrage among the Columbia crowd about the killing—as they placed the blame on Schmerler for inviting her own murder by disobeying instructions and breaking supposed cultural taboos—perhaps further suggested here by Underhill's remark that she saw the trip mainly as an excuse to travel gratis to Arizona. Lapsley, Hilary. 2001. *Margaret Mead and Ruth Benedict: The Kinship of Women*. Amherst: University of Massachusetts Press. Pgs. 206–207.

Would I! With my fare paid to Arizona and someone else to take my classes? My answer was, "When?"

~

So I found myself in a grim-looking hotel in Globe, Arizona. This was before the days of easy plane travel and before every large town in the Southwest had something like a luxury hotel. Our hostelry was the haunt of mining men and occasional commercial travelers. I remember its oilcloth-floored halls and dining room, the wide, uncarpeted stairs, and the dismal little sitting room with ancient mining magazines on the fringed cloth of the center table. For Globe was a copper town. Beside its main street ran a deep gulley. Overhead bridges ran across it to the formless buildings and the slag heaps draped and smothered with earth-colored dust. I don't remember any streetlamps on that main street, but I remember how night after night I trod its uneven surface with one or another of the prosecution witnesses. We were instructed never to discuss the trial, and in the hotel we did not, but how could we keep completely still about it? After our supper of tough steak and boiled potatoes, I would catch the eye of one or another of the varied little group caught there like flies in a web.*

"Ma'am, do you feel like taking a walk? I wonder if I could talk to you."

So I would hear how the eager girl from Brooklyn had accosted these working people of the West with an impact as strange as that of some unknown poisonous insect.

First, the superintendent of the reservation, a kindly, round-faced Swiss, who stuttered.

"Wh-wh-why we would have let her stay at our employees' club. Sh-sh-she could have seen Indians coming to the office and to school."

The club at the agency was far from the Indian wickiups, and I could picture the brushed and combed Indians who came there, murmuring their English monosyllables. It was full of kindly, middle-aged employees whose interest was in the day's routine. Of course,

---

* One of these witnesses may have been anthropologist Clara Lee Tanner, based on a conversation Nancy J. Parezo had with her around 1984 (personal communication with Parezo, February 25, 2013). Tanner was an expert in southwestern Native American arts who taught at the University of Arizona for more than half a century. See: Thompson, Raymond H. 1998. Clara Lee Tanner (1905–1997). *Kiva* 64(1):53–59.

Henrietta would have none of it. As for the old couple to whom
Boas had recommended her, she revolted against them on almost
the first day. Like most Indians, they did not talk freely, as a slashed
maple tree gives out its sap. A smiling patience is necessary to one
who would hear Indians talk, and Henrietta's patience, if she had
any, would have been fierce, almost suffering. So she walked away
from the old couple, seeking to penetrate the center of Indian life.

There was a group of wickiups not too far from the agency. She
must have seen the people sitting before them and staring quietly, as
Indians do. No one greeted her, for they did not know her, and the
Apaches, at that time, were not too familiar with whites. No hope of
entering one of those families. Not too far away was a little building
used as a storehouse for tools and grain. It had an earthen floor and
no furniture, but it was weatherproof. I do not know how Henrietta
got possession of this storehouse, though one witness thought she
rented it from an Indian family. What they all knew was that she
brought her suitcases and piled them on the floor.

"And M-M-Miss Underhill," the Swiss agent told me, round eyed
and shocked, "There was a pile of wheat in the corner, and she
j-j-just piled her suitcases on the wh-wh-wheat. Can you think of a
lady doing that?"

Of course I could. I could imagine Henrietta feeling as glorious a
thrill of possession as I felt the first time I camped alone in a mountain hut, and I could feel her excitement at being on her own in the
midst of a group of Indians, but she did not know the next move.
An old hand would simply have settled down and waited for the first
investigators, possibly children, but Henrietta was alive with purpose.
She went visiting. She asked questions. She did not sit through the
silences that are a part of Indian communication. So the Indians,
suspicious and offended, said my informants, just pulled down their
wickiups and moved off. Who was there for Henrietta to use as basis
for an article on Indian behavior and especially that little-treated part
of behavior, sex life?

As I heard it, there was only one element in the Apache population that would have anything to do with the intruder. That was the
young men just out of government boarding school. We all know
the plight of these youths, adapted partly to white man's life, partly
to Indian, and at home in neither. For years they have been forced

to speak English and to wear white man's clothes, yet they have had no friends among the whites, save a few teachers whose ideals of morals, manners, and religion were so different from their own that they always remained mysterious. The language they used with the teachers went in a few well-defined grooves. With each other, they spoke an Indian tongue or else the slang and the forbidden words they picked up from such casual workers as they met. A talk with a female that was not about lessons or proper conduct was, to them, an undreamed-of adventure.

Henrietta invited such talk. She, too, was unused to comradeship between the sexes. Never had she dreamed of being able to ask a boy about his sex life, but here there were no rules. When some awkward youth strolled to her granary in the evening, she must have felt like a hunter watching his first deer, nay, perhaps his first black bear, walk straight into his line of fire. She greeted the boys jovially. She asked them to sit down, and she brought out her notebooks. Of course, that was a queer item, but her frank gay talk was not like that of a teacher, and she talked about things that no Indian mentions to a maiden. In fact, Apache etiquette demanded that boys and girls should never be alone together, even if they were brothers and sisters. The wooing was done by shy smiles as a girl came from fetching water or by a boy's posturing as he dashed on horseback past the wickiup of his inamorata.

The reservation employees, including the English-speaking teachers, were to go in a big bus, but she didn't want to go with them. They were very respectable ladies. They asked her to go with them and sit in the bus and see what they were allowed to see, but not try to pry into the Indians' privacy. So she refused to do such a thing, which she considered thoroughly unpleasant and uninteresting.

Finally one of the boys said to her, "Well, I'm going and I will go on my pony. Would you like to go? You'd have to ride on my pony with me."

"Oh yes," she said, likely full of excitement and ready for adventure, "I would love to do that."

So he came on the morning of the day set and had only this little pony. It was a small one and not too well trained. They left with her sitting in the saddle, in a skirt showing her legs, while he sat behind with his arms around her. Now, that for him was an amazing, exciting experience such as no boy would expect to have, unless it was with a bad woman. They got on the horse in that way and took quite a long ride.

They finally got to a canyon that he had picked out, a box canyon with only one exit. He steered the horse into the middle. Then he got down and lifted her off. He expected that they would immediately go into a love act. This must have been a tremendous shock and horror to her, because she'd had no such idea. She really thought that she was going to ask him some questions and hear a little more about the Apache love arrangements, and that all would be very respectable and would make a nice article when she got home. But he was moving straight toward proper sex.

She was frightened and screamed, but he thought her screams were just acting. He proceeded and began to kiss her and let it go further. Finally she yelled loudly, "I'll tell the white people! I'll tell the white people!" When he heard that, he was scared and quite wild, and he killed her with a knife.

Nobody was there as a witness. Later some cowboys found the body and found him sitting on the ground beside her. He looked at her and said, "Why did you make me kill you?"

He was put in jail. There was to be a court session, deciding whether he deserved the death penalty or not. He was found guilty and sentenced to prison, although I had heard he was quietly released not long after the trial.

Chona and the O'odham

WHAT BOAS HAD FOR ME was $500 and the Tohono O'odham Indians.

"They are down in southern Arizona, where few whites have come since the days of the Spaniards," Ruth Benedict told me, with her beautiful dark eyes fixed as usual on a point that seemed to lie beyond me. "We ought to hurry with our study of simple cultures like that, for very soon all the field studies will be acculturation studies."

Of course, the prospect of plunging into an unknown "primitive" culture was to me endlessly exciting. Hesitantly, I asked Boas, "What am I to do there?"

He gave me his quick little smile and said, "Just find out how those people live and come tell us about it."

I know how nearly fatuous this sounds today when we have $40 books instructing anthropologists on every phase of fieldwork. Now the holistic approach and the single anthropologist without a definite problem are ghosts of the past as much as palmistry. To be fair to Boas, I do not think he would have given such instructions to all students. Perhaps my age and the simplicity of the culture chosen for me led him to think I could not come to much harm. Perhaps, too, it was an inexpensive way of testing my ability to mingle with strange people and to plan my own work for three months. It is true, though, that Papa Franz liked to use indefinite preparation as preliminary work with a trustworthy person. Later, when I was planning fieldwork for others, I said to Dr. Boas, "Should we not get ready some preliminary instruction for all new workers so they can avoid the worst mistakes?" He said, in his abrupt way, with a German burr, "If they do not know what to do, they should not go."

So I went to find out how those people lived.

❧

I settled down at the Place of the Burnt Seeds, otherwise known as Santa Rosa. For a while I had a room at the government boarding school. (More of that later and of the kindly teachers who had never been trained to deal with people of another culture and another language.)

Soon enough I learned that the Tohono O'odham are a small division of the larger Uto-Aztecan language group, spread over Mexico and the western United States. When America wished to level off their southern boundary, they just drew a line straight across from west to east, and that cut off this little tiny point of O'odham country. Despite this, they were quite united. Many people had not visited them at all since the Spanish priests had come, so I found that to ask one person about their religion or their social customs really gave me a great deal.

Immediately I decided I would like to deal with the women rather than the men. I'd known women to walk straight up to a male chief and say, "Here, I've come to study your people. Now, will you help me?" That looked pretty difficult. Instead I got started through the teachers at the small local school. The teachers were kind to me and said that I was somebody who liked Indians. I was introduced to the children, and they introduced me to their mothers and said, "This is somebody from way off east, and she likes the O'odham."

The women were a bit offish for a while. Then they found that I really did like O'odhams and that I didn't ask questions at all. In fact, my social training had been to the effect that you mustn't ask questions of strangers—it's very rude. Instead of saying, "What's your name? Where do you live?" and so forth right away, you sit quietly with them and when they're making something, you say, "Oh, what is that? How pretty!" and they tell you about it. Little by little you get to knowing where they live and what they do, but you do *not* ask direct questions. I found that that was a great advantage for me, because the boys in my class had never had that social training. The boys would fire right away with questions to anybody and would be met with a suspicious look. I simply went into the houses and sat down as a neighbor to talk. I would explain that I didn't know any O'odham but wanted to learn the language quickly. "Oh, please tell me how to say, 'please,' how to say, 'but,' how to say, 'where.'" They very eagerly told me all of those simple things, and then the children came home and taught me too.

Figure 21. Tohono O'odham children and women at home, circa 1931–1935.

But mostly I was silent and receptive and didn't ask many questions at all. The women would begin to talk. I would listen with all my ears and now and then allow myself to say, "Oh please, I couldn't understand what you said just then. Would you tell me what that means?" So they would tell me, and I'd have a little O'odham, which I'd scribbled in my notebook. And so I began to settle myself with the Tohono O'odham, who turned out to be deliciously quiet, gentle, and earnest people who had worked all their lives.

❧

I just happened to meet Maria Chona. She was all alone in Tucson making baskets. I thought one way to approach her would be to just ask her if she'd teach me basket making. I just asked her that. She said she would be quite glad. Then I came and sat with her for several days, until she found out that I had a car, and then she invited me to take her around. It all worked, even though I didn't really have a plan at first. I'd never done this. In truth, I didn't have anything called a method, nothing that I regarded as a method at all. It just happened; these were the early days of anthropology in America, and we were just feeling our way, all of us, at first. Little by little, I

Figure 22. Maria Chona, circa 1931–1935.

came to see why this business of the women was the right thing. I was getting a lot more than I would with the men, and I decided to keep right on with it. Then, it became my specialty, but not until I'd found it by chance.

I spent many of my days with Chona, and I was well repaid for it. She was almost seventy at this time. She had had two husbands, but now her near relatives and relatives-in-law were all gone. Comfort in the O'odham world means having relatives to stand by you, work for you, and speak up for you. Chona, a self-respecting woman, and independent for her day, was lonely. It was not long before she found that I would be glad to have an Indian sister. Soon she was calling me by an O'odham word for younger sister, while I adopted her as my elder. My objective of pushing myself and exaggerated respect for other people and their gifts came in here very handy. It was no trouble for me to make Chona feel that I had the deepest respect for her knowledge of the O'odham and their country. I let her smile at the flagrant ignorance of the younger sister in not knowing in which direction to walk at the ceremony or how certain relatives should be addressed. She was not interested in the things I did know, which were a mystery to her, so we communed famously on the basis of my inferiority. Our language was a weird mixture of English, Mexican-Spanish, and O'odham. As time went on I came to know other people who would help with the translation. I confess that I never learned to speak O'odham too well. There were so many other problems prodding in my mind. I tried to get the important terms, such as those for relatives and ceremonies. Also, the queer verbs that told in what way a thing was done and whether it was past or future. "Many verbs in primitive languages express aspect rather than time," I used to tell classes later and was surprised when they did not find it natural.

To go back to my first days with Chona, I soon found that I could not ask her any clear-cut general questions. Maybe some field-workers get an informant to answer the query, "What is a marriage custom with your people?" Chona could tell me only about herself and her friends, but when I had enough examples of these, I had pretty useful information. I soon adopted the plan that I used in all my time with the O'odham. That was to let the informant talk and never puncture his discourse with questions. Of course, I had a set of the usual chapter headings in ethnologies in mind, but I never thought of pursuing one to its end before starting another. So a two-hour conversation might range over the whole vista of O'odham life. Suppose I had gotten around to the subject of family life. I might ask, "How old were you when you first married, Chona?" Chona would begin the story. I sat with a small pad on my lap consisting of three-by-five-inch cards. I used dozens of such pads every week.*

"Oh," Chona might say, "I was young. I had just finished my maiden ceremony." So I would write on one pad sheet, "Adolescent Ceremony." Chona goes on to describe it, drifting off to the kind of food she used at the time, the paint she had at the dance, the story of the medicine man who officiated there, and back to how the paint was made. Furiously, I would tear sheets off the pad, putting a heading and perhaps one sentence under each. That evening I would lay the sheets out like a pack of patience cards and try to find how many chapters I had dipped into. As details came in one conversation after

---

* These cards are in the DMNS Archives. See: Jabrocki, Aly. 2012. Finding Aid to the Ruth Underhill Papers. Ms. on file, DMNS Archives.

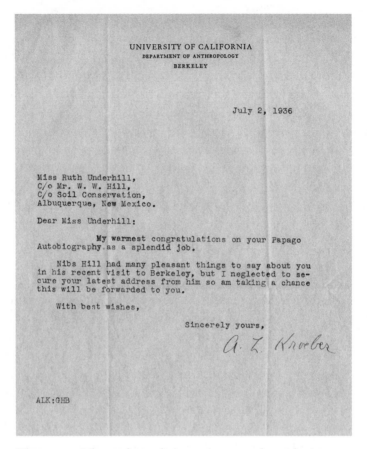

Figure 23. A letter from the prominent anthropologist Alfred L. Kroeber, congratulating Ruth on the "splendid job" of her book on Chona's life.

another, the number of headings increased. Soon I was able to look them over and decide where the gap in my knowledge was and what conversation I should start next.

It meant constant scribbling, but fortunately I was able to get absolution from Chona for that. I explained very early in our friendship that I had a perfectly dreadful memory. I hope this will not sound too subservient, but I certainly did say to Chona and to others, "It is wonderful how you remember so many details from long ago. I am so stupid that I have to write such things down." Chona and other informants were willing to admit that I was stupid, although they did it affectionately. As long as I wasn't troubled by false pride in the matter, I could say to an informant, "Oh, dear, I cannot remember all you told me about that ceremony." I would be rewarded by a glint in the informant's eyes. Yes, we both knew how stupid I was. Charitably, the story would be given to me again, so that I could get further details not mentioned in the first version. Sometimes I got a ritual repeated four or five times, each time with some addition that I needed. As talk went on, sheets came off my pad like a shower of snowflakes. I soon needed two or three shoe boxes for filing them.

Sometimes our conversation would be interrupted by long periods of silence. I learned to sit these out peacefully and even enjoyably. O'odham do not want to talk all the time. They get satisfaction from sitting, smiling in one another's company, feeling each other without touching, I might say. So my informant would sit quietly, mulling over what he or she had been telling me. In the meantime, I watched the children playing around us or enumerated all the furnishings of the one-room house. Suddenly, the informant's reverie would come to a head, and he or she would burst out with a piece of information I would never have dreamed of looking for.

～

I was very much interested in the personal stories of all of the people I knew—who got on with her husband and who did not and all that. I didn't set out to write an anthropological biography. I was just trying to follow Boas's guidance to "find out how they live." Well, Chona's life impressed me so deeply that I thought this must be written. This will be one estimate of how they live.* That is how I ended up with *The Autobiography of a Papago Woman.*†

---

* Franz Boas seemingly considered life histories of "limited value," but Ruth Benedict encouraged Underhill's biography-cum-ethnography, even writing a foreword that was eventually published in the 1979 edition. Benedict argued that "life histories are important because from them one can study special cases of the kind of impact this culture has on individuals. . . . Life histories are data on all kinds of problems of behavior in a tribe." See: Babcock, Barbara A. 1993. "Not in the Absolute Singular Sense": Rereading Ruth Benedict. In *Hidden Scholars: Women Anthropologists and the Native American Southwest.* N. J. Parezo, ed. Pp. 107–128. Albuquerque: University of New Mexico Press. Pg. 117.

† Underhill, Ruth. 1936. *The Autobiography of a Papago Woman.* Washington, DC: Memoirs of the American Anthropological Association No. 46.

I can think of some things, just the simple ones that explain why I was so attracted to Chona. One thing is she wasn't at all afraid of me. Chona was a person of such personal power; she was a chief's daughter and had magic. Nobody was going to put anything over on her. Also, many women worried that I could go and tell the superintendent. I told many of them that I never told the superintendent anything, that he was not my friend. They were glad to hear that, but they didn't really trust me. But Chona did because Chona wasn't afraid of the superintendent—what the heck! If he wanted to tell her he didn't like her smoking or whatever she did, well, that was her business and she'd tell him. Chona didn't mind a bit if I wanted to write about her life. "Well, the white people ought to know these things" was her attitude. "Too bad they don't. They're stupid people."

Finally, it was partly her own character that she sought me, and she wanted to know the foreigner because it would be interesting. Although we used the term *sister* when we spoke to each other, in fact I let her boss me all she wanted to! So it wasn't a sisterly relationship really. It was more like she was the chairman of the committee and I, one of its good members! But we opened up to each other. I told her a whole lot about my family, and she told me about hers. Of course I'd had no children, so I couldn't compare notes with her on that. Men we could talk about. She would ask me, "Are you going to take a husband, sister?" "No, I don't think so," I would say. "You are right," Chona would answer. "Men are work. Men are work!" That became one of my real maxims.

A rapport wasn't established the first year, which was sort of a trial time. They found out that I was harmless, a bumbling creature that didn't know much about what O'odham life was like. Of course, I didn't know about life. I had to be told. I took the telling very meekly and said, "Oh yes, now I see. Why do you do that?" I just waited until it came up. I would say, "Oh, you had a new chief? How did you get him?" Slowly, slowly I worked.

❧

We were eating roasted caterpillars. The children had collected a basket of the fuzzy fat things with green and brown fur, and their mother had impaled them on sticks and cooked them over the campfire. The fuzz soon burns off, leaving crisp tidbits about an inch long with a peppery, acid taste.

"Tonino," I ventured to the youth who was still helping out my babyish knowledge of the O'odham language, "could we perhaps find some old men who could sing war songs?"

There was silence. The brown faces gathered around me under the ironwood tree looked impassively into the distance. Big brown hands continued quietly to shred bunches of caterpillars from the green sticks that served as skewers. Scuffed cowboy boots of the two men, stone-colored sneakers of the women rested motionless on the stone gray canvas sheets that O'odham always spread before sitting down on the desert with its sharp stones, its thorny debris, and its scurrying ants. I had learned to carry such a sheet myself.

"Could . . . ?" I started to interrupt the silence, then remembered that O'odham never give an immediate answer to an important question. So I tried to sit motionless, as I had been taught to do long ago in Quaker meetings. I watched a cactus wren burrow into the green depths of a tall, dilapidated saguaro. Finally, with slow care, I produced my argument.

"You see, I have been here now almost a year. And there hasn't been any flood."

Slowly the heads nodded.

"And no big sickness."

Nods again.

"And no one I talked to has died."

Tonino looked at the others. "Yeah," and finally he spoke, "we was saying that last night."

An important checkpoint had been passed. I could move on in my study of O'odham Indian ceremonies.

This happened, it must be understood, in the days before World War II, before organized teams of specialists were a regular thing in ethnology, before any study expected masses of information from computers and punch cards, and before researchers could command masses of money for the production of such results. My story of three years' work among the O'odham should be classed among those journals of early travelers who wandered alone into sparsely settled country, observing and recording every sight and every experience that passed through one human mind, without benefit of machinery

---

for recording and testing. Such travel books must be read in connection with others of wider scope, but sometimes they cast a cozy, intimate light on home scenes or the motives of individuals.

My revered professor Franz Boas had thrown me out into southern Arizona to sink or swim. Here was I, an easterner who had crossed the Atlantic Ocean several times but never the Mississippi. I was no dewy-eyed babe, though. Some years of climbing tenement stairs in several eastern cities had supplied me with a panorama, though a little one, of human behaviors and human problems. So I set out to look at O'odham problems, as blithely as those female travelers of the eighteenth century who set out for Tibet with notebook and umbrella in hand. They did get to parts of it. And on this afternoon of the roasted caterpillars, I felt I had finally set foot in the real country of the O'odham.

The men were the guardians of the religious ceremonies. They had some beautiful ancient ceremonies that had been with them for generations, and they were all in O'odham. A certain old priest was in charge of each ceremony—nobody else knew it—and so you had to make your way with this old priest. Most of the priests, of course, lived at home with their families. I had my car and a walled tent. I would travel to them and get friendly after a good many visits. Then I'd tell him that I wanted to understand his ceremonies, and might I come and listen to him recite some of those songs to me? "Well, I'll think about it," was the usual reply. He would think very carefully, and finally he would send word that I might come, and then I would come and sit on the floor with my notebook in that very hot country. So hot that my notebook had to be protected with a bath towel or else my sweaty arm would melt off what I'd written in pencil. I would write down as quickly as I could the text of the very beautiful songs and recitations that would bring the rain to this dry country. And in this way I discovered that they were poets, speaking in a language not unlike that of the Psalms.*

You see, at about the end of my first year, after I'd been with the women a lot and really felt I was getting into the tribe, then I felt

---

* See especially: Underhill, Ruth M., Donald Bahr, Baptisto Lopez, Jose Pancho, and David Lopez. 1979. *Rainhouse and Ocean Speeches for the Papago Year*. Flagstaff: Museum of Northern Arizona Press.

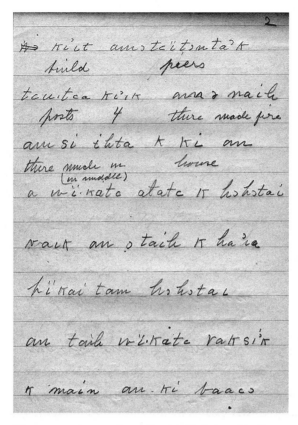

Figure 24. A page from Ruth's Tohono O'odham field notebook, working out O'odham phrases.

I'd have to have a male interpreter because some of these things are known only to men. I got recommended to me a young man named Rafael—I called him Ralph—although I was warned that he was a bootlegger and had two wives. I had no objection on either count, and he turned out to be wonderful. He was a beautiful creature, really, much younger than I, with flashing dark eyes, long, thick, curly hair, and a soft voice. I think he was interested in me because he was so anxious to get away from his own community! It was so confined, all of them together. In me he found a person so entirely different. But by that time I'd been married and divorced. I wasn't going to get into any sex trouble on the job.

He worked for me like a beaver. Sometimes two or three days before I wanted to see an old man who I knew was a keeper of some of the sacred things, I would send Rafael as an ambassador because the old man would not want me to come and see him. "A middle-aged American lady?" he might object. "Oh, that's intrusive and disgusting, I won't have it!" But Rafael came and said, "This is a woman who very much reveres our religion and is interested to tell her people about it." Then the old man would consent, usually.

We particularly had four or five different old men whom we'd consult one by one. We had to be in some place where the other O'odham couldn't tell that it was being done, because they would have thought that their language was being stolen. The old man would quietly recite quite an amount from the ceremony. I would write down just what he said, and it would have strange words in it. The old man would use old-time O'odham words. I'd say to Rafael, "Do you know what those words mean?" "No." So I'd write it down as carefully as I could with the spelling as exact as I could, then I'd say to the old man, "Now, what does that mean?" And he would tell me what he thought it meant, and then Rafael would learn what that was. Finally, he'd say, "That's all I remember now, but I will think again, and when you come again I will know more."

If we still couldn't understand a word, Rafael would go along all by himself and ask the old people and try to get the meaning of the word and come back and give me some idea. Then I might get a whole lot of O'odham all together and get two or three words and use them, and say, "Now which of those seems to you right?" They'd all talk among themselves, and we'd get a meaning that they all agreed was probably correct. There was a great deal of discussion about my vocabulary, you see, compared to later ethnographers, who just got theirs helter-skelter from whoever was talking.

Even then, the women would help me understand the men's world. I didn't sit in any of the men's ceremonies. At one big drinking ceremony the men sit in the middle, and the women can stand up behind if they want to (where I stood) and watch them drink. We weren't given any drink, although when you got home you could have a drink. The women had ways to get around most everything! I had to remember everything, because they didn't like it a bit if you took notes in a ceremony. They thought that was pretty irreligious. I went home immediately after and wrote down what I recalled. Then I would consult with the women. "Did they say it this way? Then they do that next?" They would correct me. "No, no, they didn't do that, sister. Don't you know? They wouldn't do that." They would explain what was done and why. I didn't pay the women. I just got along with them as a friend and you shared their activities and they were glad to do it. I helped with the activities, but old ceremonialists I paid a dollar an hour. They felt that was proper dignified pay. I paid Rafael, I recall, a dollar a day.

Rafael really had a brain, and he wanted an education. There was nothing but an elementary education on the reservation anywhere, and in Phoenix there was an institution called the Cook Bible School, which taught Indians English and also ordained them as ministers.[*] They could not learn English without wanting to be a minister! So Rafael told them he wanted to be a minister. He became a minister, an ordained Presbyterian minister. Funnily, he really was, and a polygamist and bootlegger at the same time!

When I was leaving, he said, "Now, what will I do when you are gone? How will I get another job like this?"

"Oh, Ralph," I told him, "probably somebody else is going to come and want to do the O'odham ceremonies."

"Who will do that?" he pressed.

"I don't know," I admitted.

"Oh, but what will I do? I've spent my time learning these things that are so important, so useful to me. Can I go somewhere and get a job about it?"

I asked various people in the universities what could they do with a young student who really didn't even know O'odham and had to learn it from the old fellows. They said, "Well, that's a difficult matter. We could get him into college, but that would be forty years until he paid for it." That was the trouble. So I left. But very shortly a beautiful lady (who was really as old as I was, but didn't look it) came to study basketry.[†] She fell for him immediately, and he was only too glad, and they married.

---

[*] A decade earlier one book noted, "In Phoenix now is maintained the Cook Bible School, where a score or more Indians, mainly Pimas [Akimel O'odham], are training for the Christian ministry, to work among their tribesmen." McClintock, James H. 1916. *Arizona: Prehistoric-Aboriginal-Pioneer-Modern, the Nation's Youngest Commonwealth Within a Land of Ancient Culture.* Vol. 1. Chicago: S. J. Clarke. Pg. 34.

[†] This may be Mary Lois Kissell (1874-ca. 1944), author of *Aboriginal American Weaving* in 1910 and *Basketry of the Papago and Pima* in 1916. She studied at Columbia University with Boas and seems to have been first sent to Arizona to study the

But it killed him. What could he get out of that? I knew her fairly well, not too much. She told me it was a little hard to get him adjusted to her. She had a private fortune and got a house in Tucson. I don't know if she was writing up her material or not. People told me that when they went there she would greet them with joy and they'd have all their friendly talk, and then she'd say, "Now, come and see my Indian husband." Then there would be Rafael sitting by the fire, if it was winter, and he looked so sad and woebegone, and he couldn't talk. He could talk English, but he didn't know how to make conversation, and they had no idea how to make conversation with him. So he was exiled, a tragic end. He drank and drank until he died.

⌒

Eventually, the O'odham said they felt that I belonged with them. I was white. I was one of those queer people. "But it's all right," was their general attitude. "They're just crazy. Won't do us any harm being with a crazy person for a while."

Then again, I was thought to be a little crazy from the other view, too. My family even thought I was. I was willing to sleep outdoors night after night, have no bath with water sometimes for up to three months, and instead use sand to clean myself. To be isolated. The wish to be completely integrated with the O'odham. But if they knew the O'odham my family would understand why I wanted to be with these people who were so delightful, sincere, friendly, and strong, and always joking, always spending a great deal of time laughing.*

O'odham in 1910 by the American Museum of Natural History. See: Jacknis, Ira. 2004. A Berkeley Home for Textile Art and Scholarship, 1912–1979. *Textile Society of America Symposium Proceeding,* Paper 448. http://digitalcommons.unl.edu/tsaconf/448 (accessed March 4, 2013); Woman Will Study Indian Basket Work. 1910. *New York Times,* 23 October.

* As one observer has noted, "Today, more than sixty years after Boas first suggested that she study the Papago, Underhill's research in this field stands among the most highly respected and widely admired anthropological efforts at documenting Native American culture and society." Staub, Michael E. 1994. *Voices of Persuasion: Politics of Representation in 1930s America.* Cambridge: University of Cambridge Press. Pg. 71.

Columbia, Part 2

THERE WERE FEW ADDITIONS to our graduate department my second year. Perhaps the shadow of Henrietta's death was hanging over us, but it had to be forgotten as we plunged into the sea of new information and new ideas about *Homo sapiens*. By this time the "steadies," those who meant to shoulder their way through to a doctorate, had been separated from those who had come merely to take a look, then drift off to marriage or a paying job. I could almost feel the tide take hold of me as when a ship leaves the waters of the harbor and is lifted by the first great swells of the Atlantic. The ship had a captain. A little stooping man, with a German accent and a scar on his face, but he knew exactly what the course was and how to keep on it.

Now I knew what my life's work was to be. Of course, I had not found what was the matter with the human race except being human, but you grow patient when you think of problems in terms of millennia rather than months. Sitting in my cubbyhole in the darkened library, I could picture the good old earth rolling along for billions of years with continents breaking up and floating away, mountains popping up and down, one species of animal after another making a trial run and then disappearing.

At the beginning of the second year we all made speeches and told what we had been doing. Boas wanted to know very practical things, something about government and social development. How long had they been there? What was the attitude toward Spain? Lots of things like that. Ruth wanted to know: how did they feel? I told her a great deal about the marriage system and the bringing up of children because that was what I was interested in, too.

Ruth became very enthusiastic about what I could provide because the other students did not have anything like that to provide. Ruth saw that I had some of the poet in me, which she had also. I guess

173

she told Boas and he thought, "Well, perhaps this is something we'd better encourage." Boas accepted what I had done. He did not praise me, but acceptance was enough. He even tried to get me to take on some of the work he was doing with one of the northern tribes. But I said I wouldn't go to the northern tribes. They weren't picturesque. I'd already sensed the poetry of the O'odham, and I wanted to stay there. He was very kind about it. He saw that I was deeply interested and didn't interfere; he let me have the O'odham. It was all just a beginning, feeling your way at first, with them and with me both.

I worked another nine months of classes and seminars. In that second year at Columbia, I was at home, busy as a robin pulling worms out of the wet soil. Anthropology was that soil, soaked and ready for me. Once it had looked impenetrable, and its worms—Bastian, Boule, Keith—had seemed not only sunk beyond my digging but probably indigestible.* Now, my beak yanked them out with gusto, chomped them into pieces, and stowed them in a notebook.

Boas had no work for me that second summer, nor for anyone. We, among our books and our arguments—dug in like prairie dogs in our own particular burrows—were forced to become aware that the Depression was growling outside our doors. Such things as money and positions still seemed far away to most of us as we chased ideas through volumes of fact, wrote papers, grasped new concepts. I, for one, took my disappointment in stride. I had saved a little from my pay of $1,000. I would see more Indians and grasp more ideas by touring among the Navajo with Gladys Reichard.

～

---

* Bastian was noted previously. Marcellin Boule (1861–1942) was, during his day, an important French paleontologist and physical anthropologist. Sir Arthur Keith (1866–1955) was also once a leading paleoanthropologist, having published in 1911 *Ancient Types of Man*, among other influential books. He was a principal advocate for the veracity of Piltdown Man, a series of fossils discovered near Sussex, England, in 1912 and which were thought by many to be the "missing link" between ancient and modern humans. Through the application of the newly developed technique of fluorine dating, in 1953 Piltdown Man was proven to be the result of a clever hoax, the fraudulent combination of a medieval human skull, a orangutan jaw, and chimpanzee teeth, all of which had been stained with chromic acid to suggest common origin in antiquity. Keith remains a suspect in the Piltdown hoax. See: Oakley, Kenneth P., and J. S. Weiner. 1955. Piltdown Man. *American Scientist* 43(4):573–583; Langdon, John H. 1991. Misinterpreting Piltdown. *Current Anthropology* 32(5):627–631.

Through Gladys, I made friends with various Navajos, and I forget whether it was that summer that I went to a wedding. Gladys was elsewhere, and I was with a young, ambitious Navajo who spoke English and was anxious to be part of the New World. He was a relative of the groom's family. The ceremony took place under a shelter out of doors. There sat bride and groom, side by side, all his relatives in a row on his side, hers on her side. A basket of corn mush was brought, and they dipped their fingers and ate, he first and then she. On the east of the basket, the southwest and north. This sharing of the sacred food was the ceremony. After it, the relatives on both sides spoke, giving advice to the young couple. It was all very dignified, I gathered from my escort, whom I will call John. The husband was told to work hard, the wife to spin and weave and to feed her family. John was one of the younger relatives of the groom, and as time went on, his moment to speak arrived. He got out of the car where he had sat with me, translating the speeches. He took his place on the groom's side and undertook a wild project.

"My relatives," so he told me later he had said, "you are young and I hope that you can give up the old customs. You [to the groom], do not avoid your mother-in-law. She is a fine woman. You could learn much from her. Speak to her. Do not be afraid." Everyone knows, of course, that with the Navajo the groom goes home to live with the bride, and he is forbidden to speak to his mother-in-law, I suppose, lest quarrels ensue.

I imagine that the statement "God is Dead" made in church would not have had a more appalling effect. Murmurs began. There was a movement, like a ground swell under the sea. John came hastily back to the car, got in, and told me, "We go." So we left the wedding, and we did not see the feast that followed.

That summer I also spent a little time with the Maidu of northern California and saw a sad modern ceremony with dances in blue jeans around a glaring arc light instead of a bonfire. I was with our new professor of linguistics, trying to grasp the special sounds and the intricate grammar of a group very unlike the O'odham. One has no idea of the different grammatical schemes human beings can think up until he has tried to work out several unwritten Indian languages. I liked the Maidu idea of using a special particle whenever the subject of a sentence was to be different from the last one. How I have

wished since that I could make my students do such a thing. About
the spelling, though, I moaned a complaint.

❧

Another person I had a very interesting visit with during this period
was Paul Radin.* Now, Boas for some reason took a great objection
to Radin. If Boas didn't like a person, then you knew all about that.
I think that Radin, who was quite a poetic person—though forgetful,
as poets are—had been somewhere and maybe had not paid his debts,
his board. I don't think he'd done anything worse than that, but Boas
took an extreme dislike to Radin. When he found that I had sat at
Radin's feet for two or three weeks, Papa Franz was rather leery about
what I might've learned. Of course, Radin had a great imagination
and very poetic attitude, so that a good deal of what Boas would have
neglected I did get from him.

Radin was thinking in the same lines that I thought in, except that
Radin was often too quick and made his conclusions too suddenly, so
that you couldn't quite rely on even his translations. But you could feel
very much enthused by his attitude of open-hearted joy in American
Indian beauties. You got that from him very definitely, but as to just
which beauty it was and how do you translate it and where did you
get it, he wasn't always careful about that.

❧

When I returned again to Columbia I was now, as I have mentioned,
an assistant in anthropology, on the Barnard staff, with my name in
the catalog. I had not told my family of this little honor, and when
I visited for a weekend, I gathered that they were resting uneasily in
the hope that I was keeping quiet for a while within college walls.
They were taking a European trip, and Father, with real generosity,
proposed that I should take my place in the group.

"But I have a job," I said.

"Those underpaid social work things are always open," said Father.

---

* Paul Radin (1883–1959) was a Boas student who went on to write nineteen books and
become a prominent folklorist and cultural anthropologist in mid-twentieth-century
America. See: Diamond, Stanley, ed. 1960. *Culture in History: Essays in Honor of Paul
Radin.* New York: Columbia University Press.

"You'd be with nice people for a while if you came with us," he added.

"You don't think the Columbia faculty is composed of nice people?"

My poor father just couldn't understand where I was and what was the matter with "the dirty Indians." He always spoke of them as "dirty Indians." I tried to tell him they're *not* dirty; in fact, the O'odham rub themselves with sand. But he couldn't accept it.

Oh, what an utter job it was to show them the catalog with my name, right on the cursus honorum. I can realize now the extreme relief the poor dears felt at the knowledge that, of my own accord, I was doing something respectable. They must have had a bad time as parents everywhere are still having bad times. Can poor *Homo sapiens* never do any better?

My job was taking Barnard girls twice a week to the American Museum of Natural History. In those days, before additions and revisions, it was a prim reminder of Balmoral Castle, with its white-bordered windows and topping of gables.* How delicious it was to lead my troupe into the huge marble entrance, where the Pygmies were dodging under the elephant and I could explain to excited maidens how they really did kill the beast that way.

≈

Those who wanted to take a Master's of Arts degree had an examination, and I asked Boas whether I should take it.

"Is that the thing?" I said. "I wish to go on to a PhD, but should I take this?"

"Oh no," he answered, "it would be a great deal of work for us in the department. We'd have to make up an examination for you, and then we'd have to correct it. Don't give us that much work!"

So I did not take the MA examination. I just waited for the PhD and finally took that.

≈

I still had the farmhouse up in the country where I had lived with my husband in the 1920s, and Father hadn't been able to rent it or

---

* Balmoral Castle is a large estate house in Scotland, one of the residences for the British royal family.

sell it. I did not want to go near the big house where I had lived with Cecil, but the farmer's cottage was comfortable, with two or three tiny rooms, and its stove could be made gloriously hot. I got my old car from the farm, garaged it outside New York, and drove it up to the country on weekends, when the gang of students liked to huddle.

We used to have a very good time. We talked freely then, and we gave silly names to the people we'd read about or the authors we'd read. One time Ruth Benedict came, too. It was one, I think, where the boys had brought several bottles of gin and the cocktails were strong. I remember that Ruth just relaxed like anybody and was a girl having a good time. We hadn't known she could do it, but she just sat on the floor with the rest of us. We all told dirty stories, and Ruth told some, too.

After that, I lost my picture of her as the ageless priestess Cumaean Sibyl, seated on a pedestal and holding her books of prophecies.* Instead, I saw her as a stimulating, well-bred friend. We were both from New York State. Both had country, early-settler backgrounds; both crossed out the same impossible people. She became a person to share thoughts with. At first, she was Dr. Benedict and I, Miss Underhill, but then we just called each other Ruth. Actually, she was just four years younger than I. She treated me on that basis, and we even shared gossip. I have read Margaret Mead's account of her as a haunted person, but I was not equipped to see that side.[†] She was getting a divorce at the time, and she knew I had had one.[‡] We spoke about husband difficulties and about which students were fools and which astute.[§] Although it may well be that so much light was now shining into my life that I could not observe the shadows in Ruth's.

---

* The Cumaean Sibyl is the mythical Greek goddess presiding over the oracle to Apollo at Cumae, an ancient Greek colony near Naples, Italy.

† Mead's obituary does not have such a tone (Mead, Margaret. 1949. Ruth Benedict, 1887–1948. *American Anthropologist* 51(3):457–468). Perhaps Underhill is referring to her interpretation of the tone in Mead's 1959 book *An Anthropologist at Work: Writings of Ruth Benedict.*

‡ Ruth sought a divorce from Stanley Benedict around 1931. See: Banner, Lois W. 2004. *Intertwined Lives: Margaret Mead, Ruth Benedict, and Their Circle.* New York: Vintage. Pg. 131.

§ Elsewhere, in her interviews, Underhill states that she and Ruth never actually spoke about their divorces with one another even though this shared experience made them feel "drawn together."

Whenever, now, I have what I think is a possible idea in anthropology, my feet yearn to turn to that dark little office. I can scarcely keep from bursting out, "What would you think of this, Ruth?" My last book would have been twice as good if only Ruth could have looked it over.

❧

In my third year at Columbia, funds were short. I lived in a little room with a corridor full of screaming girls. Once I was forced to show my age.

"Is it really more fun to scream?" I once demanded, interrupting one girl's fun.

She looked at me witheringly, as though I had asked why people have hands and feet.

"Were you ever a girl, teacher?" she impishly asked.

"No!" I snapped. "But I was a Papago." *

---

* Underhill told this same story elsewhere, with slight variations. See, e.g.: Lavender, Catherine J. 2006. *Scientists and Storytellers: Feminist Anthropologists and the Construction of the American Southwest*. Albuquerque: University of New Mexico Press. Pg. 104.

The Fruit of the Saguaro

WITH THE O'ODHAM, I stayed two weeks in the house of Crooked Lightning. In these days of social reform I have heard people rail against the horrors of a house without plumbing. "It is," they say, "an insult to human dignity. And as for a dirt floor! We should abolish such things from our civilized country."

Those critics could never have gone camping. It was fortunate for me that I had camped since girlhood and that I had gotten used to employing the face of nature as a substitute for indoor plumbing. I had spent nights in mountain lodges lying on the dirt floor and paid for the privilege. Moreover, in those mountain lodges men and women had stretched out on separate sides of the room without a thought of impropriety.

We stretched out in that way in Lightning's house. The arrangement was that the father and mother lay side by side in the center of the room. Next to the father were the males of the family, the smallest first and the oldest near the wall. On the mother's side were the females, and here it was my place to be next to the wall. I had a sleeping bag in my car, but since no one in the Lightning family used such a thing, I felt it would be pretentious, so I lay on my rubber ground sheet, which wrinkled. Later I followed the example of the O'odham, who each had a huge sheet of cotton. In old days this was all woven. It served as bedding at night, sheets during the day, a raincoat or cloak when needed.

The lack of plumbing means, of course, that there is no water for a bath. The O'odham tell, with smiles, about how the clouds can be "pulled down" in midsummer before planting begins, but in June, when I lived with the Lightnings, there had been almost no rain since the previous October. Crooked Lightning, once a week, took his horses and cart (for this was before the days of pickups) and brought a barrel of water from a tank set up by the government two miles away.

Figure 25. An elegantly simple structure used by the O'odham for domestic tasks, circa 1931–1935.

We all rushed out when we heard the wagon coming. The barrel stood in it as a permanent fixture, with a spigot toward the bottom, which let water out into a pot. The big earthen pot was of the ancient O'odham style, red clay and not watertight. It was stood up under shade outside the house in the crotch of a small tree; breezes blowing across it as it slowly leaked kept the water cool, and the sign of hospitality was to give a friend a drink. Anyone arriving picked up the gourd that hung beside the pot and helped himself to a drink as a sign that he knew he was trusted. We had to be careful of that. The hostess brought out a fry pan that was filled with water to a height of about two inches. I, as the guest, was given first wash, though in later days I refused such honor. Then the family washed in order. Old Chona first, as the elder, then father, mother, and each child. It was all in the same fry pan, which of course became pretty full of sediment, but there did not seem to be many germs in O'odham country. That year I never had any trouble. Of course, going without a bath at first seems a little strange, and I remember at a luncheon of the Women's Faculty Club

later I sent myself almost through the roof by explaining that I had
gone without a bath for three months. The gasps of horror were so
amusing that I did not tell them one can rub oneself with sand and
that, combined with perspiration, makes a pretty good cleanser.

I stayed two weeks this time with the Lightning family and had
a beautiful time. We ate dried squash, cooked over an open fire in
a saucepan from Woolworth's. Squash, I learned, was one of the
ancient O'odham foods, which grew luxuriantly after the midsummer
rain. When the yellow crooknecks were ripe, they were peeled like
an apple, the long rope, two inches wide, being wound into a ball,
dried, and preserved. It was dumped into the cooking water without
salt, though sometimes desert sage or some other herb could be used
as flavor. Salt with the O'odham was an expensive and sacred thing.
Once they had had none but what they brought on the pilgrimage
from the Gulf of California. In my time, of course, it could be bought
from the trader, but somehow that did not occur to people used to
going without it. At this time in late June, the hard desert soil was
impregnable to the shovel, so Crooked Lightning and his neighbors
were not farming. They hunted rabbits and they had village business,
while the women went out after the first green shoots to be found in
shady places. The cholla cactus at this time of the year has little hard
yellow buds that will someday be flaming red flowers. Angela, the
lady of the house, told me that in old days, these buds, boiled, were
sometimes their only food in spring—the hungry time. She and her
daughters went out daily to look for buds and other sprigs of green
while Chona and I did the babysitting. We had a companion, an old
male relative of the house. Chona called him brother, for all cousins
of both sides were brothers, no matter the degree of relationship.
This brother was nicknamed "Salt in the Coffee," and that name was
an unending joke. It seemed long ago at the traders' that he had seen
white people put a white powder in their coffee. Never having seen
sugar, he decided this was a wonderful and expensive salt that white
people could get and made a point of obtaining some.

O'odham are endlessly kind to people and to the incompetent,
but nevertheless are outspoken with their jokes. Salt in the Coffee
had borne this name for most of his adult life. He and I and Chona
sat on our ground sheets in the shade of the house, for the sun was

already almost torrid. The two old people, in their mixed Mexican and English, began to tell me what O'odham life had been in the old days. Grim, I thought it, but they talked with peaceful smiles.

"You see," began Chona, "we have no water but what comes from the skies."

"Out of the clouds," began Salt in the Coffee, and Chona told him sharply, "Silence. She knows that."

"But the clouds, and the rain, and the planting, that is for men." The old fellow was stopped with a glare.

So there was rivalry between these two ancients, although O'odham seem never to raise their voices and seem to be always smiling. I gathered I must look out for some of the little thrusts and pitfalls I had known among whites.

"You see," explained Chona, "you see, before there was a government, well, we could not live here at this time of the year on our earth—our flat land." No one will speak the name of his country with more love and reverence than O'odham spoke that phrase "the flat land." It meant the desert country where they made their little farms because, as I soon learned, they could not live there until the rains came to make it habitable.

"But, oh, how beautiful it is," said Chona, "when all this land flows with water."

"The water washes down trees," contributed Salt in the Coffee. "It could even take your car."

"Silence," said Chona.

By jerks and degrees, I learned that early O'odham life had been seminomadic. It was a planned wandering on a circuit, that flat land in summer when the rains came and they could plant, the hills in winter where they camped near springs, the men hunted, the women sought materials for basketry, and they kept alive as best they could.

In these later days I have been hearing about people who are poor, who live on less than $5,000 a year. It is taken for granted that such people must be depressed, incompetent, and rebellious, but Chona, and even Salt in the Coffee, smiled as they told me about the "hungry days."

"Sometimes," said Chona, "we lived only on cholla buds." Then she nodded with her placid smile. "Cholla buds are very good."

However, I will confess here that earlier I had done underhanded things. There were some chocolate bars that I had not presented with my other offerings on the first night. I had planned to leave them for a special treat, but of course, with the heat, they melted. I secreted them in the depths of my baggage, and soon there was only a gluey coating on the inside of a paper bag. Of course, the Lightning children would have licked that bag with pleasure, but I shall reveal the fact that I licked it myself. Dried squash, without salt, did get tiresome, and there were times when I sneaked to the car alone for a taste of that wonderful chocolate.

After two weeks I needed a breathing spell. Also, it was necessary for me to go to the government headquarters, get registered, and make some definite plans for the summer. So I bounced the car over bumpy graveled roads to the government agency at Sells, Arizona.

It is the custom now to decry the work of the Bureau of Indian Affairs, but no one could do that who has seen those tired, hard-working people going through the corridors of their flimsy buildings, doing their best to interpret orders from Washington, which they cannot make Indians understand and sometimes they do not understand themselves. Why should they, its orders? None of them spoke O'odham. Few of them knew as much as I did about the old O'odham life and its reasons. They had jobs such as seeing that the wells were kept in order, the cattle watered, schools provided, and all of this was properly reported. They were breezy and friendly with the Indians who came to them, slapping them on the back and calling them "Joe," but that the O'odham way of life was different from their way was something to be mentioned with a smile and otherwise disregarded. It happened to me later as I was talking with the cattle supervisor, who had just refused an O'odham's request for appointment as his assistant.

"The man doesn't know English," he told me with a tired smile. "Not even simple English, enough for the job."

"Have you tested him?"

"Well, his application was enough," said the tired white man.

He gave the name of someone who had recommended him, and the relationship was his "cousin-brother."

"Well! Nobody can be both of those things."

"Be he can," I began to protest. "In the Papago family system, cousins are brothers."

Figure 26. Mr. Garcia, a foreman at the Sells Agency, circa 1931–1935.

The white man shook his head. "That's too deep for me. I have a job to do, and I must have an assistant who speaks enough English to understand me. We are told to give these people jobs, but if they won't take the trouble to learn the language . . ."

I did not ask why he did not learn O'odham. It was plain that I was just an interloper, barely tolerated.

Teachers were different. I have reverence and affection for those hardworking women thrust into a situation for which they were not prepared, given a job that was impossible, to make good Americans of desert Indians within the generation. They learned as they could, and gladly they told me of their experiences, which sometimes we had to decipher together like a statement in code.

Here I want to pay tribute to a Mrs. Bennett, a jolly, sloppy south-erner who loved O'odham and was loved by them. Of course, she did not try to speak O'odham, no teacher did, and her idea of teaching them English was somewhat fantastic. The verse she gave her children to learn was:

> The year has been dawning, another new day
> Thing will thou let it, slip useless away.*

Whatever English an O'odham child in her grade failed to learn, he or she could always recite that. It was like an abracadabra, quite devoid of meaning, but it was Mrs. Bennett who told me about the summer cactus gathering, and it was she who arranged that I should go to the Saguaro orchard with one of her pupils, Ella, and the girl's family.

~

After a time, I needed a break from Santa Rosa. I took my sleeping bag to another village where I hadn't been yet. I wanted to know the people. I went there with my car. The tent was generally strapped on the side of the car; it stood on the running board and was strapped across the roof.

When I got to the new village, everybody had heard about me and the young boys thought I was fun, so they liked to hear me talk. When I said an O'odham word it sounded so queer to them, the way I pronounced it, that they would keep asking me, "Say it again! Tell us things in O'odham." I said, "All right. You tell me things. Tell me how to say something, and I will say it for you. You can laugh at me, and I can learn how it's said." We got along very well that way.

One afternoon I had spent the whole day at a new village. Every-body had been to my tent. They had been telling me some stories, even though they traditionally believed that a sacred story should be told only in the winter when the snakes are underground. They all wanted to talk, so they'd been telling me some stories, and I'd enjoyed it tremendously. Then they all went home as the sun went down. I got out my sleeping bag and laid out under the moon. I

---

* See Thomas Carlyle's 1840 poem "Today."

thought to myself, "This is the life! Why do I ever do anything but this? I'm going to live this way until I die."

I didn't go to sleep at all. I stayed looking at the glorious light at night and the wind blowing softly down from the mountains. You could just barely see them in the moonlight.

But then I began to think, "Now, what do you suppose Hitler's doing at this time? Is it really as terrible as the papers say?" The more I thought about it, the more I just couldn't bear not knowing. Suddenly I said to myself, "I can't live like this. I've got to find out what's doing in Europe!" I jumped in my car and took the sixty-mile drive to Tucson. I went into a hotel in Tucson. We had no liquor at that time, so I got an ice cream soda and a New York newspaper and gorged on them both! Filled, I drove back to the O'odham, and everything was all right.

～

"You see them long things on top of saguaro?" Ella, my fourteen-year-old guide and interpreter, pointed to the one scraggly giant cactus growing near her house in Santa Rosa, the Village of the Bright Seeds, where I was camping until the cactus expedition.

The giant cactus is a weird and impressive item of vegetation, growing nowhere in America but in southern Arizona and adjacent Mexico. The huge trunks are sometimes thirty feet high, ribbed like a marble column, and each studded with clumps of thorns long and sharp as a darning needle. Toward the top they branch like candelabra. Though sometimes the branches are stubby and awkward looking, like the arms of a deformed child, at a distance the towering green structure looks like a tree, but when touched it turns out to be made of pulp, tough but still penetrable by a knife or by the bill of a desert woodpecker, who scores it into wool to make her nest. At the very tips of the branches I saw, in this late June, forms that might be perching birds, or sometimes they were white flowers like water lilies.

"You see," Ella told me gleefully, "the liquor is growing."

That meant the cactus fruit, which grew from a white flower to a swollen green form like an avocado, but hard shelled and studded with long thorns. These were now almost ripe, Ella informed me, and the People would soon be going to gather the fruits and bring them to their ceremony that would "pull down the clouds." For it

Figure 27. An O'odham woman prepares to gather saguaro fruit with a long piece of dried-out saguaro rib, with children playing in the background.

seems that in mid-July clouds do gather in the blazing blue sky of O'odham country, and with proper ceremony they can be "pulled down" so that rain will wash the hard desert land. That end of the "hungry time" is a holiday season for the People. I could feel it as I went about the village with Ella, a burbling expectation that reminded me of childhood times when we counted the days to Christmas. I recall Ella's father, Steve, and his wife, Valalia, for those were their agency names. Steve had various other appellations, among them "Two-Bits" and "Horsetail," coming from exploits of his in the past. Steve had a wagon, as most fathers of families did, and I was to ride in it, the roadless hills being no place for my car.

I ventured to take my sleeping bag this time, for there are no houses in the cactus orchard, although there would be no rain until the blessed and wonderful moment when the clouds appeared and summer life could begin. I was wise enough not to take chocolate this time, but I decided, as raisins and cheese would keep, that these might be a desirable addition to rabbits and cholla buds. Dried squash, by this time, was all used up.

We jolted over the track toward the hills while the family pointed out rocks and ravines where something had happened, perhaps a battle with the Apaches when the old people could talk. Of course, those people could talk still, Ella tried to explain to me, although she was not sure just how this was.

~

It was dusk as we started up the hillside toward our particular camping area, and Ella grabbed my arm, panting and pointing and whispering, "Our Comrade"—Nyi Wrnaglii. This is a rough spelling of the O'odham pronunciation of the beloved term *Comrade*. I was about to speak when the stern, staid expression and the hushing of the children made me understand that this was a special event. A coyote was crossing the track at dusk, his hunting time. Later I learned that the Tohono O'odham tribe was divided into halves, or moieties, called "Coyote" and "Buzzard." I never managed to meet anybody from the Buzzard half, but, like my friends, I learned to revere the Comrade, when we saw his long figure slinking in the distance. Often his head turned back to look at us, which they told me was the Comrade's smile.

We were up in the hills now, low ridges really, and ahead we could see the cactus standing in ranks like an army. The children were pointing excitedly to the tops where the fruit could be seen clustered. Valalia was breathing with happiness, and Steve began a song.

"How thick they are," I told Ella, for I, too, was catching the excitement, and just here, nowhere else.

"Oh, that's because of Nyi Wrnaglii," said Ella.

Little by little I got the story, and, oh, what patience it took me to get those stories one by one with pauses, and questions, and fumbling for words, but what pleasure when the tale showed up clearly in my mind.

It seems that when Earth was being arranged, the Great One often used Coyote as a helper, he being very busy with all the details. So when it was time to plant the giant cactus, he gave Coyote the seeds in a bag and told him, "Spread them evenly so all the people can get them without crowding each other," but Coyote—people usually said with a tolerant smile—he never did anything right. He would forget or he would play jokes, so with the cactus seed he got to the south side of the hill and there found something he wished to chase. So he dropped the bag and scattered the seeds all on the south side, none on the north. I used to say placidly, "That was Coyote's way." And today that is where is where most of the saguaros grow.*

Every family had its particular cactus orchard, and thither they repaired, from the hills or from any other refuge where they had gone through the winter. By early July, the flowers had developed into large, thick-shell fruit, whose pulp and seeds had, for me, the look of raspberry jam. This was boiled every day, the liquid saved in a jar, the seeds dried and ground into flour. When the first spatter of rain came, loaded wagons converged from every direction toward the beloved flat land, which would soon be habitable again. Houses were cleaned and cache pits opened. The dried food from last year must sustain the families until the new crops were ready.

At the council house, the juice contributed by all the families was poured into large jars with an equal quantity of water added. There it was to stand, in the warmth and dark, for two nights and a day. A group of old men kept guard over it, to sing the fermenting songs and keep witches away. If fermentation did not take place on time, it would be known that there was evil in the village.

---

* A Native observation that corresponds with scientific observation (see: Yetman, David. 2007. *The Great Cacti: Ethnobotany and Biogeography*. Tucson: University of Arizona Press. Pg. 25).

At dusk that night, the headman called from the roof of his arbor, summoning all to sing "that the corn may grow, the beans may grow, and the squash may grow!"

We gathered in the open space before the council house. There, old men were sitting against the wall, softly intoning the words of the rain songs, so that the singing might be correctly done. In the center of the space, a small fire had been lit, and there the medicine man stood to see that all went well. Around it, the song leader moved slowly sideways, shaking his gourd rattle, and soon the men joined him, then the women. All night, with intervals, they stepped slowly in a circle, singing ancient songs that told how the rain left the earth "lying beautifully smooth and finished." Next day the men hunted rabbits for a feast that would entertain the whole neighborhood, and the next night all sang again. On this second night the morning star had not yet appeared when the medicine man came to the center of the circle to announce, "The liquor has fermented. Go home and sleep. When the sun is high, come to the sit-and-drink."

The men came, in all their cowboy finery. The women stood behind to watch, as watertight baskets of the red cactus cider were passed ceremonially with songs and speeches. The rains now were assured. Meantime, there was a day of gaiety when the ceremonial jar of juice fermented in every house must be consumed. It was done with feasting and singing. For days after that, every man in the village and many women lay about under the sun, rousing only to sip a few last drops and to sing sleepily. Then the clouds began to gather. Men took off their finery. The guests went home, and work on the fields began.

Indian Affairs

I OFFICIALLY GRADUATED from Columbia University.* I had spent two years altogether with the Tohono O'odham, and I would have spent my life with them if I could have gotten the money. But in those days students didn't get huge grants before they'd done any work, which apparently they do now. So when my grant gave out, there was nothing for me to do but to leave and tell the O'odham, "I'll be back to visit, but I really can't stay any longer."

I happened to meet some government official with the Mojave of California and Arizona who told me the tribe hadn't been well studied, and he thought it would be nice if I would come and do it. They would pay me, but they didn't offer a very large salary. It was a very modest kind of a job, not meant to be a complete study. That was all I had for the moment, so I took it. They were very different people from the O'odham—so different that although it wasn't far geographically, it was far psychologically.

Down with the Mojave I had what they called a wall tent, a great big thing with straight up-and-down sides and gabled roof, maybe ten feet long, that I lived in. I would go to the village and get friendly with them and say, "I wondered if you would mind if I brought my tent here. I don't want to interfere with you, but would that be all right?" After they agreed I'd give them a lot of soft soap: "I'm so interested in the way you live, and so many Indians don't do it anymore. I would like to see this *real* Indian way of living. I'll be very careful not to say anything against you when I write it up." "Oh well, then," they would say, "yes."

---

* Different sources give different dates for Underhill's graduation, varying between 1934 and 1937. But, as Underhill stated earlier, it seems that she did not have her degree officially conferred until *Social Organization of the Papago Indians* first appeared in print in 1937.

Of course, I always made friends with the women first, because it seemed so much easier. Then I would get to know the men. The women did not always approve. One time a woman came to me.

"Now look here, Ruta"—they called me Ruta instead of Ruth— "you want to be careful about that man called Raw But Burned. I don't think he's a very good medicine man, but he is a medicine man. He would be able to make himself into a badger, go underground, and come up in your tent and rape you. You want to be careful about that."

"I'll look out for that!" I said. He never did anything of the sort, of course. I mean he didn't even show that he would like to rape. I was really not an attractive mortal for that purpose.

Anyway, there's no one person that's the focus for the story of my time with the Mojave. You would have to move from one little incident to another. The Mojave work is not quite as absorbing as my work with the Tohono O'odham, although I think it could have been if I'd stayed long enough. Of course, the government never used my Mojave stuff. When a new administration comes in, everything done by the old administration is no good. It's just as if it had been done in the dark ages. They simply throw it away. So that's what happened. I began to see that this was no real job. This was only just a fill-in.

~

There was a little period of broken rhythm that I don't need to go into. I went to look for jobs and talk to people, and it was discouraging. Finally everybody said to me, "You better go into the Indian service. Why don't you try?"* So I tried, and they told me to take an exam, which I did and was all right. I found myself appointed as a kind of cultural expert. I was in the same rank as the teachers and so was in a group of very nice women teachers; they were really awfully good women. I wish to lay myself out in praise of those unselfish, intelligent women.

I proceeded immediately to Washington, DC. I thought it was going to be very exciting. We were all put up and told that we were

---

* Underhill loosely speaks about the "Indian service" or "Indian bureau" when she is referring to the U.S. Office of Indian Affairs, renamed in 1947 as the Bureau of Indian Affairs. See: Fixico, Donald L. 2012. *Bureau of Indian Affairs*. Santa Barbara, CA: ABC-CLIO.

to travel, probably, among the Indian groups and do our stuff. One
girl was to do domestic teaching, tell them how to cook. (Of course,
they knew how to cook what they liked, but that didn't matter.)
And another girl was to teach them sewing and how to put on nice
clothes. (Meaning to teach them not to dress the way they did.) And
then there were two or three teachers just to teach them reading and
writing. I was to investigate Indian life and try to tell people about
that. I thought that was delightful.

The big boss, Willard Beatty, was a very nice man.* "Now, Miss
Underhill," he told me when we first met, "I have come new to this
job, but I find that the people in America do not really know the
Indians. They do not know their customs and their behavior, and I
think perhaps they ought to know it. Now, I've decided that we'll
get out a series of pamphlets describing life of the Indians in different
tribes. Now, you will write the pamphlets." At which I sort of fluttered
and thought, "Pretty good." "And I will sign them," added he.

All of a sudden my heart sank. I replied, "Mr. Beatty, I don't believe
I can take this job. I am now a PhD. I've had years of training on
Indians. I'm accustomed to writing. I know how to write books, and
I don't feel that I could be subordinate in that endeavor." I think nine
men out of ten would have said, "Well, then, you're not for me." But
Beatty thought for a few moments and conceded, "I believe you're
right." He said, "We'll arrange then that there shall be a series of
pamphlets, and they shall be as informative and authoritative as we
can make them. But you will write them and you will sign them. I have
other ways my name can be before the public." He was a gentleman,
you see, so we decided on that.†

Generally, each summer I'd go to a reservation to do the research,
and then I'd sit down and write a whole pamphlet in the winter.
Writing was easier in Washington, DC; with the Library of Congress

---

* Willard Walcott Beatty (1891–1961) was appointed director of Indian education for
the Bureau of Indian Affairs in 1936 and immediately implemented a reformist agenda
to train Indian children with skills appropriate for rural life, rather than urban life, as
had been emphasized by his predecessor, W. Carson Ryan. See: Philip, Kenneth R.
1977. *John Collier's Crusade for Indian Reform*. Tucson: University of Arizona Press.

† These were published as the Indian Life and Customs Series by the US Department
of the Interior, Office of Indian Affairs (and later Bureau of Indian Affairs), Branch
of Education.

Figure 28. Ruth (lower right) and an unidentified group in the field, during her years with the Bureau of Indian Affairs, circa 1940.

and the Smithsonian right there, I could go over and get any book I wanted. I also got pictures from the Smithsonian and told my boss, who would decide how to fix them up. He'd do all the editorial work.* Yet an awful thing happened, and it ought to have made me much more of a cynic than I am. The teachers just disregarded my pamphlets. I worked on them a year, tried to get the best of the facts I could, and the teachers just said, "Oh, she's one of the office people. We don't want to bother with them." They then went ahead in the same way they'd always gone.

In addition to my writing, I taught different courses to the teachers who would head out to the reservations. I had had quite a responsibility trying to give the girls as much as I could of interest. Every night when we sat around, I would tell them what I'd heard about from the Indian homes where I'd visited, and they were so excited to know how those Indians lived. These were girls who had come for

---

* Beatty is often listed as the editor in the Indian Life and Customs Series. See, e.g.: Underhill, Ruth. 1945. *Pueblo Crafts*. US Office of Indians Affairs.

adventure, and they weren't getting very much of that in Washington! I can remember once, when I had a course in Indian home life, a girl came to me and asked to be excused so that she could take a course with someone whom she thought was a young male teacher. She was starved for a sex life, for something. That poor girl was starved for excitement; it really impressed me the starvation those girls had had in their lives. They were to teach the Indians how to be good, fruitful citizens, and yet they'd had no lives themselves.

I continued on for eleven years in the service. It was a job, you see. I'd come at that time to the point where I had to have a job. I had gotten established there, and I felt very pleased to have a title. I had a place of my own, where the employees stayed, and it was furnished with nice maple furniture. I didn't need to write home for money anymore. I could just be an independent businesswoman. I was somebody, and it was grand.

～

When I was employed by the government, I worked with the Navajo, but it was not along very spiritual lines. It was along the lines of, "What can the government do for you? Why do you not accept what the government is willing to do?" It was pretty practical material.

I tried to make a difference, especially when I was with the Sioux. I really thought these were very intelligent, active people and they were feeling by that time the complete loss of the buffalo and being just struck by it. It was awful, but they'd been cattlemen, although at first all they did with the cattle was just to chase them around as though they were buffalo and then eat them. So I decided they really could be taught to be good cattlemen, and some of them became so. I started on that.

I got the men together and said, "Now, let us form a cattle association, and you'll all belong to it. You'll all be given cattle, and the one who takes the best care of his cattle and has them for sale and can help the government by selling and bringing in money will perhaps get special consideration and a way for getting more cattle." Then I thought, "If I stay here I can really work something out," and I decided that we would have a great certificate, which could be colored. I also told them, "Every time one of you sells an animal and gets money for it and is able to give that money to the government, we'll have a great ceremony." They thought that was pretty good. So we did all that. I would see that we got a special place at the school and a table, and we'd get some hamburger and we'd all march around the table singing the man's name and give him this certificate.

Really I thought that if I could have stayed there long enough, I could have gotten that thing settled. I thought, "If this could go on regularly and they could get the idea that the more certificates they have the bigger man they are, we may really change the attitude of the Sioux." But the next thing happened to me was that I was transferred. But that project with the Sioux was the only really practical thing I did during that time besides writing about them.

The bureau was not always so practical minded. Mr. John Collier, the famous commissioner of the bureau, for one, was a very different proposition.* He was a poet, a real poet, I think. Some of the verse that he gave me I thought was very beautiful. He had his own idea, not based on any fact, of what the Indians were and what they wanted. He had just gotten ideas out of his own poetic head. If you disagreed with him, that was too bad.

There was one time when I was producing the little pamphlets and I wrote one about the Paiute.† The evidence suggested that the Paiute didn't really have much culture. They didn't have clothes in the beginning. They had very few ceremonies. In writing about the Paiute, I did say their customs were among the most "primitive" that we find among Indians. That was absolutely true, but Collier read it and was offended. He said, "The Paiute must not be insulted so." He didn't know what their customs were, of course. He just considered that they were Indians, and they must be talked of as if they were something special. Collier went to my boss, Beatty, and said, "You'll have to dismiss Underhill. We can't take a person like that in our organization." Beatty decently said, "Why, I can't do that. She's one

---

* Underhill's work at the bureau was part of Collier's "Indian New Deal," which sought to empower Native American tribes. See: Lavender, Catherine J. 2006. *Scientists and Storytellers: Feminist Anthropologists and the Construction of the American Southwest.* Albuquerque: University of New Mexico Press. Pg. 103; Philip, Kenneth Roy. 1977. *John Collier's Crusade for Indian Reform, 1920–1954.* Tucson: University of Arizona Press.

† This, in fact, was the first pamphlet Underhill produced in the Indian Life and Customs Series. See: Underhill, Ruth. 1941. *The Northern Paiute Indians of California and Nevada.* US Office of Indian Affairs.

of the experts whom I rely on." I was not dismissed. But that was the sort of attitude that went around among Collier's people.[*]

I made quite a study of Collier.[†] I guess he was a genius. He had this tremendous emotional interest in Indians, but no knowledge about their ways and no desire to find out just who they were, what they did, and why. They were people, and so he loved them. Also, he liked the white women very much. When any interesting woman came around his way, he would suddenly take her right into the Indian service, often without the civil service exams, and promise her a great big salary. Well, Collier had several ladies whom he took in in that manner. One of them, I remember, got very excited and said, "Why, these poor Indians, they don't have any fun." Just imagine! Indians play from the time they're born till the time they die! But this woman said, "They don't know *how* to play. Why, they don't even buy bean bags!" Picture that.

When Collier really got into his stride he took in this woman Laura Thompson.[‡] She was quite a good-looking woman from Hawaii. She had a lot of material about the old doings on the Pacific Islands. He just took her into his heart and gave her the Indian bureau, just simply gave it to her! Well, you can see how people who worked hard and slowly crawled up one by one began to be a little disaffected.

Another time, suddenly all the people in my grade were told that Mrs. Allen was going to be the head of our unit. "Well," I thought, "she must be quite an important person. I wonder what she's done." It turned out Mrs. Allen was the niece of somebody in the bureau. She

---

[*] Reportedly, Underhill had strong disagreements with Collier even earlier. In 1935, Underhill was hired by Indian Affairs to help review the proposed constitution for the Tohono O'odham Nation. Underhill argued against the draft for not reflecting O'odham economic, social, and political organization. Underhill was soon removed from her post and not permitted to work on government projects concerning the Tohono O'odham. Shortly after this experience, Underhill was again unfairly removed from her post, this time with the Soil Conservation Service. Griffen, Joyce. 1989. Ruth Murray Underhill. In *Women Anthropologists: Selected Biographies*. U. Gacs, A. Khan, J. McIntyre, and R. Weinberg, eds. Pp. 355–360. Westport, CT: Greenwood Press. Pg. 358.

[†] On Collier's encouragement and support of women anthropologists in the BIA, see: Halpern, Katherine Spencer. 1993. Women in Applied Anthropology in the Southwest: The Early Years. In *Hidden Scholars: Women Anthropologists and the Native American Southwest*. N. J. Parezo, ed. Pp. 189–201. Albuquerque: University of New Mexico Press. Pgs. 190–193, 197–198.

[‡] See: Parezo, Nancy J., and Rebecca A. Stephenson. 2001. Laura Maud Thompson (1905–2000). *American Anthropologist* 103(2):510–514.

was a charming woman, and she knew how to say, "Thank you" and "Please" and all the nice things, but she knew nothing about Indians and didn't expect to. I remember one night we all went to see an "Indian show," but it wasn't Indian at all. It was just made-up stuff. So I said to Mrs. Allen, "Well, that was hardly Indian, was it?" She said, "I suppose not, but I wasn't in the mood for Indian things." And I thought, "My God! This is my boss. This is the one who tells me what to do!"

The bureau is the most discouraging organization one could well have contact with. They don't see *anything*. They only see all the papers that must be written in quintuplicate and put somewhere. Where is another question, because most of them got lost. Underneath the Indian office there was this great, solid, branching tree of people who'd been in the office following their fathers and their grandfathers—just an amazing, big, solid, old, gnarled tree it was. The old fellows had been in the Indian bureau almost since World War I. I had a lot of new ideas, and when we sometimes met I explained my ideas to them, but they would always say, "Yes, yes, that's very interesting, but our present organization doesn't admit of it." And there was just nothing going to be done! It was pretty sad.

I would never get very far in the Indian service. They thought, "Oh, she's an old woman. She can't do anything. She hasn't got a high status in the service." And I didn't. I was only one of the ants on the anthill. They always just called me "Miss Underhill." They didn't even think to use the title "Doctor."

❧

I think it was my second year in the service when I was staying at the Indian school in Santa Fe, where the offices of the investigating group were always allowed to stay. It was during this time that I worked with Velino Herrera from Cochiti.* He and I became very great friends. He was a young man, in his late twenties, though married.

---

* For an example of their collaboration, see: Underhill, Ruth. 1951. *People of the Crimson Evening.* US Office of Indian Affairs. Underhill says that Velino is Cochiti, although he is often referred to as being from Zia Pueblo. According to one source: "Velino Herrera, formerly known under the name of Velino Shije and who now signs his works by his Keres name Ma Pe Wi (Oriol). He was born at the Sia pueblo but his family come from the neighboring pueblo of Cochiti." Alexander, Hartley Burr. 1932. *Pueblo Indian Painting.* Nice, France: C. Szwedzicki. Pg. 18.

I remember one experience with Velino. I had to go to some Indian camp and had to start very early in the morning. Velino often went with me because he liked to visit the Indians, too, and I, of course, loved to have him because I questioned him all the way along. Whenever we were driving somewhere, he would always go on instructing me. I just insisted on getting instructions wherever I was.

We got up very early to a morning of mist and cold. We were both sleepy, and we didn't say anything. We got into the car, and we both sat there rather glum. We drove for something like two hundred miles, and then Velino turned to me and said, "How was the world begun?" That was his first remark! I took advantage of it and started in on the science we get in the books. I told him about how the earth developed and how it got its orbit and all the other stars and things around. He listened very respectfully, and when I was through, he said, "Then, how do we get power?" He was talking about the spirits. I said, "I don't know, Velino, you tell me." Then he gave me a long lecture about how the spirit makes itself available.

It was also in Santa Fe that I met H. Marie Wormington.* The anthropologists had a yearly meeting in Santa Fe, and for lunch one day they were going to gather at a restaurant. I had been at their meeting, so I said, "Come on over to the Indian school. Nobody's there now but me. They allow me to use it as my own." They all brought things, tomatoes and bread and so forth, and we all went into the school kitchen and got ourselves lunch. Then, I met Marie. She told me that in her making of salad she never skinned the tomatoes, and I had been taught to skin the tomatoes. I felt she was quite modern about that! That's my first recollection of Marie, making her statement that you need not skin tomatoes!

We became very friendly. We found that both of us were far worldlier than other anthropologists. She told me her life history, and I

---

* Wormington served as curator of archaeology at the Denver Museum of Natural History from 1936 to 1968. Her myriad archaeological contributions, strong and (usually) supportive personality, as well as her centrally located position in Denver, established Wormington as a gatekeeper of Paleo-Indian and Archaic archaeology of the American West, and indeed the Americas as a whole. See: Cordell, Linda S. 1993. "Women Archaeologists in the Southwest. In *Hidden Scholars: Women Anthropologists and the Native American Southwest*. N. J. Parezo, ed. Pp. 202–220. Albuquerque: University of New Mexico Press. Pg. 214–215; Nash, Stephen E. 2013. Hannah Marie Wormington: Woman, Myth, Legend. *Kiva* 78(3): 247–277.

Figure 29. Ruth peeling potatoes on the Cheyenne Reservation, circa 1945.

told her mine. We helped each other for years, until our careers got too different. She was a magnificent organizer and manager. (I'm no such thing; I can't manage anything. As soon as it's put up to me, I give the secretary the responsibility and tell her, "You go ahead and do that, and I'll report on it.") Marie was much more interested in digging. She wanted to get a few arrowheads out of the soil. I thought that was wasted time. I said, "You get the arrowheads, and I'll think about what they're for. You don't have to do it!" We used to disagree about that sometimes.

Marie was employed at the Denver Museum of Natural History.* As soon as she got out of college in 1935 or so, she went to the museum, which was run by an educated man named Jesse D. Figgins, who liked her very much and was impressed by her European background and

---

* Now called the Denver Museum of Nature & Science.

the knowledge she'd already unearthed.* He thought she had courage and determination and brains—and he was right. The museum was still crude, and they didn't know much about what anthropology was, so he employed her right away. Lots of the people there didn't want to employ a woman. There was quite a fuss, quite a cabal against her. She had a hard time. You can just imagine what she would be up against. Nevertheless she got through with it all right. But then the next museum director, Alfred M. Bailey, didn't want women.†️ He just took against Marie from the beginning. Though I think she took against him, too!

~

When World War II began, I was already in the Indian bureau. We were all told, "Now this is a very serious business. The men have got to go to war, and you women have got to carry the Indian bureau." So we all felt very responsible. We were told, "Therefore, you're not going to have any Saturday afternoons off. You're going to work six days a week." Then it turned out that the work we were going to do was just what we had always been doing. It was nothing new. Here we were working extra time. We did get paid for it, though not wonderfully. I got awfully discouraged by that.

We got thrown out of Washington, DC, when the war really reached high proportions. Washington had to be emptied of all the people who were not directly involved in the war. So I was sent to Chicago. And I liked it. I spent all my free time at the University of Chicago and had tea in the afternoon with the students and faculty.

---

* Jesse Dade Figgins (1867–1944) was the first professional director of the Denver Museum of Natural History, serving in that capacity from 1910 to 1935, and was instrumental in the institution's early efforts to engage the public in science. See: Wormington, Hannah Marie. 1946. Jesse Dade Figgins (1867–1944). *American Anthropologist* 48(1):75–77.

† Alfred M. Bailey (1894–1978) was the director of the Denver Museum of Natural History, serving from 1936 until 1970. An ornithologist by training, Bailey emphasized scientific research and museum expansion during his tenure. While it is true that he and Wormington had a strained relationship for more than thirty years before he abruptly fired her in 1968, the reasons were more complex than simply Bailey's lack of tolerance for female scientists. See: Nash, Stephen E. 2013. Hannah Marie Wormington: Woman, Myth, Legend. *Kiva* 78(3): 247–277; Phillips, Allan R. 1981. In Memoriam: Alfred M. Bailey. *The Auk* 98(1):173–175.

My associates in the Indian bureau just melted away from me. Some of them were concerned with getting clothing and whatnot for the Indians, but I had lost enthusiasm.

At the university they were all male. It's taken a long time for the males to realize that a female could do anything. Some of them were nice to me, but I was a female, after all. Although the university's publishing department accepted what I did and told me to publish with them, the boys there felt that I was sort of a butt-in. We had lots of parties and lots of drinking. After I had been at the office all day, I went out to dinner with the Chicago people. But there was no talk whatever about Indians. Then there was only talk of Hitler and war.

～

I had sometimes thought about getting out of the Indian service, but I was fairly stuck. Before, Boas was the one who got my money and saw that I was sent to the field.* But he died in 1942, and when he was gone, I had no pull anywhere. I hadn't worked to get pull. It hadn't occurred to me that you ought to. I just had a lot to write, and I sat down and wrote it without trying to get money or connections. Before, it was all too simple.

There were some old, old fellows who were the executive officers of the bureau, and they were firm and stiff and straight, and they had kept their jobs no matter what. Yet again I went to meet with them to see what could be done about putting some new things into the bureau. One of them decisively said to me, "Now, Miss Underhill, I know you're interested in changing the method of Indian education, but it can't be done now. The plans have been made for a long time, and the people are all in place. We're not ready to accept any of these theories that you have. If you have offers from anywhere else to get out of the Indian service, I think you'd better take them." So I finally thought, "Well, yes, I guess I'd better."

---

* It has been noted that despite Boas's at times marginalized position in the broader academy, he "was instrumental in finding jobs, obtaining fellowships, and acquiring research funds for all of his students. . . . He was particularly protective of his female students, taking a kindly paternalist stance towards them." See: Lamphere, Louise. 1993. "Gladys Reichard Among the Navajo. In *Hidden Scholars: Women Anthropologists and the Native American Southwest*. N. J. Parezo, ed. Pp. 157–188. Albuquerque: University of New Mexico Press. Pg. 161.

Around the World

I HAD AN OFFER FROM the University of Denver. I recall Arnie Withers made me the offer.* But I had never had any contact with him previously. I believe Marie Wormington engineered it, as she was based in Denver and she was such a builder. I accepted the offer. I crawled out from Chicago and went to Denver.

I wanted to go to Denver, though. I wanted the contact with students, for one thing. I hadn't had much contact with intelligent students. I'd had the Indians, who were a different kind of audience, and I'd had my bureau colleagues, who didn't care about my sort of stuff at all. They cared about the practical side of Indian service: "Can we get them food? Can we get clothes?" But what do they *think*? They didn't care about that. So it was quite a new atmosphere I sought, and I was very interested to try it.

When I got to DU, such a change! Like getting out of Champagne and into milk! It was all too wholesome. Everybody was nice. I liked all the DU people, but I had to begin so low with anthropology, begin at almost nothing and take them a few steps and that was enough. That's as far as they wanted to go.†

---

* Arnold Withers (1916–1993) attended Columbia University in the 1940s after serving in the Army Signal Corps during the war. He joined the University of Denver faculty in 1947 and remained there until his retirement in 1976. His contributions were archaeological and included extensive work for the Smithsonian Institution's River Basin Survey. See: Holt, Laura. 1994. Arnold Withers. *Anthropology News* 35(6):73.

† However, in at least one case, Underhill likely made a difference in the life of a young woman who would become a professional anthropologist. Cynthia Irwin-Williams grew up in Denver and in high school started an archaeology club. For her advisors, she recruited H. Marie Wormington, Herbert Dick, and Underhill. Irwin-Williams would go on to an impressive career in the field. Irwin-Williams once said, "That I ever became an anthropologist is largely due to the influence of Dr. Ruth Murray Underhill throughout my life. . . . Almost from the beginning she has been a kind of beacon— lighting up the wonderful world of the quest for man's nature." Irwin-Williams, Cynthia. 1983. SWAA Distinguished Scholarly Award for 1983 Presented to Dr. Ruth

Figure 30. Anthropologists Clara Lee Tanner, H. Marie Wormington, and Ruth, 1980.

There weren't many people in anthropology; it was an awfully small department. Nobody knew what anthropology was, and they didn't really care. They liked the nice big word, they liked to throw it around, and I got elected to all sorts of committees because they needed an anthropologist. But what I had to give them, they didn't want to hear. That was just boring and out of their picture. I was astonished at the lack of information white Americans have about Indians. So I said to myself, "All right, I'll just put all my time into writing." I built a charming little cottage for myself in Denver and set down to write.

I was then nearly seventy years old and thought I would die pretty soon. I thought, "This will be about the end of the time I have on the earth. I'll take it in writing, getting what I know on paper so it's not lost." I thought that was enough. Then, I went on living. Time went past, you see. It was a surprise. It's ridiculous. I really didn't suppose I'd live this long.

Murray Underhill. *SWAA News* 22(2/3): 17–18. Pg. 18. See also: Cordell, Linda S. 1993. Women Archaeologists in the Southwest. In *Hidden Scholars: Women Anthropologists and the Native American Southwest*. N. J. Parezo, ed. Pp. 202–220. Albuquerque: University of New Mexico Press. Pg. 217.

Figure 31. Ruth at her typewriter, circa 1965.

One of the first things I wrote was *Red Man's America*.* I didn't believe there was any good textbook on American Indians, and so I wanted to write one.†

The book led to a television program of the same name, from 1957 to 1958. I enjoyed it very much indeed. Of course, the shows covered material I knew. I didn't have to look it up at all. I knew the stuff, and I knew how to be simple and direct and put things in such

---

* Underhill, Ruth. 1953. *Red Man's America: A History of Indians in the United States.* Chicago: University of Chicago Press.

† Although the evidence is certainly tenuous, it may be that Underhill's inspiration to write popular textbooks in part came from her friendship with Wormington, whose best-selling texts included her 1939 volume *Ancient Man in North America* and the 1947 book *Prehistoric Indians of the Southwest*, both of which went through multiple printings and editions.

Figure 32. *Red Man's America* on television, circa 1957.

a way that people could get them. I didn't even have to write it. I'd talk it straight out of my head. People always like what I say out of my head, so I just went ahead like that.

Dick Conn, who became such a grand man down at the Denver Art Museum, was my assistant.* I would just say to Dick, "Now, I'm going to talk about the Plains next time. I'll want the horse equipment that the Indians use so I can display it. I want the costume that they had and the drum and the various things they used." Dick would get all of those things very competently. Now and then I'd get an Indian to dress up in the proper clothes. They always liked it, and the people liked it.

---

* Richard Conn (1928–1998) served in the Denver Art Museum from 1955 to 1959 and again from 1972 to 1993. He specialized in the artistic material culture of Plains and Plateau Indians and curated many critically acclaimed permanent and temporary exhibitions. See: Blomberg, Nancy. 1998. Richard George Conn. *Anthropology News* 39(9):23.

The show seemed like a success from all sides. I thought that would
lead to other jobs on television. I really expected it. It seemed good,
but they didn't ask me again. That would have been quite a new career.

◆

I found I had saved up a little money and I thought to myself, "What
is it worthwhile to do with this money?" I decided I would go around
the world alone.* And it was a very good time to make that decision,
because the events of World War II were still more or less obvious.
People still looked toward America as one of their saviors, so they
were kind to Americans at that time. Once I decided, I just went right
to the plane company and bought a ticket for Israel.

In Israel, I stayed two months in a kibbutz. I did not come to be
a spectator. I wanted to do things. I told them I would work. They
said, "No, no. We'd much rather have you go home and write a piece
for us in a New York newspaper telling what the kibbutzes are like. It's
not crazy, and it's not silly sex or anything like that. It's a thoroughly
useful way to live." So I promised to do that and wrote something,
though I don't remember whether it even got published. There
was lots of prejudice in America against the Jews, and the kibbutzes
were thought to be shocking. I met Arabs, too. The Arabs were so
charming, you know, with their sweet moustaches and their beautiful
clothes and their long, flowing costumes. I stayed in Israel as long as
my passport would allow, which was three months.

From Israel I went to India and stayed three months, and then
to Australia for three months. I ended the trip with visits to Fiji and
Hawaii. I worked to avoid anthropologists during these travels. I
thought I would leave all the "civilized" people I knew behind.
Instead, in each place I tried to get to know the local people. Often
I was invited to stay in people's houses, and if not, sometimes I
boarded so that I could really see how the local white people were

---

* In another version of this story, Underhill offers a different explanation for her
desire to travel the world. She said that she was at a yearly anthropology conference
and realized that she had just traveled a long way to see people she already knew.
Instead, since she was done with work, she wanted to have some fun and see new
things. Both versions are compatible; most likely there was not only one reason that
Underhill took this trip. Cf.: Underhill, Ruth M. 1985. *Papago Woman*. Originally
published 1936. Prospect Heights, IL: Waveland Press. Pg. x.

Figure 33. Ruth traveling in Egypt, 1963.

living. I wanted to see new people—not the Italians, not the French and Germans, whom I'd seen before. And I was much impressed with the kindness and gentleness of the new people I'd met. It was a lovely year of travel. I enjoyed it to no end.

When I returned to Denver I was just tired. I didn't want to bother with other people's affairs any more. I was through teaching. I did a few more projects, like write about schools in Gallup, New

Mexico, and I would be invited here or there to speak or to stay for some months.* I traveled some more. But all of a sudden I finally wasn't interested even in anthropology. I just thought, "Yes, these little arrowheads, they show that people lived here and they did this stuff and then they died. Oh, what of it? That happened everywhere."

So I took a quite a long rest.† Perhaps it was too long, but I just got so tired of trying to move the world around. I wanted to move it, and the world wouldn't do as I asked at all.

---

* See: Underhill, Ruth. 1971. *So Many Kinds of Navajos.* Gallup, NM: Gallup-McKinley County Schools.

† It seems that Underhill finally found some emotional shelter with a man late in life, having a relationship in her eighties and nineties with a professor named Colum Gilfallan. Lavender, Catherine J. 2006. *Scientists and Storytellers: Feminist Anthropologists and the Construction of the American Southwest.* Albuquerque: University of New Mexico Press. Pg. 105.

We're Going to
Live This Year

I'M NINETY-EIGHT YEARS OLD. Well, I suppose I'm ready to be snuffed out.* I would rather not be, of course. I would love to know what's going to happen in the next century. I wish I could. On the other hand, maybe I would rather just be gone and not have to live through all this readjustment we're going to have. Oh, what a bother it's going to be! Change is a good thing, but it's so, so tiresome, such hard work. Yes, I think I've had enough change in my lifetime.

❧

Looking back, I know that I didn't want a family. I really didn't. The amount of self-sacrifice that I saw my mother doing was something I decided I would never do. She just didn't exist in the presence of her children. Whatever her husband and her children needed, she would just die to produce it. I decided I didn't want to do that. I think I would have done it for a man I really loved, but I didn't find the one whom I thought was the kind I'd like.

Now, of course, having children is a perfectly wonderful thing, and so many women who do it don't come up to the requirements. They don't teach their children how to live at all. We ought to, if we could fix things, set it up so that such women who choose not to have children could go off and really make something out of their lives. That would be a third sex, I suppose, a human who does not add to the earth's population. I would like to belong to such a sex. I didn't

---

* Shortly after Underhill's death in 1984, her longtime secretary, Mary Cohen, said the cause of death was "old age—she just finally wore out." Eicher, Daiane. 1984. Ruth Underhill, Noted Writer, Dies. *The Denver Post*. 16 August: 6A.

Figure 34. Ruth in her final years, 1977.

have to have children and nourish them and feed them. I didn't want to do that, goodness knows, although I do like them when they get to be a little intelligent.

I'm amazed at what those Indian women I've met do. They don't seem to feel the tremendous subjection that white women feel. They have their part; they have to do it. They cook the meals and scrub the huts and burn the rubbish and all that, and the men get the fame. One time I was talking to a group of Cherokee women who were cleaning up the huts and cooking the meals, and the men were praying all the time.

"Why aren't you in there praying?" I said. "You have just as big a right as they have."

"Oh, we don't have to pray," they replied. "What makes you think we have to? Why, the men pray to *get* power, but we *have* power."

I met so many Indian women, and they are pleasant, nice old things. They're calm and gentle. They're not struggling for power at all. They just know they already have it.

~

It's quite a while since I really felt that the Christian religion explained things very much for me. It didn't seem to me a reasonable picture at all. So I had to give up the Christian religion.

I recently dreamed that I'd had it out with God himself. I didn't want to just leave him without words. It was so impolite. I wanted to meet with God and tell him why I gave him up. So I did. I went to heaven. He allowed nonbelievers to come to heaven. If you were a good thinker he was glad to know you. So he invited me to come and have an interview.

We sat on a great long bench made of one log, the kind you see at little stops for trolleys, only it was made of gold. We sat on this gold bench, and he was a very handsome person. I liked him immensely. We got to talking, and I explained to him that I just couldn't take all this stuff he gave the Hebrews.

"Well, my dear," he said, "I had to do that. It was thousands of years ago. Don't you know? And the people were simple, and they were just coming out of the agricultural stage. I had to give it to them pretty clear about what you must do and must not do. That's why I did it."

"Well, I can understand that, God," I said. "I think that was all right. But now, you haven't anything to tell *me*, have you?"

"I suppose not. I've told everything there is to tell. You don't seem to find that enough."

"Well, you better turn your face away from me, then. I can't worship you."

He was this really handsome old gentleman with a beautiful white beard. He turned his head away and showed me his elegant profile.

Then I looked before me, and there was a woman with long, flowing chestnut hair.

"But God," I asked, "what good is she to me?"

"Well," he answered, "she's all I have to give."

⌒

I never sought a bit of material wealth. I didn't think of fame either. Although when I didn't get fame, I felt sort of disappointed and thought, "What's the matter with those people? Can't give me anything?"* But, in truth, I didn't work for fame, so why should I have gotten it, really?

Now people tell me that while the colleagues from my Boas story all achieved a certain amount of status, I didn't achieve status at all because I didn't take a teaching job and have students who would be my charioteers and talk about what I'd done and advertise me to the world. My colleagues got somebody like that, but they didn't do anything very much afterward. They simply had trumpeters to advertise them. I always just wanted to do something.

⌒

The O'odham were mostly uninterested about my other life, away from them. I would tell them whenever they asked me, but they didn't care. Once I had to go back east, and I took a plane because I was in

---

* It would be an overstatement to say that Underhill received no acknowledgement at all. As noted in the introduction, Underhill collected several honors starting in the 1960s. Additionally, in 1985 the Denver Woman's Press Club established the Ruth Murray Underhill Award "to honor the memory of one of the DWPC's most distinguished members" (http://dwpconline.org/scholarships/ [accessed 28 March 2013]). Also, the University of Denver has presented the Ruth Murray Underhill Teaching Award since 1999 (www.du.edu/facsen/facultyhonors.html [accessed March 28, 2013]).

a hurry. So I told them what the plane was like. They listened, then said, "Oh yes, our people used to fly through the air like that. We don't do it now, but we used to."

I then told them about the meals we had on the plane. In those days they served the meals in cardboard dishes. I had potatoes au gratin and hash. "Oh!" they exclaimed. "Aren't the Americans wonderful to think of cardboard dishes." You see, that was all that appealed to them! As for flying through the air, that's nothing. O'odham used to do that. They knew about flying. But cardboard dishes, they had never heard that! It was kind of a strange revelation—for both of us. How difficult this is, isn't it, to understand other people, to really understand them?

◆

I'll tell you. The song that I love to sing is the bean song.

In the very farthest west part of the O'odham country, it is so hot nothing grows but beans. Corn will not grow; squash will not grow. Those have to have a little moisture. Only the beans will grow.

The song is simple: it just means the beans are here. They have escaped thefts. They have escaped rotting. They have escaped winter frosts. The beans are here, that's all it means. And those little, ugly plants are just two or three inches off the ground. They're not beautiful, they're not impressive. The beans are very small profits, but they are the food of the O'odham race, and if those beans don't grow, the O'odham will die or have to leave their beloved country. Those beans are what keep the people alive.

In the song, the beans sing together, "We are here." The beans are here, the beans are singing, they are singing all together. I find that a perfectly wonderful picture of hope because that means we're going to live this year. That is all we have. That is all we need. I think that is quite a glorious statement.

Acknowledgments

THE EDITING OF RUTH M. UNDERHILL'S memoir would not have been possible without the generous assistance of many people. We first thank Aly Jabrocki for her diligent efforts to organize the eight-five linear feet of Underhill archival materials at the Denver Museum of Nature & Science, under the vital funding of a Save America's Treasures grant (ST-03–06–0024–09). Aly's assistance was crucial for this project, and all subsequent researchers will be thankful for her industrious, focused, and highly capable work. We are also glad that Underhill had enough prudence to charge Mary C. Coen with donating her papers to a museum archive; and we are in turn obliged to Ms. Coen, who chose the DMNS as the final repository for these materials.

This book also would not have been possible without the farsightedness and dedicated labor of Joyce Herold, Mary Cytrynbaum, Dave Baysinger, Skip Neal, Kris Haglund, and Steve Rich, who conducted a series of interviews with Underhill as she approached her final years. Carla Bradmon was a great help to us in transferring all of the interviews in the archives into digital format; transcribing Underhill's tentative efforts at an autobiography; and researching background information for the footnotes. To Carla we are deeply grateful and indebted.

We also thank the University of Arizona Press for taking on this manuscript, and particularly Allyson Carter, Scott De Herrera, Kristen Buckles, Diana Rico, and three anonymous reviewers for their efforts. Additional assistance and essential support was provided by Kirk R. Johnson, Kris Haglund, René Payne, Nancy Parezo, Linda Gregonis, Soumontha Chanthaphonh, and Carmen Carrasco. Bruce and Dorothy Dines and Jean Saul provided subvention funds that allowed us to lower the purchase price and make this volume accessible to as many readers as possible.

Figure Credits

Index

Sing Sing (N.Y.), 59
Sioux: and Bureau of Indian Affairs,
196–97
Smart Set: A Magazine of Cleverness,
103
social work, 9, 10, 88n, 89, 93n,
94–96; in New York City,
100–102, 121
Soil Conservation Service, 12, 198n
Southern California: Indian tribes
in, 12
Spier, Leslie, 147n
squash, 182
Stokes, J. Stogdell, 87–89
stories: published, 103–4
suffrage movement, 18, 106
Sunday school, 47–49
Switzerland: trips to, 69–70

Tanner, Clara Lee, 155n, *205*
teachers: at Sells Agency, 185–86; US
Bureau of Indian Affairs training,
195–96
television: *Red Man's America*,
206–7
Thompson, Laura, 198
Tierney, Dan, 32, 51
Tohono O'odham, 192, 214–15;
anthropological study of, 10–11,
17n, 18; fieldwork, 150, 159–72,
181–86; honors by, 14, *15*; proposed constitution for, 12, 198n;
pulling down the clouds, 190–91;
saguaro fruit gathering, 186–90;
water and, 180–81
travel: European, 69–70, 89–92;
world, 208–10
Trento (Italy), 114
Trieste (Italy), 114–15
Tyrol, 92

Underhill, Abram Sutton (father),
ix, 8, 17, 63, 64; family dynamics,
30, 31–33, 36–37, 42, 49–50, 52,
55–56, 59–60, 95, 97, 124, 176–77;
finances of, 56–57, 63; law studies
of, 58–59; marriage of, 54–55;
religion and academic knowledge,
74–77
Underhill, Anna (aunt), 47–48, 53
Underhill, Anna Taber Murray
(mother), ix, 8: death of, 63–64;
family dynamics, 30–32, 34, 36–38,
42–43, 49–50, 59–60, 78–81, 94,
96, 124; marriage of, 54–55; personality of, 61–63; Quakerism of,
65–67; religious views of, 76–77
Underhill, Elizabeth Sutton (sister),
ix, 33, 44, 45, 61
Underhill, Eliza Sutton (grandmother), ix, 47–48, 53
Underhill, Helen F., 33n
Underhill, Jesse Haight (grandfather), ix, 52–53, 57
Underhill, John, 57–58
Underhill, Margaret. *See* Barton,
Margaret Underhill
Underhill, Robert Lindley Murray
(brother), ix, 32–33, 37–38, *44*, 45,
81, 96, 132
Underhill, Ruth Murray: as anthropologist, 19–20; birth and death
of, 6, 8; marriage and divorce, 10,
119–22, 125–26; photos of, *7, 9, 15,
22, 30, 35, 70, 79, 97, 109, 118, 149,
201, 205, 206, 207, 209, 212*; on
religious education, 46–49
Underhill Award, Ruth Murray,
214n
Underhill Collection, Ruth M., 5–6,
21–22
Underhill family, 58; dynamics of,
8, 29–46, 49–50, 55–57, 59–60,
64–65, 96–97, 123–24
US Bureau of Indian Affairs (Office
of Indian Affairs), 12, 184, 193;
nepotism in, 198–99; pamphlet
writing for, 194–95, 197–98;

in Santa Fe, 199–200; Sioux and,
196–97; teaching teachers for,
195–96; during World War II,
202–3
US Department of Agriculture, 12
US Office of Indian Affairs. *See* US
Bureau of Indian Affairs
University of Chicago, 202–3
University of Denver, 13, 204–5
University of Munich, 92n

Vassar College, 9, 16, 86–88
Victorian era: gender roles in,
15–16

Wagley, Charles, 134n
water: Tohono O'odham and,
180–81, 183
wedding: Navajo, 175

Westchester County: farm in,
120–21, 177–78
Wesleyan College, 58
White, Leslie, 134n
White Moth, The (Underhill), 16, 104
Withers, Arnold (Arnie), 204
women: Mojave, 193; as researchers,
19n, 153–54; role of, 15, 211, 213;
Tohono O'odham, 160–61, 170–71
women's movement. *See* suffrage
movement
Wood, James, 53
World War I, 10, 18, 63–64; end of,
113–16; Red Cross service in, 108–13
World War II, 202–3
Wormington, H. Marie, 13, 204n,
205, 206n; at Denver Museum of
Natural History, 201–2; friendship
with, 200–201

About the Editors

Chip Colwell-Chanthaphonh is curator of anthropology at the Denver Museum of Nature & Science (DMNS). He received his PhD from Indiana University and his BA from the University of Arizona. Before coming to the DMNS, he held a post-doctoral fellowship with the American Academy of Arts & Sciences in Cambridge, Massachusetts. He has published more than three dozen articles and book chapters, and has authored and edited eight books. He is a recipient of the 2009 National Council on Public History Book Award.

Stephen E. Nash is curator of archaeology and chair of the Department of Anthropology at the Denver Museum of Nature & Science (DMNS). He received his PhD and MA from the University of Arizona and his BA from Grinnell College. Before coming to DMNS, he spent nine years at the Field Museum in Chicago, where he served as head of collections in anthropology and as a post-doctoral research specialist. He has published more than two dozen articles and book chapters, and has authored and edited five books on subjects ranging from the history of archaeological tree-ring dating to museum collections.